Design Thinking

Design Thinking

Peter G. Rowe

The MIT Press
Cambridge, Massachusetts
London, England

Third printing, 1991

© 1987 by The Massachusetts Institute of Technology

This book was set in Helvetica by Achorn Graphic Services and printed and bound by Halliday Lithograph in the United States of America.

Library of Congress Cataloging-in-Publication Data

Rowe, Peter G.
  Design thinking.

  Bibliography: p.
  Includes index.
    1. Architectural design—Decision making—Case studies.   2. Architecture, Modern—20th century—Decision making—Case studies.   I. Title.
NA2750.R68   1987   729   86-8402
ISBN 0-262-18122-3

To Niki and Anthony

Contents

Acknowledgments

This book is largely the consequence of seminars on methods of inquiry that Peter McCleary invited me to give to students in the Ph.D. Program in Architecture at the University of Pennsylvania. To Peter and several classes of seminar students at Penn I owe a considerable debt for their frank criticism and constant encouragement. Without them the book would never have materialized.

I also want to acknowledge the strong support and encouragement of Anderson Todd, my former colleague at Rice, and our rather special graduate seminar of 1984. And I would like to express my appreciation to Peter Papademetriou, at Rice, for his encouragement, and to Timothy Williams, for his early contributions and support of the enterprise.

Acknowledgment must also be made of some of my new-found colleagues at Harvard. In particular, I would like to thank Richard Krauss and John Whiteman for their interest and constructive criticism. And I am grateful to Bill Mitchell, my old friend and now colleague, for his very constructive suggestions about organizing the material and for his encouragement.

Finally, my thanks to Doris Anderson and Debbie Alber for their work in preparing the manuscript and to Fisseha Wegayehu for his support on the graphic material.

Design Thinking

Designers in Action

1

The design of buildings can be viewed in a number of ways. First, it can be seen from the perspective of the historical record of production—the lines, shapes, and masses of past buildings and urban artifacts—interpreted according to various aesthetic canons, social circumstances, and technical opportunities. Second, it can be examined for its conformity with theoretical prescriptions of what constitutes "proper" architecture and "good" design. Some recent examples of this approach are Krier's *Urban Space,* Lynch's *A Theory of Good City Form,* and Rossi's *The Architecture of the City* (Krier 1979, Lynch 1981, Rossi 1982). Third, its study can take the form of observing what designers do and how they undertake their tasks. Seen in this last way, design has often occupied an ambivalent position, being characterized as either a form of fine art or a form of technical science. From all perspectives, however, design appears to be a fundamental means of inquiry by which man realizes and gives shape to ideas of dwelling and settlement. Furthermore, design is a practical form of inquiry insofar as it is concerned with making and a certain commonplace usefulness, quite apart from its more esoteric benefits (Harrison 1978).

This book is an attempt to fashion a generalized portrait of design thinking. A principal aim will be to account for the underlying structure and focus of inquiry directly associated with those rather private moments of "seeking out," on the part of designers, for the purpose of inventing or creating buildings and urban artifacts.

Although they certainly affect design thinking, other important aspects of practice, such as the organization and administration of professional activities, will be of little concern here. Nor will I be dealing with the nature of client-architect relationships or other formal and informal institutional dimensions of practice, although in other renderings of the general subject such relationships and dimensions might profitably have a central role (Kostof 1977, Tafuri 1976). Their influence on the outcome of design is undeniable in most architectural and urban design undertakings. Nor shall I dwell on the manner in which the results of architectural and urban design might be construed by some specific audience or by society as a whole, although again these are undoubtedly pertinent issues (Jencks and Baird 1969, Bonta 1979). Nor shall I advance a theory about architecture in the sense of how design should be carried out and what makes for "good" architecture. Mine will be a neutral account in this regard.

My subject is more narrowly defined. I am concerned with the interior situational logic and the decision-making processes of designers in action, as well as with theoretical dimensions that both account for and inform this kind of undertaking.

A useful way to begin the development of a general portrait of design thinking is by looking at some actual examples of designers at work. It is here, in the give and take of problem-solving situations in the real world, that we start to see the complex texture of decision making. And it is here that we discover there is no such thing as *the* design process in the restricted sense of an ideal step-by-step technique. Rather, there are many different styles of decision making, each with individual quirks as well as manifestations of common characteristics. Sometimes the unfolding of a design is strongly influenced by constraints derived from the initial setting of the problem, such as the context in which the building is to be built or its social purpose. On other occasions the process seems more determined by a designer's personal attitudes and prejudices toward such things as functional expression or modes of fabrication technology. More often than not, there is a mixture of both orientations, as designers move back and forth between the problem as given and the tentative proposals they have in mind.

Three case studies of designers in action will be presented. Each involved lengthy periods of observation and documentation, where designers described their activities in detail with the aid of sketches and other drawings. The aim of these interview sessions was to faithfully reconstruct the sequence of steps, moves, and other logical procedures that were employed. This type of reconstruction is referred to as a *protocol;* and while it omits the minute-by-minute detail and other real-time variations in design behavior, it does represent a plausible record of major events (Hayes 1981, pp. 51–57; Pohlman 1982). Furthermore, the subjects had the opportunity of providing detailed explanations of the rationale behind each step, thereby providing greater insight than might be gained from mere observation of surface activity.[1]

The three case studies were chosen, from among a more extensive collection of protocols, because they illustrate three different styles of design thinking. One protocol seems more constrained by information derived from the immediate context of the design problem. By contrast, another is almost totally dominated by the a priori use of a particular building type as a model for resolving the problem at hand. In the third example two large ideas seem to dominate the process of designing, as much through their conflicting influence as through their complementary effect. The full range of design thinking is by no means represented by these three examples, but they do provide sufficient material and variation to serve as an informative backdrop for later theoretical discussion.

Further examples of the design process, taken from various written sources, will follow the case studies. Certain features will emerge as characteristic of the problem-solving behavior of architects and urban designers, particularly its episodic structure and the fact that the designer relies on presuppositions and hunches about architecture at least as much as on information furnished during orderly confrontation with the constraints found in a given design problem. It will, I hope, be made evident that in order to clarify the essential method and style of inquiry encompassed by design thinking, we must venture beyond the traditional boundaries of explanatory theories about creative problem solving. We must engage the normative realm of discourse about architecture if we wish to gain insight into what shapes the content rather than the strictly procedural aspects of design activity.

Case Study 1: Making an Urban Place

The first case study concerns the problem of designing a commercial complex for some 1.5 million square feet of office space on a suburban site of a large American city. The area of the site is 16.5 acres, spanning roughly north-south between a major thoroughfare and a small river. The site is irregular in shape, with the widest extremity bounding the adjacent thoroughfare. Other characteristics of the site include a small area in the floodplain next to the river, extensive wooded areas, and the remnants of old buildings. The surrounding uses consist of a single-family residential subdivision to the east, a wide utility easement to the south, vacant land to the north, and an apartment complex under construction across the river to the west. The site is some ten miles from the central business district of the city, although in an area that has already seen considerable development of commercial office facilities. In short, the program of uses and the site are not at all unusual for commercial office developments in outlying suburban areas of many modern American cities.

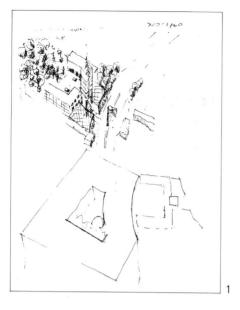

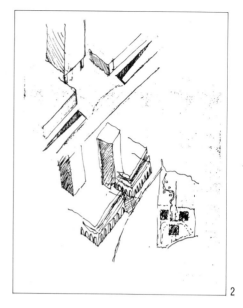

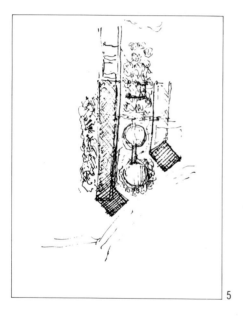

1
Case study no. 1: early sketches.

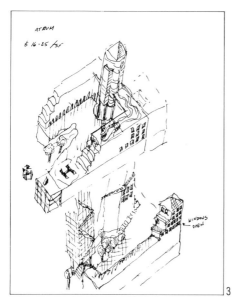

As shown by the early sketches (figure 1, parts 1 and 2), the designer began to frame his intentions with the ideas of providing a strong sense of corporate image, giving a strong sense of address on the major thoroughfare, and making use of the wooded amenity of the site. Rather than electing to explore these ideas in the more traditional manner of isolated tower buildings arranged within the site boundaries, at the outset the designer attempted to develop a strongly urban form that acknowledged the public domain of the street by pulling the building masses forward on the site and creating a plaza along the thoroughfare boundary. As we shall see, this was a persistent aspect of the design that became more highly resolved as the process unfolded. In making these moves the designer manifested an intention to establish a context for future developments in the area, especially those along the major thoroughfare next to the site.

The designer's attention then turned to the issue of the various kinds of office space and supporting commercial areas that could be provided. Here the emphasis was on the accommodation of major and minor corporate tenants and the making of subordinate spaces within the development that would give each some sense of identity. In addition, the requirement of parking some 5,000 cars was addressed, together with modes of entry and egress and the question of the appearance of the complex

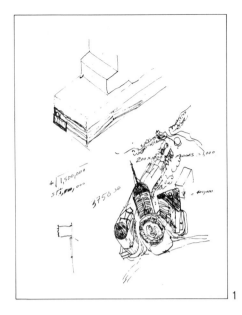

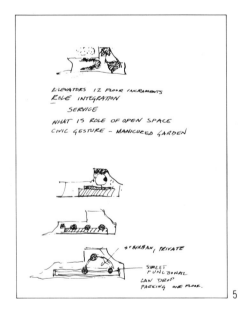

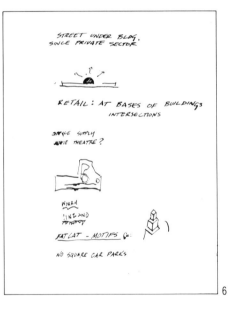

2

Case study no. 1: exploration of design ideas.

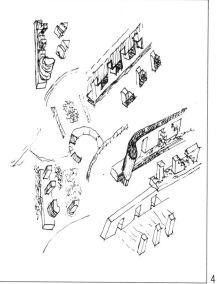

3

4

when viewed from the upper floors of the buildings (figure 1, part 4).

At this stage a linear arrangement of buildings was provisionally established, dictated in large measure by the size of the program of accommodations and the geometry of the site (figure 1, part 5). There was also an attempt to orchestrate a sequence of public spaces, emanating from the major plaza, on which each office building had an individual address, onto the street, on which the complex had a common address. Evaluation of this plan, however, indicated that the linear scheme was problematic from the standpoint of efficient distribution of rentable office space in conjunction with circulation, especially in the vertical direction. This realization on the part of the designer initiated a flurry of experimental arrangements (figure 2, parts 1–4). First, two public spaces were created and the buildings rearranged with the lower-rise structures placed at the rear of the site so as to minimize destruction of the site's natural amenity. A relatively large number of plausible arrangements seemed possible, however, and there was a sense of backtracking in the direction of the earlier linear scheme. Generally, the problem at this stage seemed to be underconstrained and lacking a specific direction.

The apparent deadlock was addressed by systematically evaluating various aspects of the scheme (figure 2, parts 5 and 6; figure 3, part 1) for the purposes of retrenching and more thoroughly

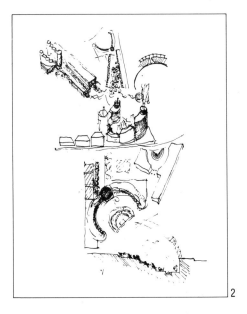

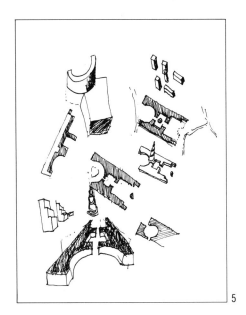

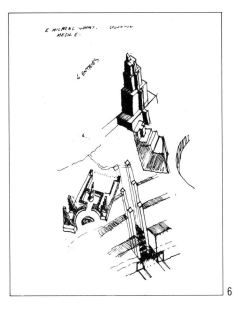

3

Case study no. 1: development of design ideas.

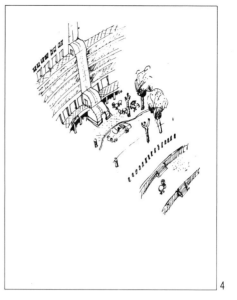

3

4

validating some of the initial design ideas. For example, the
plaza on the street was reasserted as a primary idea. The relationship of car parking to concentrations of building mass was
also reappraised. Essentially, guidelines or rules were established that helped the designer plan and prepare for subsequent
exploration. Indeed, the combination of the results from these
evaluations began to give shape to a more definitive organization for the scheme. First, harking back to an earlier proposal,
two major exterior spaces were employed, around which the
building program became organized. Each space was seen to
have a landscape quality befitting its location on the site (a
public plaza on the street and a more informally landscaped area
in the interstices of the site; figure 3, part 2). Second, the problem of providing an appropriate sense of entrance and address
to the major office components was addressed by placing the
primary vertical elements of circulation around a common base
that, in turn, defined the street plaza. This base was also used to
accommodate main entrances and retail commercial uses, with
structured car parking rising up behind, also forming a base for
the office towers (figure 3, part 3). Aspects of this general arrangement were then explored and elaborated in more detail,
including the provision of separate means of entry, egress, and
parking for office workers and visitors. The architectural treatment of the building base was also studied further, with an ac-
centuation of the vertical circulation expressed to mark the

building entrances, within the horizontal banding of the plaza's enclosure. Attention was also directed toward the landscape qualities of the street plaza (figure 3, part 4). The potential function of this major exterior space was investigated further, with the result that it became cast in the role of outdoor amphitheater and storm water detention and retention device. Parenthetically, this latter technical function was a general requirement of the development program.

Exploration of the arrangement and articulation of the building base, on which the office towers were to be placed, was continued, with special attention to the transition between the two major exterior spaces (figure 3, part 5). Generally, the base was regarded as building fabric, with the primary purpose of defining these public exterior spaces. Resolution of this aspect of the scheme involved a dimensional interplay between the shape and scale of the outdoor spaces and the planning requirements for efficient circulation and for adjacency of car parking to the office towers. It should be noted that a number of more precise and dimensionally accurate drawings, not shown here, were made to test these assumptions and to help firm up the scheme.

Having resolved the layout and formal arrangement of the lower floors, at least for the moment, the designer proceeded to investigate various methods of architecturally articulating the office towers (figure 3, part 6). Uppermost in his mind were the provision of a distinctive image quality, the making of distinctions among various tenant functions, and the clarification of entrance and address. In addition, considerable attention was paid to matters of structural design and building erection technology. The decision was made to employ lightweight steel framing for the office towers because of the economic advantages of speedy fabrication and because of a preference for the architectural qualities of the glazed fenestration and spandrel panels that would automatically follow by the same line of reasoning. At this stage a number of detailed design investigations, not shown here, were undertaken to more properly incorporate these technical considerations and to address the matter of providing a variety of efficiently planned office suites.

With the front portion of the project approaching resolution, several issues introduced by the arrangement were identified and pursued further. First, the car-parking requirements effectively dictated construction over much of the site, obliterating most of its natural character. Second, another consequence of the extension of the building base across the site was the comparative lack of acknowledgment of the "edge conditions": the perimeter of the overall building mass essentially walled off the site along its boundaries. Finally, the phasing of construction was acknowledged as potentially problematic in an otherwise unified and integrated proposal.

Recognition of these aspects of the design led to a radical reconsideration of the back portion of the complex, toward the river. The natural landscape was reinstated in the form of a terraced garden on top of the parking structure, flanked by lower-rise office accommodations relating more directly to the edge of the site (figure 4, part 2). Another office tower complex was located on an axis with this formal garden, at the back of the site, thus alleviating the problem of distributing the parking in close proximity to office circulation (figure 4, part 3). This arrangement also had the advantage of rationalizing the phasing and construction of the development, from the southern portion of the site forward to the street, in easily identifiable units. Moreover, it provided ample accommodation for the development's primary tenant in a secluded location with the most outdoor amenity but still with a strong presence, because of the reduction in the massing of the three towers on the street plaza.

Further development of this overall arrangement was undertaken, including systematic studies of vehicular and pedestrian circulation (figure 4, part 5) and the formal treatment of towers and public spaces. Incremental adjustments were made, and the scheme began to be finalized and moved forward into detailed delineation (figure 4, part 6).

In summary, we see a design scheme that developed from a few well-chosen urban concepts that were more an interpretation of what the project might be like than pragmatic responses to prevailing site conditions and program. The protocol exhibits at least three or four major sequential episodes of design activity, in which the full consequences of earlier proposals became evident and were explored. Through these efforts the framework for further design was clarified. Periods in which the problem appeared underconstrained to the designer were immediately followed by systematic reevaluation of his position and an assessment of the potential outcome of various lines of reasoning. Not all the initial intentions were completely satisfied, however, particularly with regard to the site's natural amenity.

1

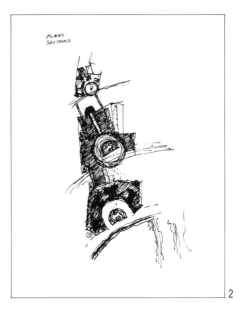

2

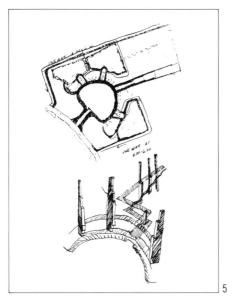

5

6

4
Case study no. 1: sketches from the final stages.

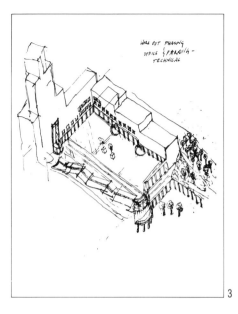

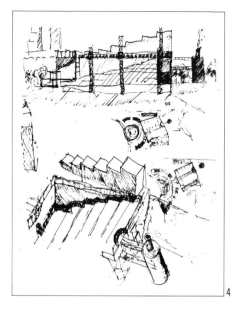

3

4

Case Study 2: Making a Building from a Formal Type

In the second case study a somewhat different approach was taken by the designer, although many shared characteristics are evident. The project called for construction of a hotel and comprehensive health facility on a naturally landscaped site in a relatively undeveloped area. The site included a lake, several wooded areas, and an existing hospital to which the proposed building complex was to be connected. The primary function of the new health facility was health maintenance through exercise, dietary control, and "clean living."

For preliminary planning purposes the designer divided the program of uses into three parts (Rowe 1982): the hotel, the health facility proper, and a third element housing shared functions such as restaurants, entrance ways, and car parking. The designer then proceeded with the intention of "addressing and preserving the lake on the site . . . as a major focus of the scheme." The first move was to create a "formal space next to the lake," but shielded from the portion of the site where the main access was to be found (figure 5, part 1). To accomplish this, a "classical villa" served as the point of departure, linking the two major programmatic elements—the hotel and the health facility—around the lake.

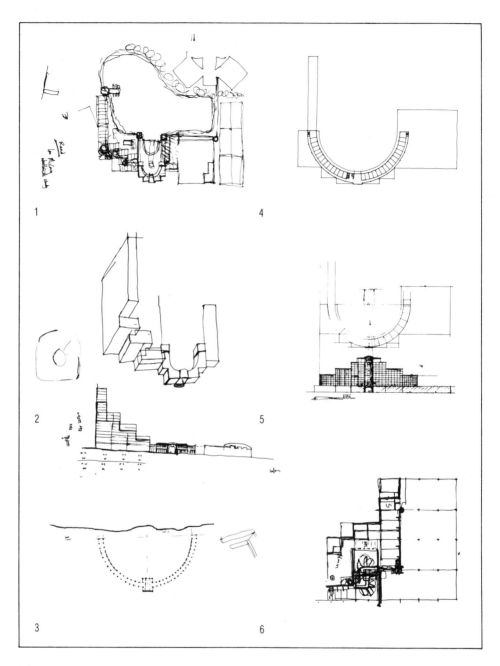

1

4

2

5

3

6

5

Case study no. 2: early concepts.

This decision to deal with a functionally subordinate element first may appear curious. The choice was made, however, because of the apparent correspondence between the villa type and the problem at hand. This correspondence was seen in terms of the location on the water, a certain symmetry and formality in the building program, and the presentation of a formal facade to the public side of the site and an informal facade to the lake. The adoption of the villa type as a model also furthered the initial intention of simply defining a special place by the lake, but the intention seems to have been derived as much from the model as from a study of the site in the absence of the model. The treatment of the space between the building complex and the lake was to become a continuing theme throughout the design.

As shown in figure 5, part 2, problems were immediately encountered with this arrangement, due in large measure to the overpowering physical presence of the two larger elements —the hotel and the health facility—on either side of the villa. Consequently, the designer generalized the symmetrical arrangement of the building form, linking these two parts into a semicircular plan (figure 5, part 3). This move also gave rise to the idea of defining a circulation path through the pieces at the base of the building masses and thus having an ordering impact on the scheme. Considerable attention was then directed toward reconciling the asymmetrical program with the symmetrical spatial conception by elongating one arm of the plan composition and shifting the inward lake front focus around to the eastern edge of the site (see figure 5, part 4).

Evaluation of the scheme at this stage revealed problems with the scale and shape of the hotel, as well as the lack of any formal difference between it and the health facility. As the designer observed, "it was a problem of thinking of it [the health facility] just as a piece in a formal arrangement, so I started analyzing it as a separate piece." At this point a shift occurred in the type of organizing principle being employed, from a preoccupation with formal composition derived from the model type to a concern with the geometrical properties of structural bays and with the abstract functional arrangement of required program facilities. To continue the narration, "Basically I was trying to take a structural diagram, a functional diagram, and a circulation diagram and combine them" (figure 5, part 5). These considerations amounted to a redefinition of the problem at hand. The result was an alternating plan sequence of large and small structural bays, within which circulation and functions of various sizes could more appropriately be accommodated (figure 5, part 6).

The same level of strategy was then used to plan the service functions of the hotel. By "working strictly in sort of square bubbles, and within an understanding of proximity requirements among the uses," the designer "tried to arrange the pieces so that they would make sense." That is, having organized the conditions of immediate interest into a well-defined problem, the designer proceeded to explore various ways by which building elements might be arranged and then turned to a more systematic form of exploration, once this initial sense of the problem had clarified certain principles and procedural rules.

With the problem of space-planning the facility at least partially resolved, attention was again shifted to the overall plan of the building complex. As the designer put it, "One of the consequences of adopting the semicircular symmetrical form was that it brought in an [implied] axial arrangement that really had no relationship to everything else that was going on. If I was going to stay with that form, I would have to develop a relationship, and so I went back to looking at the whole site." Perhaps not surprisingly, an axial composition of building and landscape elements evolved, with a progression from the site's main entrance through to the lake. Adoption of these ordering principles quickly led to a realization that a formal outdoor space was appropriate for the entrance to the building complex, both for functional reasons such as car parking and in order to complete the composition (figure 6, part 1). Further, the designer now felt that she "was dealing with two major outdoor spaces: one at the end of the axis when you arrive and the other facing the lake"; she characterized the first as "a formal public arrival space" and the second as "a more informal space"—something of a reversal of the earlier data about placing the formal space next to the lake.

These decisions made, the most pressing issue was which way the curvilinear form of the hotel should face—out toward the lake or out toward the street. The designer also realized that she "was trying to use the hotel piece to solve all problems and was having difficulty with this." At this point many different experimental arrangements were made with alternative plan shapes (figure 6, part 2). Ultimately, the designer decided on a more simplified formal arrangement for the hotel, simply running a straight slab block across the site (figure 6, part 3). This arrange-

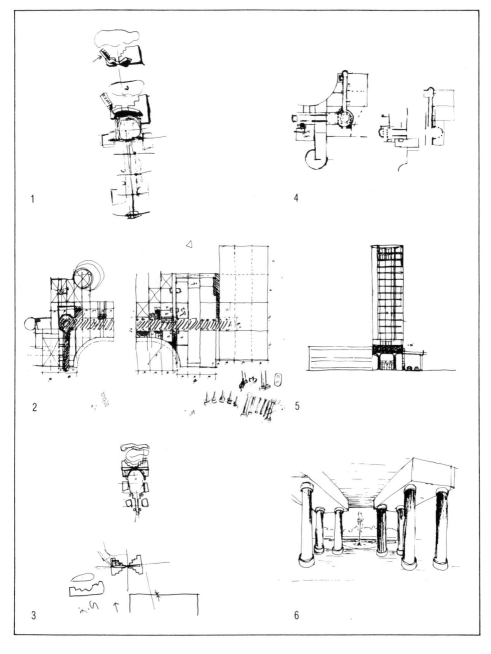

6
Case study no. 2: concept exploration.

ment resolved the overall scheme for the major elements of the project in the designer's mind.

Within the now well-established framework, solutions to more detailed problems were developed. For instance, the open-ended expression of the primary public circulation corridor, running beneath the slab block and defined by the columnar structure of the hotel, was terminated at the junction with semipublic functions in the form of an alcove (figure 6, part 4). The columns themselves and the section through the base of the hotel were articulated so as to give a sense of grandeur to the public entry space and to allow for a view through the building toward the lake (figure 6, parts 5 and 6). The northern, public facade of the building was composed from a proportional grid with intervals determined so as to diminish the apparent scale of the building, always a problematic condition to the designer (figure 7, part 1). This facade was further divided into a distinct base, middle, and top, no doubt as an outgrowth of the classical references employed earlier in the process (figure 5, part 5). A more informal textural treatment was proposed for the southern facade facing the lake (figure 7, part 2), consistent with the quality of its location, although here again the organizational properties of a grid are evident.

This process of refinement, adjustment, and embellishment continued. The only subsequent modifications to the overall arrangement of the complex arose through attempts to extend the strategy of expressing various site constraints, a strategy the designer had earlier found successful. For example, several lines in plan at 45 degrees were introduced, in order to better relate the building complex with the existing hospital across the lake (figure 7, part 3). This feature had the additional purpose of helping to organize a greater sense of informality in the architecture along the lake front (figure 7, part 4).

In this case study, several distinct lines of reasoning can be identified, often involving the a priori use of an organizing principle or model to direct the decision-making process. The use of the villa type at the outset of the process was as much a preconceived notion as it was a response to the broad array of site conditions and the building program. It functioned as a dominant organizing principle through which both the site conditions and the building program were subsequently conformed. More abstract relational models, dealing with conditions of structural organization and an expressed preference for functional proximity, were used effectively to solve specific layout problems. The

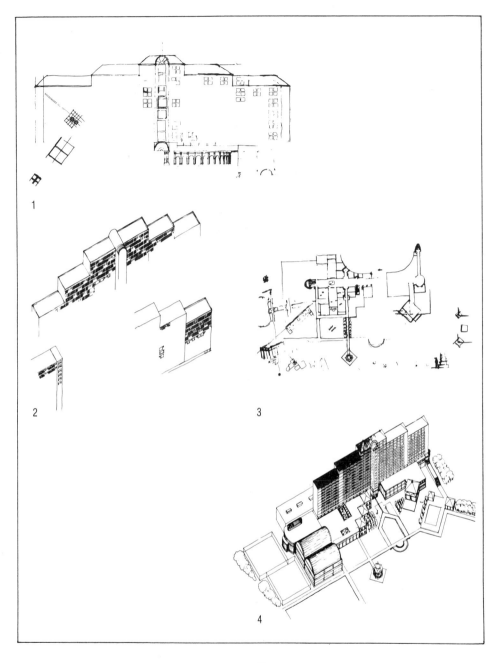

1

2

3

4

7
Case study no. 2: project resolution.

symmetrical compositional principles, apparently engendered by the earlier preoccupations, seemed to persist, exerting a pronounced influence over subsequent lines of investigation. As in the first case study, a certain amount of backtracking and consolidation of the problem constraints was evident, giving a distinctly episodic structure to the process.

Case Study 3: Reconciling Two Large Ideas

The third case study concerns a design for a world bibliographic center on a waterfront site, adjacent to the downtown area of Chicago (see figure 8, part 1). The program for the center called for a "hard-copy" library; a computer and data-processing facility, including telecommunication linkage with similar complexes in other parts of the world; and several theaters, or auditoriums. The site itself was interesting in the light of Burnham's plan for Chicago from the "City Beautiful Movement": the designers had to assume completion of the area of parkland and civic buildings begun by Burnham to the south of the site.

From the outset the designers recognized the site as a potential point of symmetry with Burnham's scheme and entertained the idea of establishing this symmetry by extending out into the lake on a pier structure, similar to those adjacent to the site on the river side (figure 8, parts 2 and 3). Attention then became focused on the overall shape that the library facility should take on the site location opposite Burnham's planetarium. Initial speculation was strongly influenced by parallel studies of Burnham's plan, at least with regard to the massing of the building in the form of regular solids, although other historical references could also be seen at work (figure 8, part 4).

This episode was followed by a more systematic evaluation of the site and its environs. For this purpose a model was constructed (see figure 8, part 2). The features of primary interest were the relatively tight grid pattern of Chicago's downtown development contrasted with the larger grid blocks of the parkway, the bounding of streets by buildings, and the presence of low-rise structures on the waterfront (figure 8, part 5). Generally speaking, the project's context was defined in these terms.

Two themes emerged from these contextual studies (figure 8, part 6). One was the creation of a landmark at the point of symmetry with Burnham's plan. The other was the development of a scheme in the form of a linear system of buildings and interstitial spaces that would thematically extend the Chicago grid pattern

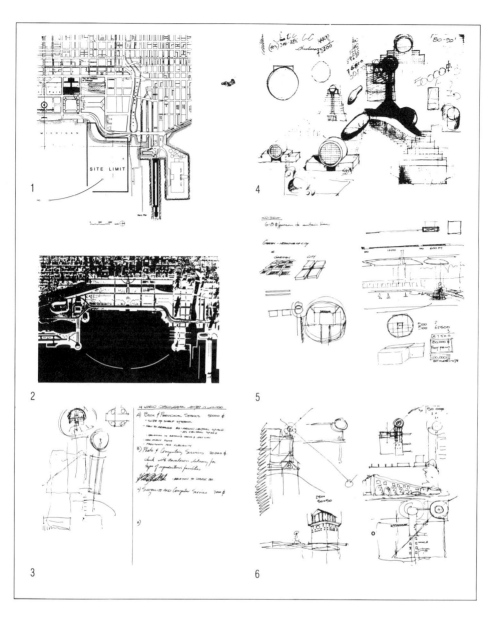

8

Case study no. 3: site constraints and early sketches.

out into the lake. In figure 8, part 6, we also begin to see experimentation with various axial arrangements of objects and three-dimensional figural experimentation that again makes strong references to the buildings of the Chicago Exposition.

The process of exploring and elaborating these two themes continued (figure 9, parts 1 and 2), with attempts to position the "landmark building" within the linear grid system and to vary the meter of the grid pattern in order to more fully understand its potential properties for "place making." Gradually the scheme became resolved as a linear form, protruding into the lake, extending the Chicago grid and terminating with a rotunda-like structure reminiscent of the regular solids postulated at the beginning of the process (figure 9, part 3).

At this stage of development, however, a programmatic evaluation of the scheme suggested to the designers that the linear proposal would both require more building facilities than were available and prove to be an inefficient arrangement for library use. Here the need for vertical library stacks and close proximity to supporting services dictated a more compact shape. Consequently, organization of the scheme became more concentrated at a single location and the linear structure began to recede (figure 9, part 4). Further concentration of the building elements followed, until a single building emerged (figure 9, part 5). Vestiges of the linear scheme can still be seen, however, in the manner in which the building mass is "flattened," addressing the drive out from downtown Chicago to the site.

Having resolved, for the moment, the matter of the dominance of the two earlier themes, or large organizing principles, the designers then began to explore alternative programmatic arrangements and formal configurations for the center's building mass. Here a straightforward proposal of vertical library stacks, in the form of a tower resting on a base of administrative and other facilities, began to emerge. In the minds of the designers this arrangement was both efficient and consistent with the idea of creating a landmark (figure 9, part 6, and figure 10, part 1). Throughout these explorations there was a conscious preference for adopting a strongly formalistic, symmetrical, and neo-classical conformation for the building. The only remaining linear plan element was a road leading from the building, on axis, toward downtown Chicago.

Other aspects of the facility's program were incorporated into the design investigations, as much to help resolve choices between formal alternatives as for the sake of comprehensive

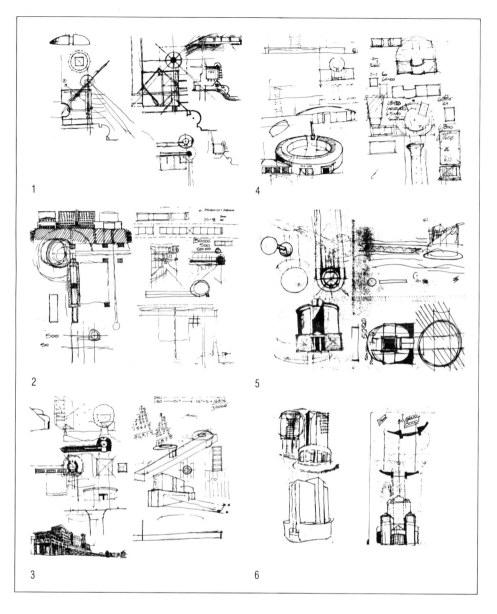

9
Case study no. 3: investigation of design themes.

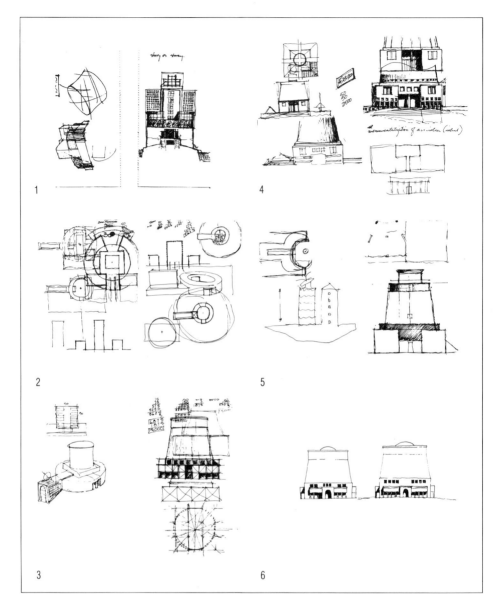

1

4

2

5

3

6

10
Case study no. 3: development of design concepts.

study. A myriad of compositional principles were invoked, as well as a separation of the library proper from the facility housing the electronic media and transmission devices (figure 10, part 2). The incipient notion of enforcing a duality between electronic media and printed matter was soon abandoned, the designers having concluded that this separation "made the computing and technical facilities stand out too much"; they once again retrenched to proposing a single building (figure 10, part 3).

The next episode of design activity, not shown here, involved extensive experiments with various kinds of structural arrangements, the accommodation of vertical circulation within the tower, and refinement in the distribution of programmatic elements. During this process a square building base with a round drum of library stacks was established. A distinction was made between "ceremonial" circulation to and through the building and "expedient" circulation. Geometrically, the square base was divided, in plan, into nine parts for the symmetry and general centering effect afforded by such an arrangement. Further subdivision resulted, albeit in a subtle form, until a "reasonable structural bay of 27 feet" was determined. Throughout this process of fitting structure and circulation and use areas together in plan, the three-dimensional consequences were also explored for the purposes of making necessary adjustments.

The organization of the facades and general external form of the building was pursued next, although to some extent these investigations had been performed concurrently with the studies of structure and circulation. To start with, the elevation was geometrically organized, within a square approximately corresponding to the outline of the plan. A vertical division of one-third for the base and two-thirds for the tower was adopted (figure 10, parts 4 and 5), at least provisionally, as representing the "right" proportions for the building mass. During this process the facility for the electronic media returned, again as a conspicuous (linear) element in the overall composition (figure 10, part 5). It was later relegated to a more minor role, although now its location became fixed on the minor axis through the library facility (see figure 11, part 2). Exploitation of geometrical characteristics, either seen to be inherent in the square building form or deriving from the plan configuration, were finally abandoned as arbitrary. Instead a more straightforward articulation of entrance, reading rooms, and library stacks was adopted (figure 10, part 6).

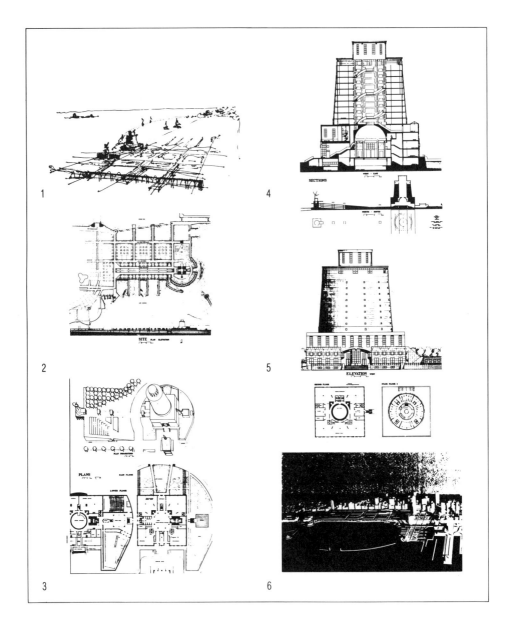

1

4

2

5

3

6

11
Case study no. 3: final drawings.

At this stage a number of sketches were made, as the designers put it, "to examine the overall effect of the proposed scheme" (figure 11, part 1). As a consequence, the theaters, formerly part of the building base, were placed underground, on the pretext that their distinctive shape detracted from the clarity of the overall composition. This placement also allowed the profile of the shoreline to be shaped in a circular manner around the building base (figure 11, part 2).

Finally, the proposal was delineated in more detail, as shown in parts 2 through 6 of figure 11. The earlier concept of a grid pattern extending into the lake returned in the guise of parkland with reserve tracts for later development (figure 11, part 2). The minor axis through the main library building was used to organize the location of the computer facility and the entries to the theaters (figure 11, part 3). The earlier formal and figural preoccupations on the part of the designers are evident in the resulting elevational and sectional treatments (figure 11, parts 4 and 5).

Perhaps the most distinctive feature of the protocol is the attention paid by the designers to the two large themes of creating a focal point, or landmark, and extending the grid pattern of Chicago, in a linear fashion, out into the lake. Throughout, these two themes seem almost to compete with one another. First one dominates, only to recede again as the process unfolds. In the end, design effort was focused on the proposal of a single landmark building, although even then its immediate site environs were clearly controlled by the idea of the grid pattern. An explicit concern with context is another hallmark of the case study. Here homage is paid to Burnham's earlier plan and to the buildings of the Chicago Exposition, as well as the general layout of contemporary Chicago.

Other Accounts

The historical record provides few case studies in similar detail involving well-known designers in action. This is to be expected, given the rather private nature of the activity and the "messy" quality of early speculations when compared to the finished designs. As Robert Venturi remarked on some recent work in progress, "One ought not to watch the sausage being made at the factory" (Holmes 1985).

Still, there are a variety of sources from which we can gain insights into the act of designing that range from spasmodic glimpses to reasonably thorough reconstructions. We have, for instance, autobiographical accounts from major designers that at least provide some outline of situational and experiential factors that have shaped their output. Frank Lloyd Wright's own account of his early years, formative experiences, and preoccupations during various projects is a case in point (Wright 1943). In a less personal vein, designers have offered retrospective analyses of projects on which they worked. At times these are more than rationalizations for the purposes of explaining and justifying a scheme and deal with what really happened—with the inner conflicts inherent in their particular design philosophies. In Suckle's recent *By Their Own Design,* for example, architects openly discuss their process of design and construction (Suckle 1980). We also have public presentations and archival material closely chronicling the design thinking that went into major architectural projects. Finally, we have numerous reconstructions by historians and design critics who have attempted to piece together the designing of various buildings.

● **Le Corbusier's Venice Hospital**

One reasonably complete account of prominent designers in action concerns the scheme by Le Corbusier and Julian de la Fuente for the Venice Hospital (1964–1967). Undoubtedly this thoroughness is the result of the project's having been completed in Le Corbusier's atelier after his untimely death, thus necessitating the explicit documentation of earlier steps and the disentanglement of the web of design ideas. After all, to faithfully pick something up where another has left off requires more than interpretation "in the manner of" that other. It requires substantiation through reconstruction of the prior thinking.

The primary themes for the project are the city of Venice and, secondarily, advances in modern medicine, particularly in the realms of postoperative and outpatient care (Julian de la Fuente 1968). The hospital is viewed less as an instrument for the efficient technical practice and institutional delivery of medicine than as part of the city, where patients and visitors alike can partake in something that, as closely as possible under the circumstances, approximates urban life. Here Le Corbusier is very explicit. When describing the more public realm of the hospital, or what he terms the *calli* and *campielli* (both words are used by Italians particularly to describe features of Venice: the narrow streets and the small squares, respectively), he states that they not only are "places . . . for circulation but are equipped with all necessary to permit social life of patients." "These spaces," he continues, "are covered and glazed in such a manner that the patient would experience the same feeling that he would have in the city" (Julian de la Fuente 1968, p. 22).

Within this broad and strongly guiding idea, the development of the scheme starts with a number of observations about the city of Venice. "Venice is formed by her plan of water," which is "one of the most favorable sustaining elements for architecture," as shown in figure 12, part 1 (Julian de la Fuente 1968, p. 8). From which Le Corbusier becomes more focused and particular in the orientation of his interpretation. "What is basic in Venice," he states, "is the ordering of natural and artificial circulation, the pedestrian and the gondola. . . . Venice [is] a testimony to functional precision" (Julian de la Fuente 1968, p. 8). Further on he describes a revelation that came to him about this circulation: "The pedestrian ways are amazingly economical, all very efficient. . . . I disentangled the puzzle of the houses, the networks of pedestrians. . . . It is like a cardiac system, pure, perfect in its workings. Nothing is straight . . . the plazas are imposing reservoirs, lakes to accommodate the throngs" (Julian de la Fuente 1968, p. 9). And so the idea for the hospital's circulation and public spaces came into being.

Early developmental sketches reveal that the scheme had another point of departure as well, deriving from the technical accomplishments of modern medicine and health care delivery. To quote from Le Corbusier's report, "The extremely profound and swift evolution of modern medicine, combined with the growing obligation to offer equally modern services to the sick, are two factors, among others, which hasten the obsolescence of existing hosptials" (Julian de la Fuente 1968, p. 20). In particular, Le Corbusier and his collaborators were concerned with the intensive care and accommodation of hospitalized patients as well as with ambulatory and outpatient care and the most appropriate environment for this service.

A three-level hierarchy of spaces and activity areas was fashioned out of the program of uses (figure 12, part 2). At the most fundamental level was the *unité lit,* or "bed unit," sometimes referred to as *la cellule,* "the cell" (Julian de la Fuente 1968, p. 21). This consisted of a private 3-meter by 3-meter space at the disposal of the patient, complete with necessary accommodations, a hanging garden, and the possibility of altering the ambient lighting of the space through the use of colored panels (figure 12, part 3). These *unités lits,* in turn, were arranged into the *unité*

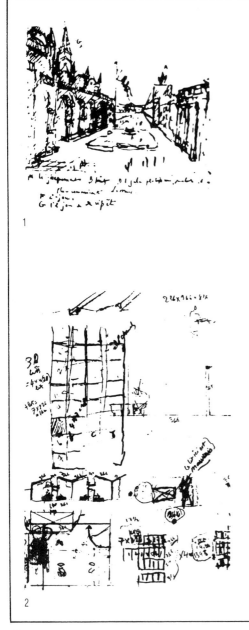

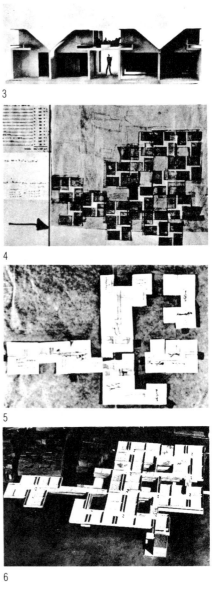

12
Le Corbusier and Julian de la Fuente's Venice
Hospital project—drawings of Venice, plan
developments, and model.

des soins, or the "unit of care." Here 28 patient spaces were organized into a single, relatively independent administrative unit under the supervision of a nursing staff. Finally, the units of care, together with other service functions, were arranged according to the principles of circulation and community spaces described earlier through the use of the *calli* and *campielli.*

In the development stages of the plan, attention seemed to be focused on the basic patient spaces and their arrangement into a coherent unit of care. Consequently the overall disposition of the plan at this stage is regular in its layout (figure 12, part 4). Further on in the process the plan becomes far more differentiated as specific site requirements begin to make their presence felt and as the interpretation of the morphology of Venice comes into play (figure 12, part 5). Instead of having the appearance of happenstance interstitial realms, the public spaces— "the domain of the upright man"—now take on a more positive and consciously arranged pattern (Julian de la Fuente 1968, p. 22). Accommodation is also made for future expansion and functional rearrangement of the facility. The final result is a building complex of considerable spatial variety and systematic order (figure 12, part 6). It is also a facility that appears to blend in with the city, not through superficial imitation but through thorough reckoning with the morphology of surrounding areas, adapted to different institutional purposes.

● **The Use of Analogy**
As we saw in the earlier case study examples, initial design ideas appropriated from outside the immediate context of a specific problem are often highly influential in the making of design proposals. Quite often references are made to objects already within the domain of architecture. On other occasions, however, an analogy is made with objects and organizational concepts that are farther afield and outside architecture. Sometimes these analogies serve a designer's purposes for more than a single project and thus become incorporated as a central part of that individual's design thinking.

In Suckle's anthology, John Johanson candidly provides an account of his basic premises in architectural design (Suckle 1980, pp. 67–77). "I have more recently come to see buildings and building complexes in terms of their parts: that is, individuation," he explains; he goes on to describe, albeit somewhat in caricature, a procedure of "place it [the enclosures], connect it [provide access], and support it [hold it together structurally]." The underlying analogy, which gave substance to the Goddard

Library at Clark University (1968) and the Oklahoma Theater Center (1970), is drawn from the field of electronic circuitry. Johanson observes, "I wanted to borrow the underlying ordering principles and their systematic logic and use them as a model for architectural methodology." The specific relevance of the analogy to architecture is seen to be sustained through the organization of three principle elements: the circuit's chassis, "representing the structural frame"; the circuit components, representing "functional enclosures" in architecture; and the circuiting system, which represents "channels for the circulation of people and mechanical systems."

Setting aside any qualms we might have about the somewhat mechanistic and strictly functional character of this analogy, Johanson does seem to use it in order to address several issues that he sees as important in contemporary building. The first is the need for "direct solutions," for an "economy of means" and an improvisational approach, or what Johanson calls "ad hocism." Here the analogy serves him well. After all, in the design and assembly of electronic circuitry these are among the major design parameters. The second issue is the impermanence, or possible impermanence, of a building's spatial and technical organization. Again the concept of open-ended planning and the provision of facilities is well modeled in the analogy of electronics. Third, there is the question of accommodating the obsolescence of certain parts of a building and the various maintenance and replacement schedules of service components. Here the "plug in and clip on" aspect of the analogy for interchanging and rearranging parts is evident. Finally, there is the modern technological prospect of dynamically changing a building envelope to accommodate different environmental conditions or periodic requirements of use. Again the analogy with electronic circuitry, at least as far as it goes, serves Johanson well. This is a technology that has explicitly incorporated notions of planned adaptation through changes in system configuration and hence function.

● **Big Ideas and Operational Constraints**
Another aspect of design thinking that was evident in the foregoing case studies is the tenacity with which designers will cling to major design ideas and themes in the face of what at times might seem insurmountable odds. Often the concept the designer has in mind can only come to fruition if a large number of apparently countervailing conditions can be surmounted. For instance, a new building technique might have to be invented, as

was the case in Utzon's Sydney Opera House, or antiquated institutional rules and codes might have to be overcome.

Again in Suckle's anthology, Richard Rogers provides a detailed and unabashed account of the give and take that took place between the central design idea and the technical requirements for the well-known Plateau Beaubourg or Centre Pompidou project in Paris (Suckle 1980, pp. 107–121). According to Rogers, the central design idea was the inversion of the traditional notion of facade and the conception of the project as a "flexible container capable of continuously adapting, not only in plan but also in section and elevation, to whatever needs should arise." In short, Plateau Beaubourg was seen as an "inside-out building." To these ends, "Beaubourg [was] constructed completely from prefabricated dry elements [and] becomes in essence a gigantic ever-changing erector set, as opposed to the more common doll's house with its precious, nonadditive, tailor-made detailing and its inherent lack of freedom and choice." Plateau Beaubourg was to be an "architecture of possibilities," in which "flexibility should be communicated by the legibility of [the] building."

An enormous amount of effort had to be invested in order to realize this architecture of possibilities. For instance, within the time allotted for completion of the project it was impossible to "debug the initial idea of moving floors held by friction clamps." Consequently the idea, though theoretically feasible, was abandoned. The prefabricated nature of all building components necessitated advances in building technology in a number of areas, not the least of which was the use of special cast-steel components (geberettes) for the building's frame. Furthermore, the hoped-for use of standardized components added to the necessity for unusual engineering accomplishment. Consistent with the theme of an inside-out building, the decision to expose the mechanical components of the building required a significant realignment of traditional attitudes among architects, engineers, and contractors. The appearance of each component became a paramount consideration, calling for unusual cooperation among all the parties concerned and ultimately for unorthodox methods of fabrication and construction.

As Rogers was to observe, however, "Probably the major flaw in the scheme lay in our inability to develop a new technique for fireproofing structural steel. . . . We actually believed that we would make a major breakthrough and find a system of making the steel itself incombustible without resorting to the considerable expenditure of creative effort required in the search of elegant ways to ad hoc fireproofing. It didn't happen." Instead, the codes and practices of Parisian bureaucracy prevailed. In order to bring the building within range of firemen's ladders, it was reduced in height by some 19 meters. Further, the allowable fire compartment size required modifications to the layout of interior spaces. Finally, a design principle of "separate and extinguish" was invoked, whereby individual components were fireproofed. For example, trussed beams of steel were wrapped in a blanket of fibrous material and further encased in stainless steel in order to achieve the required rating. Indeed, the visual effect of almost every element in the building had to be thoroughly considered from this perspective.

Quite apart from its unusual and perhaps visionary appearance, Plateau Beaubourg stands as a testament both to the design team's original ideal and to their technical and administrative prowess. "It is impossible," pronounced Rogers, "to divorce the building from its legal, technical, political, and economic context. At the same time, a major part of any design approach is the way constraints may be absorbed and whenever possible inverted into positive elements."

Observations and Questions about the Protocols

From these cases and others that have been documented (Consortium of East Coast Schools of Architecture 1981, Schön 1983, Schön 1984), several observations can be made about the nature of design thinking. To begin with, it is apparent that the unfolding of the design process assumes a distinctly episodic structure, which we might characterize as a series of related skirmishes with various aspects of the problem at hand. Usually the results of these investigations cohere into a more singular direction for the design activity, although not necessarily as a linear progression of reasoning.

This episodic structure manifests itself in a number of ways. First, there is the "to and fro" movement between areas of concern—a movement perceived at the time by the designers in our three case studies. In all three protocols there was movement back and forth between exploration of architectural form and evaluations of program, structure, and other technical issues. Second, there seem to be periods of unfettered speculation, followed by more sober and contemplative episodes during which the designer "takes stock of the situation." Third, each episode seems to have a particular orientation that preoccupies the designer. We might say that the organizing principles involved in each episode take on a life of their own, as the designer becomes absorbed in exploring the possibilities that they promise. Here a "dialogue" between the designer and the situation is evident (Schön 1983, ch. 3). In our case studies these episodes, such as the various massing exercises with building volumes, often became very speculative as the designer "pressed on," as it were, when information from another quarter might have resolved the problem at hand more economically. Such situations often subsequently gave rise to a certain amount of backtracking, as the designer retrenched to what seemed a more advantageous position. Finally, as the scope of the problem became more determined and finite for the designer, the episodic character of the process seems to have become less pronounced. During this period a systematic working out of issues and conditions took hold within the framework that had been established. This phenomenon is not at all surprising when we consider the fundamental difference between moments of problem solving when matters are poorly defined and those with clarity and sufficiency of structure.

These observations raise questions about the inherent structure of the episodes, the kind of information that is being included, and its relationship to the procedures being employed. They also raise questions about the manner and means by which one episode gives way to another. These episodes are not happenstance events. They possess an interior logic that seems determined partly by the subject matter at hand and partly by the organizational procedures being used. They also have a consequential connection with one another. Without such logic and closure among episodes the emergence of design proposals would be difficult to imagine.

Within the episodic structure of the process, the problem, as perceived by the designer, tends to fluctuate from being rather nebulous to being more specific and well defined. Furthermore, moments of "blinding" followed by periods of backtracking take place, where blinding refers to conditions in which obvious connections between various considerations of importance go unrecognized by a designer (Newell, Shaw, and Simon 1967, pp. 107–108). Sometimes this characteristic seems to have a great deal to do with the manner in which a designer represents the problem at hand. For example, in the second case study the designer was preoccupied at one moment with making a formal arrangement of the building elements in plan and then suddenly realized that one of the elements was a very large structure and not at all in keeping with the plan concept. To remedy such a situation, designers invariably seem to return to an earlier point of departure—they backtrack. We saw this in the third protocol when the designers pursued the linear plan form of the complex to what they regarded as an illogical conclusion and then turned back to considering the buildings as a more concentrated formal composition.

By contrast, during moments of clear problem definition more straightforward procedures are used. For example, in our case studies there were episodes in which variations of a particular organizing principle were systematically explored, immediately followed by an evaluation of their relative success or appropriateness. On other occasions, although the desired result was clear, the precise means for achieving that end remained a matter for consideration. When difficulties were encountered, designers resorted to various forms of reconsideration, although rarely did they attempt to break down the conditions at hand into their basic components.

Having observed these phenomena, can we identify and define certain generic problem-solving procedures? Are these procedures exclusive to design, or can they also be ascribed to other forms of creative problem-solving activity? Consider the dominant influence that is exerted by initial design ideas on subsequent problem-solving directions—another prominent feature revealed by the protocols. Designers inevitably bring certain organizing principles to a problem at the outset. Even when severe problems are encountered, a considerable effort is made to make the initial idea work, rather than to stand back and adopt a fresh point of departure. In the third case study, on the site in Chicago, this phenomenon was particularly evident in the persistent competition that took place between the two underlying design themes. We can also see some very real distortions of otherwise systematic procedures in these attempts to adhere to the "big idea." For example, there were the instances of designers seeming to cram the building program into the architectural object that they were shaping, and the attempts to conform otherwise straightforward structural systems to architectural intentions about movement and entrance. Sometimes it was as if the inherent relational structure of subproblems took on an entirely malleable quality in the face of other design prejudices. The persistence and technical virtuosity with which Rogers approached the Pompidou Center also had these hallmarks.

Clearly a distinction can be made between the constraints and opportunities that are found in the problem conditions as given and the *enabling prejudices*[2] that designers bring to bear on the situation. Moreover, the protocols discussed in this chapter showed interpretation of the context solely as given to be exercising a subordinate influence over decision making, compared to ideas and references supplied by the designers from elsewhere. This phenomenon was particularly evident during the early stages of the projects, as the designers searched for concepts around which to construct frameworks for reinterpreting the design problem. These concepts or hunches were to provide insight and direction for further information processing.

What, we must ask next, is the source of these design ideas? Why is it that ideas from outside the immediate problem context are so influential? Without a doubt design is to be seen as a normative enterprise; the resulting proposals are about what is proper. Even if the presence of such normative reasoning is clear, however, its role and character remain vague. What qualities should we look for in a normative position about architecture, and how might we adjudicate among positions that compete for our attention? In addition, what is the structure of the interplay between normative design ideas and procedural aspects of design thinking?

Finally, it should be noted that the "style" of the completed projects seems to have been determined primarily by two factors. First, there was the sustained influence of initial design ideas in the form of organizing principles, rules, and references. Second, there was the influence exerted by the particular structure of the problem-solving process itself. In this latter regard, the sequence in which design principles were applied seems to have mattered the most. Contrary to some earlier accounts by so-called design methodologists, the kind of theory we need if we are to explain what is going on when we design must go beyond matters of procedure. We need to move directly into the realm of normative discourse about what constitutes architecture and urban design in order to clarify both the inherent nature of the enterprise and the direction in which procedures are inclined. Futhermore, we need to ask how this discourse is shaped and what frames of reference are appropriated in its shaping. Definitions of problem-solving procedures are not enough. We must also explore what we can say about the service in which these procedures are placed.

Procedural Aspects of Design Thinking

Beneath the surface irregularities of designers' modes of operation, common information-handling procedures can be identified. Furthermore, theoretical developments in cognitively based interpretations of creative problem solving have provided us with tools for analyzing such procedures (Hayes 1978, Hunt 1982). In spite of variation, these interpretations all seek to explain creative problem solving under the conditions of bounded rationality that are characteristic of design. Here bounded rationality refers to the concept that human problem solvers are rarely in a position to identify all possible solutions to the problem at hand and therefore settle for choices that seem to satisfy the required solution properties of a problem, as they see them at the time. Generally, they make decisions that might otherwise be seen as suboptimal, or what Simon refers to as "satisficing" (Simon 1957; Simon 1969, pp. 64–76; Simon 1979, p. 3). This condition certainly holds for most design exercises, at least of the kind involving invention and novelty, with which we have a primary interest. As we shall see in more detail later on, the latter are invariably problems whose solutions are neither strictly true nor false.

Before continuing, it is well to address a point that usually arises as soon as the so-called creative aspect of design is introduced into a discussion of problem solving. After all, some might maintain, design is much more than mere problem solving. The veracity of this observation, however, clearly depends on our understanding of the word *problem.* To paraphrase Thorndike's venerable definition, a problem can be said to exist if an organism wants something but the actions necessary to obtain it are not immediately obvious (Thorndike 1931). It is hard to imagine circumstances under which the impetus for design is not covered by this definition, which subsumes both problems that are predefined and placed at our doorstep and those that are brought into our consciousness *de novo,* requiring definition and redefinition.

Some General Characteristics of Design Problems

In the world of design problems, a distinction can be made between those that are *well defined* and those that are *ill defined.* In the latter category further distinctions can be drawn, resulting in the subclass *wicked problems* (Churchman 1967).

● Well-Defined Problems

Well-defined problems are those for which the ends, or goals, are already prescribed and apparent; their solution requires the provision of appropriate means (Newell, Shaw, and Simon 1967, p. 70). Rittel, who refers to this class of problems as "tame," states that they can be "exhaustively formulated . . . and solved by a knowledgeable man without the need for further information" (Rittel 1972, p. 392). A common example is the solution of two algebraic equations with two unknown values. Here the aim of the exercise is to find the values for x and y, or some other similar designation of variables. The solution requires application of the rules of algebra to the specific equation structure that is given.

This class of problems can be specified under the rubric "Given a set P of elements, find a subset S of P having specified properties" (Newell, Shaw, and Simon 1967, p. 70). Other common and not-so-common examples of this class are crossword puzzles, finding the combinations to safes, and making moves in checkers and chess. In architecture and urban design the class would include the *space-planning problem,* in which a set of building spaces is prescribed, together with a site in which they are to be assembled and some expression of adjacency requirements among the spaces. Here, the problem can be formally expressed by letting P represent all possible combinations of building spaces, $s_1, \ldots, s_n,$ with a subset S of combinations that satisfy the adjacency requirements, $A(s_i,s_j)$. The object is to find a satisfactory combination, S. Other problems, such as those involving the compositional arrangement of building elements in design or the allocation of natural resources in planning, may also have sufficient clarity in their goals to be formulated in a similar manner. It should be understood, however, that when actually confronting even these problems designers must define and redefine them in a manner that is sufficient for the proposal of a solution.

● Ill-Defined Problems

For ill-defined problems, on the other hand, both the ends and the means of solution are unknown at the outset of the problem-solving exercise, at least in their entirety (Newell, Shaw, and Simon 1967, p. 71; Bazjanac 1974, p. 8). Most architecture and urban design problems are of this type. A client or a citizen group comes to the designer with the desire to build a house or improve the quality of a neighborhood. Although the general thrust of the problem may be clear, considerable time and effort are usually spent with the client in order to clarify what is required. A large part of the problem-solving activity, then, consists of problem definition and redefinition.

● Wicked Problems

Many design problems are so ill-defined that they can only be called wicked problems (Churchman 1967, Rittel 1972, Bazjanac 1974). This class has, among others, the following characteristics that are most pertinent to our discussion. First, they are problems without a definitive formulation, or indeed the very possibility of becoming fully defined. Additional questions can always be asked, leading to continual reformulation. Second, as a corollary to this first characteristic, they are problems with no explicit basis for the termination of problem-solving activity—no *stopping rule.* Any time a solution is proposed, it can, at least to some significant extent, be developed still further. Third, differing formulations of the problems of this class imply differing solutions, and vice versa. In other words, the problem's formulation depends on a preconception that, in turn, implies a definite direction toward the problem's solution. Finally, solutions that are proposed are not necessarily correct or incorrect. Plausible alternative solutions can always be provided. This characteristic follows logically from the first property—the impossibility of definitive formulation. Reformulation can take place beyond the realm of considerations within which the original proposals were made, thereby opening up avenues of approach to other solutions.[1]

Such distinctions were not always a part of our understanding of problem-solving activity. In fact, as we shall see, earlier theories made few if any references to the kinds of problems confronting designers.

Early Theoretical Positions

Without venturing too far back into history, two distinct themes can be seen at work in the development of theory about problem solving. Beginning toward the end of the nineteenth century with associationism, a mechanistic type of doctrine can be observed to recur that sought to explain problem-solving behavior through the use of irreducible lawlike relationships deemed to govern mental processes. By contrast, other efforts were made to explain problem solving in more behavioral and nonmentalistic terms.

● Associationism

At the turn of the century associationism was the prevailing doctrine in most quarters concerned with theoretical speculation about problem solving. It held that the sole mechanism of human learning consisted in the permanent association of impressions that had been repeatedly presented to the senses in combination.[2] The associationist view of creative problem solving was both atomistic and mechanistic. It was atomistic in the sense that it postulated that ideas took the form of elements, analogous to basic physical entities, and that these elements were hooked together to form thoughts or insights about problems. It was mechanistic in the sense that simple laws of contiguity, again based on models of atomic structure in the physical world, were used to account for the association of elements— ideas—to form thoughts (Newell, Shaw, and Simon 1957).

Under the doctrine, creative problem solving was seen to proceed as a stream of associations, where each association produced successive new attachments and thus new insights about problems. The source of these new associations, or attachments, was experience of the environment external to the mind. The doctrine thus embodied an empiricist view of the mind as a tabula rasa upon which experience was recorded.[3] In the final analysis, creativity was seen to be largely a matter of happenstance, a random kind of event.

Around 1900 a controversy developed between two opposing camps of experimental psychologists (Boring 1950, chs. 17–19). On one side were the adherents of many of the basic tenets of associationism, such as Wilhelm Wundt, who maintained that mental images, sensations, and feelings were a necessary part of understanding and learning.[4] For instance, after its introduction into our language a word will call up a picture in the mind of what it stands for. Having this image is what understanding the word amounts to (Bloor 1983, pp. 7–10). On the other side were those, like the Austrian Brentano, who maintained a psychological theory that stressed the role of mental acts such as intending and focusing attention. For them a word, to use the same example, has meaning not because it is accompanied by a mental image but because it is accompanied by a mental act (Bloor 1983, p. 9).

● The Würzburg School

During the first decade of this century, speculation from the Würzburg School in southern Germany, principally under Kulpe, Ach, and Bühler, began to replace the doctrine of associationism (Humphrey 1963, chs. 3–4). Although originally followers of Wundt, this group, using extended introspective methods, produced results that suggested that subjects given complex tasks such as translation, mental arithmetic, and problem solving arrived at answers without any accompanying imagery or other sensations. Thus they tended to side with Brentano and the "act theorists."[5]

From these findings a number of new and useful concepts emerged. Instead of the association of ideas, the *Aufgabe* ("task" and hence "determining tendency") was seen to be the controlling mechanism in problem-solving behavior (Humphrey 1963). Here a task gave direction to thought, especially in problem-solving situations. Creative problem solving was thus regarded as essentially purposeful and, therefore, controlled in a manner that was far more circumscribed than by pure chance.

Another major technical contribution of the Würzburg School was the use of systematic introspection as a means for describing problem-solving behavior. Subjects were asked to reconstruct their sequence of thoughts during some problem-solving exercise, while the experience remained fresh in their memories. This kind of approach toward data gathering gained wide adherence during subsequent technical developments of the field.

● **The Gestalt Movement**
The Gestalt movement in psychology, beginning in the 1920s with the work of Köhler, Koffka, Wertheimer, and others, has made a wide variety of contributions to our understanding of human thinking, not the least of which is their celebrated work on visual perception (Köhler 1929, Koffka 1935, Wertheimer 1945). In the specific realm of our interest, proponents of the movement rejected the mechanistic doctrine of associationism, although they maintained the central value of phenomenal observation of environmental stimuli in explaining problem-solving behavior. An idea of holistic principles for organizing information, embodied in the concept *Gestalten,* replaced the discrete mechanistic view of prior positions.

Speculation and experimentation within the Gestalt movement also extended the Würzburg School's idea that creative problem solving was directed behavior: from the notion of the *Aufgabe* developed the notion of the *set,* or what became more loosely referred to as the *mind set* of the problem solver in confronting a task. Clearly, this extension moved the controlling influence on the mental processes associated with problem-solving behavior beyond a singular focus on the task at hand by admitting other kinds of influences, say from related experiences, that were generally less intrinsic to the particular task situation.

A logical progression of this concept was the mechanism of the *schemata,* or organizational frameworks for structuring information. In the case of visual perception, these frameworks were overlaid on external visual stimuli, vastly facilitating the organization of these sense data into meaningful information about the source of the stimuli, namely the object being perceived. Among others, Bartlett sought to explain creative thinking in terms of the idea of schemata, suggesting that there are certain fixed arrangements within the brain, strongly associated with past responses to general types of stimuli or cognitive experiences (Bartlett 1961, Broadbent 1966). To Bartlett, imagination, or creative insight into a problem, consisted of free construction on these fixed arrangements or schemata. Once again we can see that the associationists' reliance on random mechanisms was largely rejected and that the Würzburg School's concept of *Aufgabe* was generalized into the realm of prior experience. We can also see that this position remains fundamentally mechanistic and mentalistic in its doctrine.

● **Behaviorism**

The behaviorist position began as a reaction to what proponents termed the mentalism of earlier doctrines. It was a fundamental rejection of all attempts to study inner mental processes in which distinctions were made between a concept of mind and a concept of body. Instead, the behaviorists postulated that human behavior, including problem solving, could only be adequately explained in nonmentalistic, concrete terms. By concrete terms they meant observable, measurable, and replicable patterns of physical behavior.

Investigations within the position quickly gave rise to the now familiar stimulus-response, or S-R, models of behavior, founded on the assumption that given a particular external stimulus, one could predict a certain response with complete assurance. From the standpoint of the working methods of the behaviorists, mental processes didn't matter. Questions of the "mind" were irrelevant. Behaviorism consequently rejected the Würzburg School's use of introspection as unstable and thus suspect, although adherents were strongly wedded to the use of experimental techniques. Instead, they embarked upon a far-reaching program of correlating environmental stimuli with what they could document as consistent patterns of behavioral response.

The position took strong hold in psychology and related disciplines, especially in the United States after Watson returned from Europe in 1913, bringing the central ideas out of the laboratories of Pavlov and the like (Watson 1930 [1924]). The movement reached its apogee in the work of Skinner during the 1930s and 1940s and became generalized, even popularized, into the idea that behavioral malfunctions and pathologies could be cured by appropriate environmental modification (Skinner 1953).

In the more specific realm of problem-solving theory, the behaviorist position gave rise to, or certainly supported, the development of *phase,* or *rigid-state,* models of creative problem-solving behavior (Arieti 1976, ch. 2; Ghiselin 1952; Gregory 1966). Such behavior was widely acknowledged as conforming to an episodic process consisting of distinct and almost discontinuous phases of activity. The aim behind the models was to identify and describe each phase and the sequence of phases.

Although a number of variations were developed, each model in one way or another incorporated four fundamental steps, or discriminable phases of activity.[6] They were (1) preparation for the task or situation at hand, (2) incubation, (3) illumination or inspiration, and (4) verification, involving the testing of proposed solutions. In the structure of the models the illumination phase occurs when the problem solver becomes aware of a potential solution to a problem. Such awareness can arise as a sudden intuition, a flash of insight—the so-called "Eureka!" phenomenon. It can also transpire as a result of sustained efforts at exploration involving the more systematic pursuit of various hunches. Furthermore, the awareness of a solution may not be complete; sometimes it is merely a glimmer from a propitious direction in which a more fully developed solution might be sought. The incubation phase of activity was usually defined simply as the period of preparation for illumination. It is the stage in which thoughts about the situation or task are allowed comparatively free rein. Clearly, the steps in the process could be repeated until all aspects of the problem at hand were addressed. Within the models' structure, however, the progressive relationship among the steps remained immutable.

This general view of problem-solving activity dominated the literature in the field, at least within the United States, for several decades, roughly until the end of the 1950s. We can see that the theoretical enterprise was strongly based on the observation of human behavior. There was no attempt to venture into the realm of mental processes. In fact, as mentioned earlier, the very possibility of making such an excursion was antithetical to the behaviorist doctrine.

At the same time there were, of course, some exceptions to this position. Koestler's speculations about creative thinking arising from the "bisociation of two mutually incompatible contexts" hark back to the Gestaltist idea of schemata. To summarize Koestler's view: (1) normal thought proceeds within a frame of reference, associative context, or type of logic; (2) in normal personal dealings we operate within many such frames of reference, but only one at a time; and (3) creating involves relating two normally independent frames of reference, or in Koestler's terms the "bisociation of matrices" (Koestler 1964, Perkins 1981).[7] Bruner's use of "puzzle forms" in attempting to explain problem-solving behavior has similar hallmarks. Here the problem solver, when confronted with a new and yet unsolved problem, overlays the structure of the unsolved problem with an apparently similar problem with which he or she is experienced (Bruner 1961; Bruner, Goodnow, and Austin 1967). Finally, Gordon's "synectic theory" and its associated techniques for attempting to enhance creativity by "making the strange familiar and the familiar strange" are also principally based on the use of analogy. In certain other respects, however, his position generally acknowledged a phased, episodic structure for creative behavior (Gordon 1961).

Staged-Process Models of Problem Solving in Design

In explorations that seem to have drawn heavily on rigid-state models from the behaviorist doctrine, a number of significant contributions were made that are pertinent to design. During the late 1950s and the 1960s, attempts were made to describe the creative problem-solving process at work in design by way of the logical structure of overt activities that appears to take place. In other words, design was regarded as a series of stages characterized by dominant forms of activity, such as analysis, synthesis, evaluation, and so on.

Evidence of this kind of concept about design can also be found within the tradition of architecture in the form of project organization and pedagogical doctrines that evolved in the ateliers of the Ecole des Beaux Arts and the Ecole Polytechnique during the eighteenth and nineteenth centuries (Egber 1980, Carlhian

1979). Here a rigidly formalized staging of work activities was imposed on the students by their masters during the conduct of an *esquisse*. In the teachings of Blondel this sequence took the form of a systematic reading and interpretation of the program, followed by exploration of ways in which the program could be met, culminating in a *parti*. Subsequent phases were directed toward elaboration and detailed presentation of this *parti* in plan, section, and elevation. Throughout, each episode of activity was carefully monitored. For our purposes, however, the work of Morris Asimow, an industrial engineer prominent during the 1950s and 1960s, will serve to introduce and illustrate the theoretical contributions of this kind.

● Asimow's Model

In a text entitled *Introduction to Design,* Asimow distinguished two structures in the design process: a vertical structure involving a sequential phasing of activities, and a horizontal structure in the form of a decision-making cycle common to all phases (Asimow 1962). The chronological sequence of steps, or phases, in the vertical structure proceeded from a definition of need, through feasibility study, preliminary design, detailed design, production planning, and finally production itself. Furthermore, within each design phase there was a sequence: preparation for design, design of subsystems, and so on. Overall, the general process, or sequence of activities, was seen by Asimow to advance from abstract considerations to those that are more concrete and particular. Numerous *feedback loops*—relationships between phases along which information about the design situation was seen to flow—were incorporated to account for the observable tracing back through the process in order to respond to new information or difficulties.

Asimow represented the horizontal sequence as a cycle that began with analysis and proceeded through synthesis and evaluation to communication (Asimow 1962, ch. 3). He saw this cycle as repetitious, or iterative, both within and between the various phases of activity. Parenthetically, Asimow's speculation about the structure of design activity is roughly congruent with the "iconic model" proposed in various forms by Mesarovic and others, as shown in figure 13 (Watts 1966, Mesarovic 1964). Throughout this kind of account runs the assumption that it is possible to discriminate distinct phases of activity and, furthermore, that such distinctions have relevance to our understanding of design. Here we can see the influence of behaviorist doctrine. In addition, the account exhibits a strongly deterministic posture. The very maintenance of distinct phases of activity,

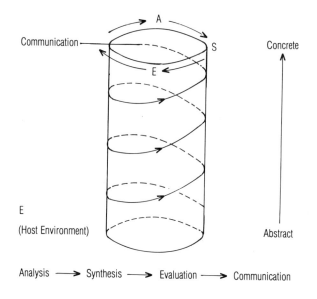

Communication

A
S
E

Concrete
↑

E
(Host Environment)

Abstract

Analysis ⟶ Synthesis ⟶ Evaluation ⟶ Communication

13
An iconic model of a design process.

with a beginning and an end, and with feedback loops among them, requires that objective performance criteria can be explicitly stated in a manner that fundamentally guides the procedure. Moreover, there is a strong implication that the eventual synthesis of information in the form of some designed object follows in a straightforward fashion from an analysis of the problem at hand together with likely performance criteria. Therefore, once a problem has been defined, its solution is made directly accessible in terms of that definition. In many ways this is also a prevalent view in "operations-research" circles, in which problem-solving activity is defined through the application of technical procedures, largely of a mathematical kind, that have been developed to solve general classes of problems.

● **Models of the Hochschule für Gestaltung at Ulm, Archer, and Others**
Similar propositions were advanced during the late 1950s and early 1960s by designers and theoreticians at the Hochschule für Gestaltung at Ulm in southern Germany (Maldonado and Bonsiepe 1964). In the work of Hans Gugelot, Tomas Maldonado, and others, various staged-process models of design were proposed and used as a basis for design education and product designs for clients like Lufthansa and Braun (Maldonado 1972, Broadbent 1973, ch. 13). Furthermore, here such speculation moved beyond description and explanation of design behavior

into the realm of idealization. Not only was the possibility of a "scientific" and totally objective approach toward design seriously entertained, it became a goal in itself. A confident sense of rational determinism prevailed; the whole process of design, it was believed, could be clearly and explicitly stated, relevant data gathered, parameters established, and an ideal artifact produced.

Advocates of the position were also very mindful of the social and political consequences of such an enterprise in allowing the esoteric and, to them, heretofore subjective realm of design to be emancipated and made accessible to many. The Ulmers' experiment proved short-lived, however: as Frampton's account makes clear, unsuccessful reckonings with both the technical and the sociopolitical issues involved in their approach conspired to force members of the Hochschule to disband the institution on the nineteenth of February 1968 (Frampton 1974).

Bruce Archer, an industrial designer from the Hochschule für Gestaltung at Ulm and the Royal College of Art in London, also proposed an "operational" model of design, although in slightly different terms (Archer 1963–1964). In a simplified form, Archer's model is schematically represented by figure 14. Here again design is seen as a sequence of activities defined by their orientation and by the general type of task involved. Whether intentional or not, strains of *Aufgabe* can be discerned. Furthermore, the process can be described in a general form, irrespective of particular circumstances. Feedback loops, or relationships between activities, are more in evidence than in preceding models, with the result that the staging of activities is perhaps less discretely defined. With the enumeration of three interrelated realms for the process, namely external representation, process of activities, and the problem solver, a distinction begins to be made between overt behavior and the cognitive realm—a departure from the behaviorist position. The emphasis, however, is still on the sequence of activities and on the behavioral realm.

Among similar proposals by other designers and theoreticians, the work of Denis Thornley at the University of Manchester deserves mention. His model, which clarifies the design process for educational purposes, was incorporated among the professional practices of the Royal Institute of British Architects (Thornley 1963).

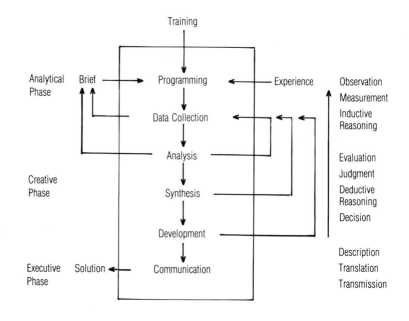

Training

Analytical Phase	Brief →	Programming ←	← Experience	Observation
				Measurement
		Data Collection ←	← ←	Inductive Reasoning
		Analysis —		Evaluation
Creative Phase		Synthesis —		Judgment
				Deductive Reasoning
				Decision
		Development —		
				Description
Executive Phase	Solution ←	Communication		Translation
				Transmission

14
Archer's model of the stages of a design process.

The Information Processing Theory of Problem Solving

From about the 1930s onward, there accumulated a body of experimental evidence that behaviorists found increasingly difficult to explain (Hunt 1982). For example, results from maze experiments involving rats and other animals—a popular empirical technique of the behaviorists for testing the stimulus-response mechanism—suggested that the animal subject paused at the choice points along the maze's pathways before making decisions about which way to travel. Under the behaviorist paradigm, the animals' conditioning should have led to a straightforward, uninterrupted traverse through the maze. It was concluded by Tolman and other experimenters that the subjects were going through a vicarious process of trial and error as they attempted to traverse the maze; they must, therefore, hold a mental map or picture of the maze (Tolman 1938, Hunt 1982). This finding seemed to call for a cognitively based explanation rather than one that was purely behavioral.

Questions also arose with reference to the phase or staged-process models. What is it about a definite progression of activities that automatically results in a specific, further activity? Through what mechanism or means do we advance from analysis to synthesis? How is it that unique solutions are often rendered to problems, when the information processing that takes place seems so straightforward? As far as they go, staged-process models do illuminate certain commonly observable features of design activity; yet the illumination is at a comparatively low level.

In 1957 Newell, Shaw, and Simon published a paper entitled "Elements of a Theory of Problem Solving" that ushered in quite a different line of explanation. This position quickly became known as the *information processing theory* of problem solving (Newell, Shaw, and Simon 1957, 1967). Instead of regarding the cognitive realm as eluding analysis and therefore irrelevant, proponents of the new theoretical perspective sought to explain problem-solving behavior by way of basic information processes. They maintained that an adequate explanation of observed human behavior can be provided by a "program" of primitive information processes that account for the cognition associated with an action. In other words, the primacy of essentially cognitive processes in explaining problem-solving behavior was reasserted.

The research agenda of this theoretical position was the description and analysis of human cognitive processes, with the aim of explaining a wide variety of observable activities, including creative problem solving (Hayes 1978, Newell and Simon 1972, Simon 1979). Proponents couched their explanations in terms of a small, finite number of basic mechanisms for processing information, mechanisms that could be grouped or arranged into strategies, or programs in the computer sense, that allowed complex problems to be solved. Considerable emphasis was also placed on experimental evidence gained from the analysis of step-by-step narrations, or protocols, provided by problem solvers about their own behavior (Hayes 1981, pp. 51–57).

● **Postulates and Directions**

The following postulates emerged from Newell, Shaw, and Simon's early work and became central to the information processing position (Newell, Shaw, and Simon 1967, pp. 63–75). First, there is a *problem space* whose elements are *knowledge states,* some of which represent solutions to a problem. Second, there are one or more *generative processes,* or operations, that allow one to take knowledge states as input, or as starting positions, and produce new knowledge states as output. In other words, the problem space, composed of knowledge states, is transformed during the course of problem-solving events. Third, there are one or more *test procedures* that allow the problem solver to compare those knowledge states that are presumed to incorporate solution properties with a specification of the solution state that is not the knowledge state itself. Test procedures are also assumed to exist for comparing parts of knowledge states to detect differences among them. Finally, there are further processes enabling a problem solver to decide which generative processes and which test procedures to employ, on the basis of the information contained in available knowledge states.

Perhaps these postulates will become clearer when connected to the following general definition of a problem (Newell, Shaw, and Simon 1967, p. 70): "Given a set P of elements, find a subset S of P, having specified properties." Here the elements of both P and S are knowledge states, and their arrangement in P represents the problem space. Finding subset S among P is thus a matter of moving, by way of generating potential solutions, from one knowledge state to another, until one having the specified properties is found or developed. Throughout this procedure the direction of search is governed by information gained from comparison of the properties of some knowledge state S_i to those of S and by the use of this information in making a selection from among a range of potential generative processes.

A commonplace example can be found in the manner in which we solve word-arithmetic problems of the type "John is twenty-four years old. His brother was half his age fourteen years ago. How old is his brother?" Here the generative processes are essentially algebraic, allowing symbols representing substantive aspects of the problem to manipulated and transposed according to acceptable rules or practices (Eastman 1969). Test procedures, in the form of questions about relationships among various aspects of a problem under consideration, allow progress toward a solution to be ascertained. Particular sequences and specific choices from among the generative processes and evaluative procedures that are available to a problem solver are also important, for they represent the overriding means by which a solution can be sought. In the course of post-hoc analysis, they also allow particular approaches to be distinguished, even for relatively simple problems. As we are well aware from everyday experience, essentially the same solution to a problem may be arrived at from a number of directions involving a variety of means. Other commonplace examples can be found in doing

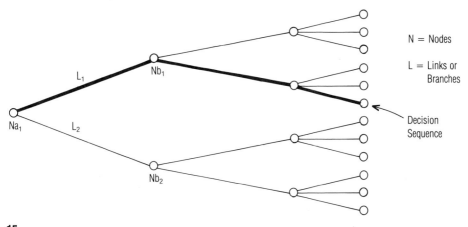

N = Nodes

L = Links or Branches

Decision Sequence

15
A general diagram of a decision tree.

crossword puzzles, arranging furniture in a room, and even such extemporaneous exercises as cooking.

Formal representation of problem space and of knowledge states is often achieved through the device of a *decision tree,* through which a search for a solution is conducted. In figure 15 the nodes Na_1, Nb_1, Nb_2, and so on, represent points at which decisions must be made, or *decision points,* and the links L_1, L_2, and so on, represent *branches*—the courses of action associated with different outcomes at each decision point. A particular problem-solving approach, or protocol, is thus specified by a particular sequence of nodes and links beginning on the left-hand side of the tree and moving toward the right-hand side.

A simple example from the field of transportation planning will serve to illustrate this conceptual scheme. Consider the various choices involved when we contemplate making a trip to work with the aim of saving time and expense. First, we may decide whether or not to go to work at all, although presumably our state of health, the traffic conditions, or some other fundamental aspect of the trip would have to be very poor indeed to prompt a negative outcome. Second, with the approval of our employer, we may decide whether or not to travel during the "peak hour." Third, depending on a variety of factors such as the availability of vehicles and of mass-transit service, relative cost, and waiting times, we may choose to take our car, travel with a friend, take a bus, or walk to work. Finally, again within the means available to us, we may choose one route over others. Using a decision tree, the choices associated with a trip to work can be arrayed as

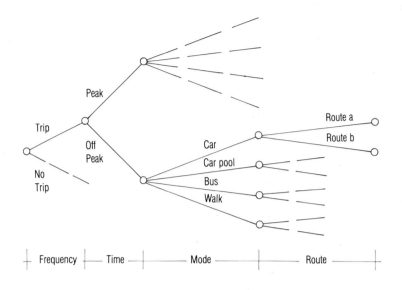

16

A decision tree of typical transportation choices.

shown in figure 16. The possibilities among the general classes of decision about frequency, time of day, mode of travel, and route of travel may be represented by as many as 12 nodes, or decision points, and 28 branches, or courses of action. Clearly the comparative advantages—measured, say, in terms of time and expense—for each combination of the available courses of action could be computed, and the one or ones that meet the criterion of minimizing time and expense could be identified. It is also apparent that when we make this kind of decision in actual practice we seldom, if ever, systematically evaluate the outcomes of all possible decision sequences. Rather, we choose combinations that are habitual, seem to offer satisfactory results, or perhaps seem to involve the least amount of risk. Furthermore, we might combine the decision components (frequency, time, mode, route) in a different order from the one represented here, say from initiation with what appears to us to be the most critical (for instance, availabililty of modes of transportation), and never really move beyond this node of the tree in our practical decision making. In other words, having once decided whether to take a car or a bus, we become largely indifferent to other aspects of the work trip. What has transpired is the application of a simplifying assumption that makes the decision process more tractable.

It should also be clear from the form of extensive representation offered by the decision tree that many ordinary tasks (such as seating people appropriately for a dinner party) may turn out to be fairly complex, requiring to be tackled in a piecemeal, step-by-step fashion rather than at a single stroke. Certainly more complex and specialized tasks, such as finding the optimal arrangement of departments in a large hospital complex, require concentrated effort and a stepwise progression through a problem space.

Considerable psychological evidence would seem to support this kind of observation and its explanation under the information processing theory. For instance, the well-documented limits on short-term-memory—the kind of memory that handles data associated with immediate recall in connection with a particular task—are placed at between 4 and 11 "chunks" of information (Miller 1956, Simon 1979).[8] Because the capacity of our short-term memory is so circumscribed, complex problem-solving activities requiring extended attention are likely to be performed in a serial fashion. Combinations of basic procedures that allow the generation of information and the assessment of progress toward a solution are applied in a directed manner, as a sequence of events rather than as a single episode or experience.

Currently, the information processing theory is the dominant school of thought about creative problem solving. As mentioned earlier, experimental research is usually conducted through the use of elaborate protocol analyses in which subjects engaged in a problem-solving task faithfully narrate, or otherwise communicate, what they are doing as they work through a problem. Unlike the introspection of the Würzburg School, the procedures are immediate, generally replicable, and external in their mode of operation. The results from these experiments are then carefully examined to discern which fundamental information-processing mechanisms appear to be involved. Often computer programs are devised that incorporate these mechanisms and allow solution of the same class of problem in a manner that is indistinguishable from that of human subjects. In a very real sense, these computer programs represent the theory and become building blocks in the advancement of the theoretical position.

A number of architectural researchers concerned with the design process have become involved with this kind of activity, or at least in this line of speculation. The information processing theory has also provided a basis for contemporary work in computer-aided architectural design, particularly for attempts to develop "complete and hospitable design environments." Here the work of Negroponte, Mitchell, and Eastman provides clear examples (Negroponte 1970, 1972, 1974; Mitchell 1977; Eastman 1975).

● Problem-Solving Behavior

Problem-solving behavior can be divided into three subclasses of activity. The first, the representation of the problem through structuring and restructuring a problem space, is known as the *problem representation problem*. The second, the generation of solutions, is termed the *solution generation problem*. The third, the evaluation of candidate solutions, is known as the *solution evaluation problem*. Those who study problem-solving behavior generally make comparisons among problem solvers according to differences in their methods of problem representation, solution generation, and solution evaluation. Clearly these three subclasses of activity are interdependent. The choice of solution generation strategy may markedly affect the manner in which a problem is represented and the manner in which solutions are evaluated. It is generally in terms of solution generation strategy that problem-solving procedures are described.

Trial-and-Error Procedures

In the strictest sense, random trial-and-error procedures involve finding a solution to a problem in an entirely random manner. It is arguable, however, whether truly random trial-and-error takes place without some sort of bounding or narrowing down of the scope of a problem. Obviously the concept of error requires the presence of some means of testing a solution for desirable properties. This indicates the operation of at least tacit methods of both evaluating and representing solutions.

The distinguishing feature of trial-and-error procedures is that successive trials (proposals of solutions) are made independently of the results of intermediate tests. In other words, information provided by tests with regard to discrepancies between the properties of proposed solutions and those deemed necessary is not used to guide further information processing. This usually means that although the problem solver can detect whether or not a proposed solution is satisfactory, the means are not available to use this information in any determinate manner.

Consider, for example, the problem of arranging furniture in a room to satisfy some specified requirements, or the problem of laying out the floor plan of a building to satisfy certain requirements regarding the adjacency of rooms, or the problem of sub-

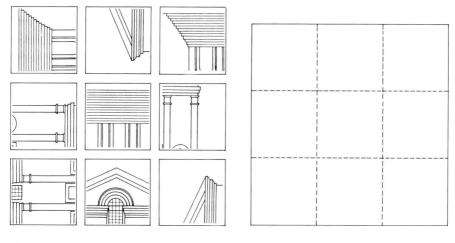

17
Pieces of a simple puzzle and the layout field.

dividing a piece of land among various kinds of uses. All three are specific cases of a class of problem in architecture and urban design that is commonly referred to as the *space-planning problem.*

Another very familiar example of this class of problem is the jigsaw puzzle. Consider a simple puzzle made up of the pieces shown in figure 17. Using trial-and-error, one would generate candidate solutions by arranging and rearranging the pieces, sometimes in a random manner. The pattern of lines and shapes that resulted from each trial arrangement would then be compared to a picture of the final solution to ascertain whether the proposed solution actually matched the picture in all its particulars. After a certain number of attempts at rearrangement the process might be abandoned and the most complete proposal or the one with the least discrepancy adopted (see figure 18).

In the hands of a young child this is a plausible strategy for solving the jigsaw puzzle, and given enough perseverance a line drawing of Alberti's early scheme (1460) for the facade of San Sebastiano in Mantua would result (Wittkower 1971, p. 52). In the hands of an adult, however, a more direct approach is likely to be taken, unless the number of pieces is dramatically increased or the picture of the solution confiscated. Under these circumstances it is likely that a considerable amount of trial-and-error would be required to solve the puzzle, at least until some recognizable pattern of lines emerged.

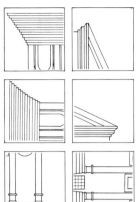

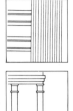

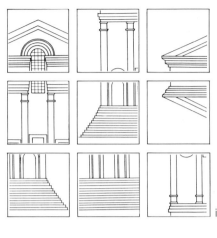

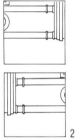
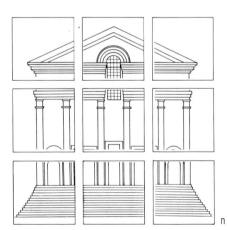

18
An example of trial-and-error on the puzzle problem.

We tend to resort to trial-and-error procedures when the magnitude of a problem—the number of parts and of interrelationships between them—is overwhelming, and especially when information from the application of available testing procedures cannot be used to direct the search for a solution. In the example of the jigsaw puzzle it is possible to test matched and unmatched lines between adjoining pieces, but the outline beyond this simple matching procedure may still not be evident. The point is that solution generation takes place, to a significant degree, independently from the organization of the problem space after a prior trial.

Generate-and-Test Procedures

The generate-and-test approach is a variant of trial-and-error, with the important difference that the results of tests are explicitly used to guide subsequent attempts to generate solutions. Again the procedure takes place in the context of well-defined, explicitly bounded problems.

Let us again consider the puzzle of Alberti's San Sebastiano facade. At first a solution is proposed, randomly or otherwise, by arranging the pieces in the field provided. The shape of lines in this arrangement is then compared to a picture of the final solution. If it does not conform, then the differences between the arrangement and the solution are noted. This testing may be done by observing whether lines match, whether they make recognizable figures, or whether the overall composition appears to be lopsided in some way. Quite commonly the piece that seems to be most out of place is chosen to be rearranged next. If the second arrangement of puzzle pieces is better than the first, then it is accepted for further improvement. If not, then the earlier arrangement is used as the basis for further improvement (see figure 19). The process of generating and testing candidate solutions continues in this manner until a satisfactory arrangement has been found.

Of course, there are several other versions of this general strategy that could be proposed. For instance, rather than selecting each time the puzzle piece that seems to be most out of place, the overall arrangement of pieces, among several candidates, showing the least discrepancy with the solution could constantly be used as the basis for further improvement. The distinguishing feature of the procedure, however, is that it makes explicit use of information regarding the conformance of prior trial arrangements to the required solution properties (here, the lines of the drawing) as the basis for directing further search for a solution.

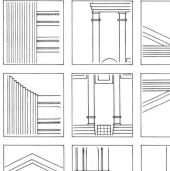

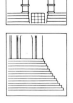

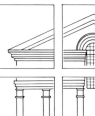

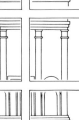

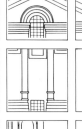
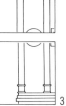
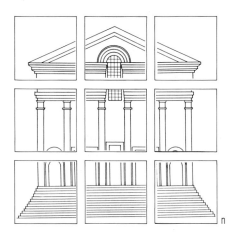

19

An example of generate-and-test on the puzzle problem.

Certainly not a random process, it involves, if in a rudimentary form, explicit decision rules for guiding subsequent problem-solving behavior (for instance, "Select the most out-of-place puzzle piece and attempt to improve its location and arrangement").

Numerous examples of this kind of approach can be found at work among architects and other designers in action. Many different manifestations of layout problems involve the constant adjustment of various parts (rooms, for example) with respect to one another and with respect to a whole (a building), in order to achieve a desired effect. Even in the resolution of formal design problems, where we are operating under the aegis of some proportional rule or compositional concept, we inevitably make these kinds of incremental adjustments.

This strategy raises the question of how a problem solver determines whether the best possible solution has been found. Until a point is reached where there is no discrepancy between a proposed arrangement of spaces and the solution properties (the criteria for arrangement), it is difficult to decide on a stopping rule and to discontinue that particular aspect of problem-solving activity. Furthermore, returning to our jigsaw puzzle example, it may be the case that several different arrangements of pilaster bays and openings are plausible, even as variations of the solution. Therefore, a totally determined arrangement of the puzzle pieces cannot in fact be reached. One obvious stopping rule in this kind of circumstance would be that the solver should quit when no further improvement in the overall arrangement can be observed under a number of successive arrangements. Nevertheless, there is no guarantee that this candidate solution is not suboptimal and that with further perseverance we couldn't find a better solution.

This phenomenon of incrementally moving from worse to better solutions is often referred to as "hill climbing," where the top of the hill is the location of the best solution. For some kinds of problems explicit techniques have been developed, allowing assessments to be made as to whether a candidate solution is suboptimal or not. For many other kinds of problems, however, no such techniques exist. In any event, the idea that successive, small, short-sighted steps can lead toward innovative results contrasts starkly with the notion of insightful leaps described earlier. Nevertheless, such procedures remain effective, especially when we bear in mind that a large number of small steps may cover more ground than a leap (Perkins 1981, p. 151).

Means-Ends Analysis

This strategy involves an extension of the generate-and-test procedure, particularly into the realm of allowing the provision of alternative decision rules so that we can explicitly meet different kinds of problem-solving situations. The three essential components of this approach are (1) a prescribed set of actions (means), (2) a prescribed set of goals (ends), and (3) a set of decision rules. In short, the approach involves the explicit definition of both ends and means and an analytical framework, via appropriate decision rules, for connecting these two aspects of the problem together.

Consider again the facade of San Sebastiano in Mantua, only this time not in the guise of a jigsaw puzzle but rather as a compositional problem framed quite explicitly by basic architectural elements such as pilasters, wall openings, a pediment, and steps, as well as by the decision rules (means) illustrated in figure 20. The ends are also quite explicit, namely to arrange the elements into a classical form after the fashion of Alberti's original composition.

Along the way toward this kind of resolution, various kinds of discrepancies, or compositional difficulties, are likely to be encountered, requiring various kinds of action and the employment of various means. For example, the use of decision rules regarding the division of the facade into bays of equal spacing and the symmetrical distribution of the facade along a vertical center line strongly indicates placement of the tallest wall opening in a central position. The rules do not, however, necessarily provide guidance as to the arrangement of the arched and squared-off smaller wall openings. At least two possible arrangements appear plausible, as shown in figure 21—a dilemma that can be resolved through the use of another rule that relates the centers of the radii producing the arched openings with the center of those producing the similar split pedimental opening, in the form of an equilateral triangle (see figure 20). The result is distribution of the arched openings in the outside bays and, further, termination of the angle of incline of the stepped base. In other words, through successive use of appropriate decision rules the compositional problem can be resolved. Clearly, other rules could and did apply to this case; it is hoped, however, that the example is sufficient to illustrate the procedure.

Without too much suspension of disbelief, we can see how the structural features of this rather simple illustration can be extended to many problems that we encounter in practice. It is

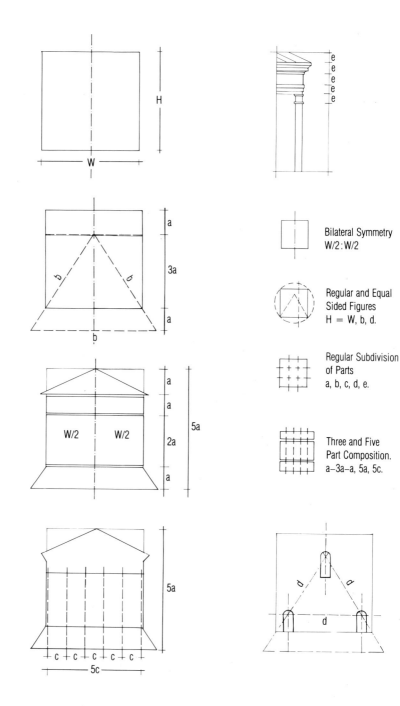

20

Rules for means-ends analysis of a facade problem.

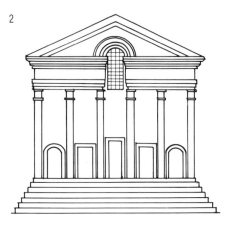

21
Alternative arrangements of openings for the facade
of San Sebastiano.

probably more likely that architectural design, within the canons of some accepted or self-imposed aesthetic orthodoxy, coupled with siting requirements and user needs, proceeds along these lines than by the use of simpler generate-and-test procedures. In fact, very strong similarities are evident between such means-ends analysis and the format of rules and prescriptive devices found in a number of theoretical works from the classical tradition, such as those of Perrault, Blondel, and later Durand, as well as other members of the Parisian *écoles* (Perrault 1683, Blondel 1771–1777, Durand 1802). Other practical guides, perhaps with less theoretical merit and import, are to be found in the work of people like Halfpenny and Morris (Halfpenny 1968 [1724], Morris 1971 [1734]). In fact, the seventeenth, eighteenth, and early nineteenth centuries are replete with such treatises (Wiebenson 1982).

Generally speaking, the resolution of appropriate architecture, from overall organization to the selection and conformation of ornament, was fastidiously documented, not in a rote step-by-step fashion from beginning to end, but through the generalized treatment of a myriad of subproblems that might be encountered and the rules by which solutions should be sought. We might quibble over the normative aspects of this approach represented by both the division of subproblems and the means for their solution. Nevertheless, an explicit protocol for performing means-ends analysis is very evident.

Still other examples of the development and use of design rules that reasonably conform to the framework of means-ends analysis can be found among more recent architectural works. For instance, in his ATBAT project of 1946, Le Corbusier specified precise guidelines ("means") concerning the resolution of conditions of spatial arrangement toward the "end" of mass housing provision, as shown in figure 22 (Le Corbusier 1951, p. 116). In many ways Habraken's concept of "supports" and "structures" is of a similar kind, specifying as it does the means for individual determination of a dwelling environment within a comparatively unified system of production (Habraken 1972).

It should be clear from these examples, and from reflection on the character of the space-planning problem mentioned earlier, that although the number of rules, or types of moves that can be made in two-dimensional space, may be quite finite in scope, each rule may result in a process that allows for several outcomes. The various concatenations of rules and means may thus lead to a wide variety of particular renditions of acceptable compositional arrangements and spatial layouts. The point is that such surface variety should not necessarily be construed as resulting from an equal variety of fundamental problem-solving procedures; nor, conversely, should it be assumed that a comparatively small number of procedures will result in a lack of compositional variety.

Problem-Space Planning

The purpose behind the procedure of problem-space planning is evident in the earlier definitions of a problem space and of the decision tree that represents its structure. To reiterate for a moment, a problem space can be defined as an abstract domain containing elements that represent knowledge states, some of which are solution states to the problem at hand. As described by the decision tree, the structure of a problem space is represented by nodes for decision points and branches for courses of action. In considering a simple case where two courses of action (1 and 2) are applied in sequence to represent an approach toward a solution to a problem, the structure of the resulting problem space can be displayed as shown in figure 23. If we say that a 2-1-2 combination, or ordering, of the two available courses of action reaches a solution, then the minimum, but not the only, path through the problem space is a_1, b_2, c_3, d_6. Thus, problem-space planning, and the procedure used to accomplish it, aims to structure the overall search process toward a solution: to help select, in advance, an appropriate combination of courses of action that leads economically to a solution. The example also

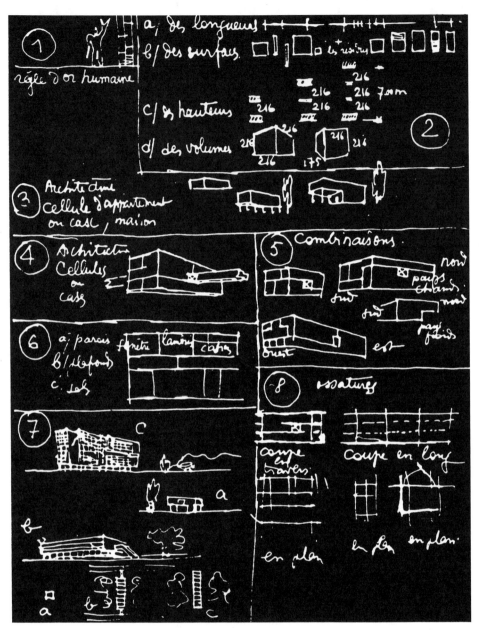

22
Le Corbusier's guidelines for the ATBAT project of
1946.

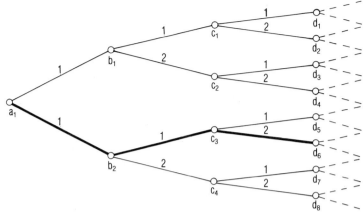

23
A tree diagram of a problem space.

illustrates just how extensive the problem space can be for a problem that appears to be quite straightforward. This further underlines the need for some kind of planning.

The relationship between this kind of procedure and those discussed earlier should also be evident. It is through problem-space planning that we define and subdivide larger problems into more tractable subproblems and find guidance in applying more specific strategies and procedures.

Two broad categories of problem-space planning can be distinguished. They are the *top-down* or *hierarchical decomposition* methods and the *bottom-up* or *hierarchical decomposition-recomposition* methods. This distinction becomes clearer under another kind of representation of a problem space (Alexander and Manheim 1962, Milne 1970).

Let us consider the elements of a problem space with distinguishable subproblems in the form of a finite hierarchical subdivision down to the (primitive) level of singular statements about specific criteria, or required solution properties (see figure 24). Reformulation and rerepresentation of the problem space can be made in the form of a hierarchical planar or lattice structure, denoted by the solid and dashed lines, where the nodes represent subproblems at various levels of detail and the links represent (implied) connections between the subproblems. Thus the node P_1^5 represents subproblem number one at the fifth level in the hierarchy of subproblems, node P_2^3 the second subproblem at the third level, and so on. As shown, nodes P_1^5, P_1^4, and P_2^3

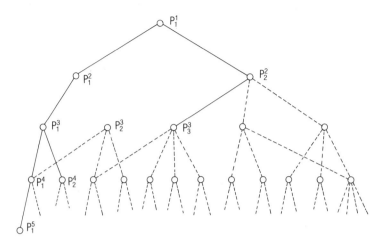

24
A hierarchical diagram of a problem space.

are linked, and therefore the subproblems that they represent can be expected to have a common or similar ingredient. For example, if the graph represents the structure of a problem about the provision of urban outdoor spaces in a downtown area, then the subproblems represented by the nodes P_1^4 and P_2^3 may concern the design of retail commercial and recreational areas, respectively. The two may be linked by concepts of pedestrian and vehicular movement. The subordinate node P_1^5, in this case, may deal specifically with something like a restaurant area in direct proximity to a street and thus related most directly to P_1^4 and more indirectly to P_2^3.

In problem-space planning of the top-down or hierarchical decomposition variety, the solver's attention is directed downward through the lattice structure, creating what tend to be broader subdivisions of the problem at first, and gradually moving into more numerous detailed subproblems (see figure 25). The overall (implicit) structure of the problem thus gradually becomes revealed as the process unfolds, through times $t_1, t_2, t_3, \ldots, t_n$, and continues toward a higher level of resolution and eventual termination (Peña 1977).

In architectural design the reasonably immediate selection of an overall *parti,* once the outlines of a problem have been presented or explained, is an example of this kind of approach. Likewise, the immediate delineation of a community planning problem in a direction such as transportation versus, say, community services is another case in point. Unless we assume a

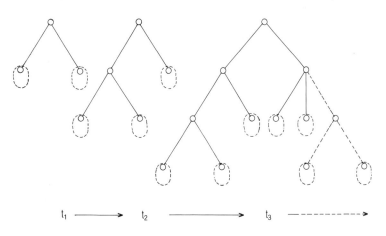

$t_1 \longrightarrow \quad t_2 \longrightarrow \quad t_3 \dashrightarrow$

25
Top-down hierarchical subdivision of a problem
space.

special status for such "big ideas," the process of discovering a problem's structure may also be initiated by "smaller ideas." For instance, the tendency to light upon a familiar or intriguing aspect of the problem, even though that aspect may prove in time to be relatively insignificant, often serves to "get things started."

Returning to the facade of San Sebastiano, the composition of which was presented earlier as an exercise in means-ends analysis, we can view problem-space planning as a method of organizing and sequencing the application of decision rules. It is the process by which we think through the problem at hand, define it further, and plan our moves. One plausible sequence, illustrated by figure 26, begins by applying general compositional principles before becoming more particular. This is not to suggest, of course, that Alberti's scheme of approximately 1460 was arrived at in quite so straightforward a manner. As Wittkower points out, the project for San Sebastiano at Mantua, as does the project for San Andrea in the same town, represents a departure on Alberti's part from earlier principles (Wittkower 1971, p. 47). San Sebastiano, with its very thin pilasters on a continuous wall surface, heavy entablature, and wall openings, represents a theoretical shift. It is, in effect, an alternative "scheme for reviving the classical temple front . . . adapted to the needs of wall architecture" (Wittkower 1971, p. 49)—hardly a straightforward design exercise. We do know, however, that certain of the compositional principles presented earlier were explicitly employed by Alberti—for example, the width-to-height ratio of 1:1, the

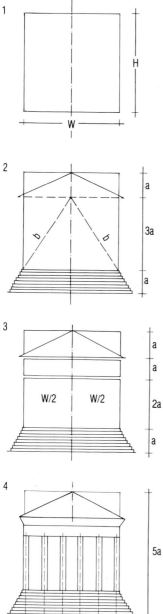

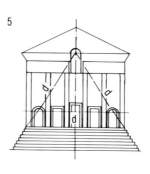

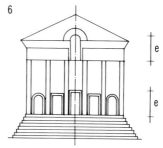

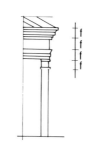

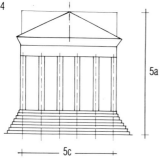

26

Sequential recomposition of the facade of
San Sebastiano.

equal division of bay widths across the front of the facade, and the general proportional system of regular subdivision of regulating lines (Wittkower 1971, p. 48). Parenthetically, the scheme was not executed in the manner described. The two pilasters next to the central bay were omitted, as well as the broad expanse of steps at the base (Wittkower 1971, p. 49).

In spite of what might be seen as peremptory, even rash decisions embraced by this general approach, in the hands of experienced practitioners it can be very successful. Fluent problem solvers make use of a large repertoire of plans and planning schemes. Consequently they appear to tackle problems "head on," or "top down." Furthermore, lack of clarity in the problem as given may render an alternative approach inconceivable.

By contrast, in the use of bottom-up or hierarchical decomposition-recomposition methods the aim is to provide a complete, or at least extensive, description of the inherent structure of a problem space from the outset by explicitly breaking down—decomposing—the problem as given and understood into its most fundamental components; that is, to the level of the kind of singular problem statement mentioned earlier. The relations among these components are then systematically identified, allowing recombination into a coherent picture of the problem-space structure.

The procedures described in Alexander's landmark work *Notes on the Synthesis of Form,* and in later works dealing with "pattern language," are essentially problem-space planning methods of this kind (Alexander 1964; Alexander 1965; Alexander, Ishikawa, and Silverstein 1968; Alexander et al. 1975; Alexander et al. 1977; Alexander 1979; Studer 1965; Milne 1970; Owen 1970). In general they proceed in the following manner (see figure 27). First, the problem as given is restated in a form consisting of numerous discrete problem statements. In other words, it is described in terms of its singular constituent elements rather than by broad organizing principles. For example, in Alexander's case of the Indian village, under the heading of social forces shaping the community environment we find simple descriptive sentences such as, "Extended family is in one house," "Need to divide land among sons of successive generations," and so on (Alexander 1964). Second, relations among these discrete problem statements are expressed, usually in the binary form of "yes, there is a relationship" or "no, there is not a relationship." For example, again for Alexander's Indian village, the problem statement "Rules about house door not facing south" is

1

Religion and Caste

1. Harijans regarded as ritually impure, untouchable, etc.
2. Proper disposal of dead.
3. Rules about house door not facing south.
4. Certain water and certain trees are thought of as sacred.
5. Provision for festivals and religious meetings.
6. Wish for temples.
7. Cattle treated as sacred, and vegetarian attitude.
8. Members of castes maintain their caste profession as far as possible.
9. Members of one caste like to be together and separate from others, and will not eat or drink together.
10. Need for elaborate weddings.

Social Forces

11. Marriage is to person from another village.
12. Extended family is in one house.
13. Family solidarity and neighborliness even after separation.
14. Economic integration of village on payment-in-kind basis.
15. Modern move toward payment in cash.
16. Women gossip extensively while bathing, fetching water, on way to field latrines, etc.
17. Village has fixed men's social groups.
18. Need to divide land among sons of successive generations.
19. People want to own land personally.
20. People of different factions prefer to have no contact.
21. Eradication of untouchability.
22. Abolition of Zamindari and uneven land distribution.
23. Men's groups chatting, smoking, even late at night.
24. Place for village events—dancing, plays, singing, etc., wrestling.
25. Assistance for physically handicapped, aged, widows.
26. Sentimental system: wish not to destroy old way of life; love of present habits governing bathing, food, etc.

2

1 interacts with 8, 9, 12, 13, 14, 21, 28, 29, 48, 61, 67, 68, 70, 77, 86, 101, 106, 113, 124, 140, 141.

2 interacts with 3, 4, 6, 26, 29, 32, 52, 71, 98, 102, 105, 123, 133.

3 interacts with 2, 12, 13, 17, 26, 76, 78, 79, 88, 101, 103, 119.

4 interacts with 2, 5, 6, 17, 29, 32, 45, 56, 63, 71, 74, 78, 79, 88, 91, 105, 106, 110, 124.

5 interacts with 4, 6, 10, 14, 17, 21, 24, 46, 102, 113, 116, 118, 131, 133, 140.

6 interacts with 2, 4, 5, 20, 21, 53, 58, 61, 63, 82, 102, 111, 117, 130, 134, 135.

7 interacts with 20, 31, 34, 53, 57, 58, 59, 80, 85, 86, 94, 105, 106, 123, 124, 125.

8 interacts with 1, 9, 14, 15, 21, 22, 25, 27, 48, 58, 59, 61, 62, 63, 64, 65, 89, 95, 96, 99, 111, 112, 114, 115, 116, 121, 129, 136, 140, 141.

3

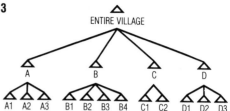

A1 contains requirements 7, 53, 57, 59, 60, 72, 125, 126, 128.
A2 contains requirements 31, 34, 36, 52, 54, 80, 94, 106, 136.
A3 contains requirements 37, 38, 50, 55, 77, 91, 103.
B1 contains requirements 39, 40, 41, 44, 51, 118, 127, 131, 138.
B2 contains requirements 30, 35, 46, 47, 61, 97, 98.

4

27

Excerpts from Alexander's procedure in *Notes on the Synthesis of Form.*

connected with a variety of religious rituals and with "Sentimental system: wish not to destroy old ways of life . . ." (Alexander 1964). In a design problem about an urban space, such as the one mentioned earlier, identifiable aspects of the problem having some bearing on pedestrian movement presumably would be related to one another. Third, very closely interrelated groups of problem statements are identified, thus defining the most basic level of design subproblems. For instance, returning to Alexander's Indian village, this may be an expression of house design criteria. Fourth, the subproblems isolated in this manner are combined, using the pertinent relational information, usually in a hierarchical stepwise fashion. This process of combination culminates in a single problem statement that is inclusive of all subordinate statements. It corresponds, then, to the root node P_1^1 of the lattice in figure 24. In short, the procedure allows decisions made by a designer about parts of a problem, and about their interrelationships, to be systematically structured so as to produce an explicit picture or diagram of the problem space at various levels of generality. Finally, this structure can be further exploited in order to identify those aspects of particular subproblems of interest that seem to have the most controlling influence over the configuration of the problem space. For example, if the problem essentially revolves around concepts of movement and circulation, this will become evident. These may not be concepts that are apparent to the designer at the outset, and their revelation may also be consequential by exposing a bias on the part of the designer that may subsequently become the basis for reconsideration of the problem's structure (Silverstein and Jacobson 1978).

Clearly, alternative representations of and decisions about the problem space are possible and may even prove more enlightening. For instance, there are procedures where the relational structure is seen as representing the "lines of communication" along which subproblems are connected. This technique allows instances of partially contradictory statements to be resolved (De Leon 1972, Batty 1971). For instance, the assertion that doors of houses should not face south may be made from one point of view, and the contention that they should face south from some other standpoint. Obviously such statements are related through the contradictory aspect. Nevertheless, appropriate resolution may not be as simple as taking them to be self-canceling. What is required is a resynthesis of the information in which the ambiguity is either preserved or resolved by reference to other more determining factors. For example, the preponderance of evidence from elsewhere in the problem space may suggest that of the two alternatives the south-facing doorway is the least detrimental to expected patterns of behavior.

We can see that both top-down and bottom-up approaches to problem-space planning apply to well-defined problems, or at least to problems for which we have sufficient definition and understanding to make the necessary planning decisions. On the other hand, the idea sometimes associated with Alexander and others' formal treatments of this issue, that the procedures are strictly a way of defining problems, is a mistaken one (Studer 1965). We can certainly say that they are techniques for structuring problems, but not that they are techniques for defining them. Clearly, specification of problem elements and of the interrelationships among them requires the use of some overarching concept or knowledgeable attitude about a problem: a knowledge that, when all is said and done, remains in some sense implicit, even tacit. In this regard it further seems inaccurate to assume that top-down approaches are necessarily inferior to bottom-up approaches because they provide, at a given moment, a less explicit structural description of a problem space. Here we must observe that bottom-up methods, although seemingly more determined, or determining, are just as vulnerable as their counterparts to shifts in understanding and orientation to a problem. The desirability, even the necessity, of explicit problem structures, according to Alexander and others, lies in the critical judgment that can be brought to bear on the biases and misinformation that are revealed when a problem is explicitly and comprehensively stated (Silverstein and Jacobson 1978).

Finally, the formal accounts of problem-space planning that have been discussed are altogether idealized forms of the procedures, just as were the earlier examples of other problem-solving approaches. In actual practice, designers rarely if ever adopt one extreme or the other. Nevertheless, at least implicitly and at particular moments, our problem-solving behavior can seem to lean one way or the other.

Heuristic Reasoning and Design "Situations"

One aspect in this discussion that has been alluded to but so far not really addressed is the class of devices variously termed decision rules and overarching concepts. Particularly in connection with generate-and-test procedures and means-ends analysis, the ability to invoke an appropriate rule for relating the results from an evaluation of solutions to further courses of action was fundamental. Also, rules and principles are necessarily invoked when one is pursuing the task of problem-space planning. Such behavior introduces us into the realm of *heuristics* and *heuristic reasoning*.

To Newell, Shaw, and Simon, a heuristic is any principle, procedure, or other device that contributes to reduction in the search for a satisfactory solution (Newell, Shaw, and Simon 1967, p. 78; Simon 1969, p. 80).[9] Perkins in his account is less emphatic about the results. For him, "a heuristic is a rule of thumb that often helps in solving a certain class of problems, but makes no guarantees" (Perkins 1981, p. 192). It may be compared to the exact procedures of an algorithm in that regard. Similarly, for Polya, the term again applies to "rules of thumb," or provisional procedures that prove useful in solving problems (Polya 1957, p. 37). In short, *heuristics* is a term that is applied to specific problem-structuring devices ranging from explicit decision rules of the type discussed earlier to a wide variety of analogies, analogs, and models. It is also applied to general kinds of procedures for guiding the search for solutions. For example, the "heuristic of reducing differences," apart from its particulars that may vary from one application to another, lies behind the concept of means-ends analysis (Newell, Shaw, and Simon 1967, p. 87). As we have seen, the specific decision rules are aimed at reducing the difference between the properties of proposed solutions and those of the goal set. In the foregoing accounts of problem-space planning, the underlying concepts enabling decisions to be made (that is, the heuristics employed in the overarching concepts) direct specific decisions and thus are instrumental in the manner in which a problem becomes defined in the first place.

The term *heuristic reasoning* refers to a problem-solving process in which it is unknown beforehand whether a particular sequence of steps will yield a solution or not. Consequently, it involves a decision-making process in which we do not know whether we actually have a solution until the line of reasoning is completed, or all the steps are carried out. Heuristic reasoning is part and parcel of most solution generation strategies, may be characteristic of an individual problem solver, and guides the overall organization of search through a problem space. So far, however, it is an area in which no general theory seems to exist. In fact, there is considerable disagreement about the emphasis that should be placed on heuristic procedures in the realm of human problem solving, particularly with reference to what is known as "heuristic technology"—the development of procedures that are superior to those routinely used. Skeptics assert that the broad organization of problem-solving behavior almost takes care of itself, once a person masters the contributing performances that are required. Knowing various techniques for solving layout problems, for example, more or less guarantees that the overall approach to this type of problem will unfold appropriately. On the other hand, Perkins, among others, presents evidence and arguments that suggest the importance of heuristics in matching already familiar methods with problems during the pursuit of more efficient problem-solving performance (Perkins 1981, p. 196).

This picture of episodic rule making and application does not entirely convey the nature of the act of heuristic reasoning, at least as it occurs in the design process. For one thing, the rules may or may not be explicit and repeatable in the sense of something objectively acquired and learned. The term *heuristic* is used here in a broader sense than in heuristic technology, where subjects learn the application of various problem-solving techniques in order to improve their performance on specific tests. The heuristics employed by designers may be quite subjective, having evolved from prior personal experience. They are certainly explicit, but only in the contexts with which they are associated in the designer's mind. Further, rule making and rule application have a certain congruence with the concepts of "framing," "frames of reference" (Schön 1984), and "appreciative contexts" (Vickers 1983), although heuristic reasoning is less potentially contemplative and more immediately associated with action. Useful knowledge of a rule is as much a matter of the purposes to which it is to be put as it is a matter of the rule's external existence.

This concept of heuristic reasoning, when it moves beyond the objective and perhaps mechanistic realm of problem solving theory, bears a striking resemblance to aspects of Merleau-Ponty's concept of *situation* (Merleau-Ponty 1962). As interpreted by Mallin, Merleau-Ponty uses *situation* to mean "involvement in circumstances" or "active concern with sets of natural, cultural, or human problems" (Mallin 1979, p. 7). A situation occurs when an individual becomes totally absorbed in something, relates it to himself, and begins to understand it (Mallin 1979, p. 7). Quite clearly, various episodes of design presented in chapter 1 have these characteristics about them. To Merleau-Ponty, when we are in a situation neither the objective realm of those things outside ourselves nor our own subjectivity is primary (Mallin 1979, p. 8). Both are founded in the situation.[10] Therefore, in the matter of heuristic reasoning it is not simply a case, as the information processing theorists would seem to suggest, of isolating problem-solving circumstances and setting them over against a similarly abstracted set of actions and purposes. By the same token, it is not a case of subjective idealism either (Mallin 1979, p. 12). For how could we explain the very evident struggle that took place in the first chapter's protocols to reorganize, manage, and be accountable for objective aspects of problem-solving contexts?

The rule aspect is also present in Merleau-Ponty's concept of situations. In a creative endeavor such as designing, an attempt is made to overcome the situation's novelty and make some sense of it. This process leads to the acquisition, as Mallin puts it, "of a sort of general principle . . . that is habitually reapplied." Thus the acquired principle becomes "sedimented," allowing one to "learn how to act in certain kinds of circumstances" (Mallin 1979, pp. 12–13).

The open-ended aspect of heuristic reasoning finds a parallel in Merleau-Ponty's definition of situations as being ambiguous. They are said to be beyond complete and perfect grasp; further meditation can always lead to "a more specific and deeper comprehension" (Mallin 1979, p. 14).

In summary, the design process may be seen to be marked by a sequence of episodes or situations that are, in turn, coincident with periods of heuristic reasoning through which problems are defined and solutions sought. During each episode a particular heuristic device or set of devices can be said to be in operation and in general control of the reorganization of a problem space. Further, the orientation of this operation is neither entirely objective nor entirely subjective. It is both. Between episodes, control is relinquished, so to speak, from one set of organizing principles to another.

● **Logical Structure**
In simple form, the logical structure behind the application of heuristic reasoning would seem to be, "If problem X is encountered or perceived, then take action Y under conditions Z" (Akin 1978, pp. 27–34; Akin 1982 [1979]). In the case of architectural design, action Y might take the form of a specific design response, such as the prescription and manipulation of the compositional qualities of some building elements in response to a perceived problem and its surrounding or auxiliary conditions. For example, the problem might be construed as one of satisfying the requirement of a distinct and grand formal entry to a

building complex, given the available components of the building program and the features of the site (the auxiliary or bounding conditions of the problem). Here, action Y might be an
arrangement and massing of the elements of the building in
which major public areas are combined at the termination of a
principal thoroughfare leading into the site. It would thus resolve
both the problem at hand and specific conditions inherent in the
building program and site configuration, such as adjacency requirements among functional areas and accessibility.

On the other hand, with the earlier definition of a wicked problem in mind, the logical structure of the reasoning process might
also be seen as, "If conditions Z obtain when viewed from the
perspective of the application of action Y, then problem X is defined." In other words, a problem becomes defined in response
to a perceived set of conditions by way of a concrete proposal.

At first reading this may seem to be a perverse state of affairs.
Nevertheless, it is the framing and self-referential qualities of this
kind of logical structure that allow more comprehensive judgments about the scope and thrust of the problem-solving situation to be suspended for a moment, permitting problem-solving
activity to proceed. This logic characterizes the "hunch making"
so often observed in design behavior, without which it is difficult
to imagine how any kind of solution could be reached. For example, in the first of the case studies presented in chapter 1, a
preoccupation with resolving the street plaza on the front portion of the site allowed the design scheme to be advanced, with
an almost complete absence of concern for any other aspect of
the problem.

● **Problem-Oriented Constraints and Autonomous Constraints**
In connection with the logical structure of the heuristic reasoning process, a question arises about the manner in which a
particular action Y becomes associated with either the recognition of a problem X or the perception of conditions Z. To put it
another way, how is it that the ensemble of problem X, action Y,
and conditions Z becomes recognized in the first place?

Although other aspects of this question will be tackled later, for
present purposes it is useful to distinguish between two types of
problem constraints. According to Simon, these are "problem-
oriented constraints" and constraints that are autonomously
(that is, independently) provided by a designer in order to organize a problem space (Simon 1970, 1973).

Problem-oriented constraints are those that are primarily derived from consideration of a problem X that has been previously defined. In other words, as far as the problem solver is concerned, the necessary and sufficient conditions for taking action Y are determined solely within the ambit of problem X and related conditions of the task environment Z. A form of means-ends analysis may take place, in which the means are defined and specified in terms of clearly identifiable ends. For example, the point of symmetry with Burnham's planetarium, which became such a determining factor in the third case study in chapter 1, was essentially part of the problem as given. So too was the location and shape of the existing hospital in the second case study, which subsequently constrained the location and orientation of building elements along the lake edge.

By contrast, autonomous or independent contraints do not derive from the problem as given and understood. They are, however, not arbitrary, as their application may lead positively to a reformulation of the problem in a different light—a reformulation that greatly facilitates further problem-solving acitvity. In essence, information about the ensemble of $X, Y,$ and Z is introduced into the problem-solving process from somewhere else, rather than by direct consideration of problem X under conditions Z. An example is the use of the Chicago grid in the third case study, for the purpose of providing constraints for the overall layout of the site. While the grid was certainly present in the area adjacent to the site, there was nothing in the problem statement, or brief, that required that any reference be made to it. This constraint, introduced by the designers, usefully transcended the givens of the problem situation.

It is the "covering" characteristics, yet lack of complete correspondence (isomorphism) between autonomous constraints and their problem-based contexts that renders them so useful in providing a basis for further problem-solving activity. For unless the entire problem at hand can be solved using strictly problem-oriented constraints, we have to step outside the known problem context in order to continue problem-solving activity. In the vein of Merleau-Ponty, the "otherness" of the independent facts surrounding the problem can only be broached by the use of "sedimented principles" known to the designer (Mallin 1979, p. 13).

One way of describing the kinds of heuristics that are employed
to constrain problem spaces in architectural and urban design is
with reference to the type of information that they provide. At
least five classes of heuristics can be distinguished, in the guise
of common types of analogy, "solution images," and form-giving
rules. They are as follows: *anthropometric analogies, literal
analogies, environmental relations, typologies,* and *formal
languages.*

● **Anthropometric Analogies**
The use of an anthropometric analogy involves employing a
mental construct that describes man's physical occupancy of a
space. Such constructs can often be seen at work in the deliber-
ations of naive designers or in problem-solving situations where
a designer has little or no experience. For example, a person
without any architectural background might produce a design
for a staircase based entirely upon the act of imagining someone
ascending into a room in a certain manner. The result might be a
graceful form for which the designer in question appeared to
have no prior reference. Almost anyone who has experience
with moving, sitting, standing, and so on, yet no special knowledge, would seem capable of devising and exercising such a
construct.

Recently, in the face of what they see as an abstract and non-
body-centered architecture, Bloomer and Moore have attempted
to reexamine the significance of the human body in architecture.
In their words, "We believe that the most essential and memo-
rable sense of three-dimensionality originates in the body
experience and that this sense may constitute a basis for understanding spatial feeling in our experience of buildings" (Bloomer
and Moore 1977, p. x). Certainly in other eras the body and anthropometric qualities were more central to architectural
thought (see figure 28).

● **Literal Analogies**
This kind of heuristic involves borrowing known or found form-
giving constructs as a point of departure for structuring a design
problem. Literal analogies are so termed because in all cases the
resulting architectural forms match very closely the conformation of what the designer sees as the key features of the analog.
Here a useful distinction can be made between what we might

28
An elegant stairway with anthropometric qualities
(the main stair of the Benedictine monastery at
Götweig, by von Hildebrandt, 1718–1739).

call *iconic analogies* and *canonic analogies* (Broadbent 1973, ch. 2).

The scope of references for the development of iconic analogies is extremely broad. Objects from the natural world may serve as sources—the shell of a crab for the roof of Le Corbusier's Ronchamp Chapel (Le Corbusier 1958), hands folded in an attitude of prayer for Frank Lloyd Wright's Unitarian church (Broadbent 1973, pp. 40–45; Wright 1943), sails for Utzon's Sydney Opera House (figure 29), in a milieu steeped in yachting (Ziegler 1973).[11] Iconic analogies can also include imagery from some scene, painterly conception, or narrative account of real or imagined circumstances. As Waldman clearly demonstrates in his commentary on "narrative design problems," we can and do make use of story lines as metaphors in solving design problems (Waldman 1982). Hans Hollein presents the elements of such a scenario in his design for the Ringturm Travel Agency in Vienna, which incorporates the motifs shown in figure 30. Artifacts and elements from more squarely within the realm of architectural experience represent a third major resource.

In all cases the analogy appears useful to designers by virtue of the symbolic or iconographic qualities that they attach to it. It is a physical representation of an intention that, when applied, provides additional structure to a problem.

Canonic analogies have as their basis "ideal" proportional systems or formal geometric properties. They are usually manifested as somewhat abstract geometrical patterns or shapes. Configurations such as "Cartesian grids" or "Platonic solids" have quite a venerable history in the shaping of design problems, although the proposed ideal may show considerable variation. For example, the Hellenic urban grid layout of the fifth century B.C., as at Priene, had a modular order of more or less equally spaced blocks and streets with a central area set aside for special functions. By contrast, the later layout of Alexandria, by the Macedonian architect Dinocrates (c. 331 B.C.), accommodated variations in both site conditions and local functions. One of the features of the Alexandrian grid was the deployment of multiple subcenters, each within an ethnic quarter of the city, linked together in the form of a hierarchical functional system (figure 31).

A particular literal analogy may, of course, be capable of simultaneously expressing both iconic and canonic qualities. In actual application the final distinction must be regarded as a circumstance of the moment and clearly both a matter of degree and a

29
A form with the visual quality of a sailing vessel
(original elevations for the Sydney Opera House, by
Jørn Utzon, 1957–1973).

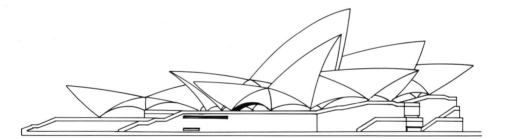

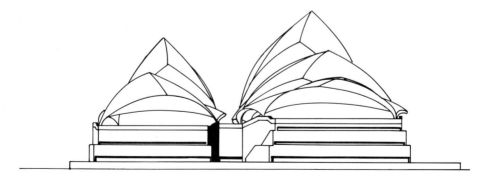

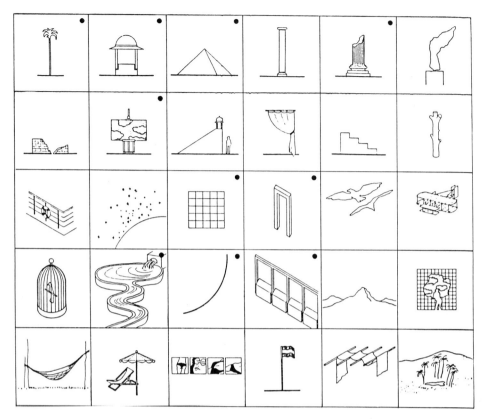

30
Elements of a narrative scenario (the Ringturm
Travel Agency in Vienna, by Hans Hollein, 1979).

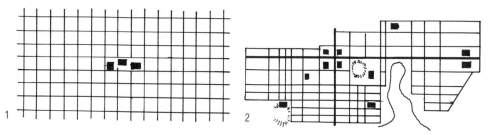

31
Two variations on the grid system of town layout
(1. Priene, 2. Alexandria).

matter of the purposes to which the analogy is put by the
designer.

● **Environmental Relations**
Here use is made of a principle or set of principles, often derived
empirically, that represents what appear to be appropriate relations between man and his host environment and among components of the building fabric itself. Special information is
typically incorporated about human behavior as a determinant of
form; about the influence of environmental factors such as climate, physiography, and resource availability (see figure 32);
and about engineering factors affecting structural and material
performance.

This kind of heuristic is apt to be highly problem oriented. The
principle involved creates a bridge between a perceived problem
and an ensemble of form-giving characteristics representing its
potential resolution. For example, the application of "bubble diagrams" in the arrangement of spaces in accordance with given
formulae about human behavior—such as how far apart people
prefer to sit in a waiting room—rarely moves beyond the constraints of the problem as given.

● **Typologies**
Typologies embody principles that designers consider unvarying
(Colquhoun 1967); as heuristics they allow us to apply knowledge about past solutions to related architectural problems. For
this discussion it will be useful to divide them into three subclasses: *building types as models, organizational typologies,* and
elemental types. Again, a long and venerable history is associated with their use (Vidler 1977).

A building type used as a model represents characteristics
worthy of emulation. It seems to provide for the perceived needs,
uses, and customs found in the design situation under consider-

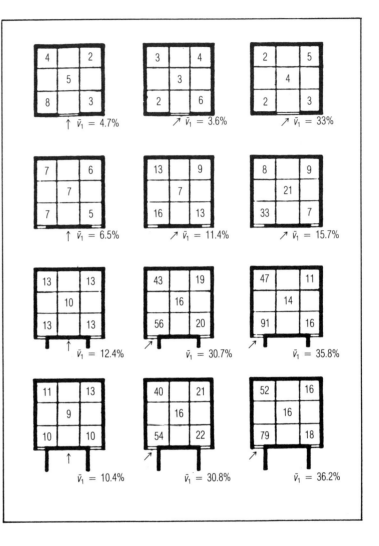

32

Environmental principles for energy conservation
(planar view of the effect of vertical projections and
openings on interior ventilation patterns).

ation. For example, a courtyard house, a French *hôtel,* or a basilican church may be closely followed in arriving at a design solution. Vidler in his apologia for the neorationalists sees our cities as a typological source of design ideas (Vidler 1978).

The organizational typology is primarily used as a framework and reference for solving problems concerning the spatial distribution and conformation of functional elements. It may also be used for the underlying rules of formal composition that it offers. A case in point would be the use, without complete or literal emulation, of those organizational principles at work in a classical villa facade.

Finally, elemental types are prototypes for solving general classes of design problems—the problem of entry into a building, for example, or that of rendering the transition between the ground plane and the rise of a building, or that of resolving the needs for both a sense of community and a sense of privacy. The corpus of architectural production and theoretical writing provides a repertoire of approaches to such problems.

The foregoing classification is, or course, rather arbitrary. A building, or part of it, may be used as a prototype in all three regards, serving at once as model, organizational type, and provider of elemental types. Again, the particular orientation of the use of a typology in design is largely a matter of the moment and of the designer's intentions. Furthermore, typologies implicitly possess both the iconic and the canonic qualities of literal analogies—but with the important difference that these qualities are confined to the realm of existing architectural expression and thus can be considered "tried and true." This property is not necessarily applicable to literal analogies. As with other heuristics, however, the effectiveness of a borrowed type hinges ultimately on its demonstrated appropriateness to the design problem at hand.

So far, in this as in many other discussions of typologies, there is a distinctly reverential tone. The types referred to are usually those with time-honored pedigrees from the point of view of contemporary historical-theoretical preoccupations. Yet other types must surely be admitted: organizational principles stemming from current practice or lore, without overt historical references. Sometimes these arise out of a sober, practical reckoning with current needs and prevailing circumstances; on other occasions they might stem from forward-looking polemical positions. In modern urban design enterprises both these latter strains are often evident among the principles presented to rationalize a

scheme. Organizational diagrams manifesting such contemporary preoccupations as circulation, market forces, and prevailing
institutional mechanisms of development are cases in point
(figure 33).

● **Formal Languages**
These are generalizations of information from other heuristics,
especially from typologies and environmental relations. They are
languages inasmuch as they possess guiding structures or rules
that explicitly direct decisions about the "correct" functioning
and "meaningful" ordering of formal design elements. For example, treatises on the "classical language" provide a repertoire
of architectonic elements and rules for their composition that
undoubtedly incorporate fundamental aspects of relevant typologies but go beyond the realm of particular types in both scope
and generality (Wiebenson 1982, Summerson 1979). Such works
present the "semantic" and "syntactic" ingredients of an internally consistent architectural expression.

Alexander's "pattern language" (Alexander et al. 1977) represents a heuristic repertoire that is also of this kind (figure 34).
Furthermore, it is a no less deterministic method of reasoning,
although ostensibly concerned in a different manner with the
problem of architectural composition (that is, with behavioral
determinism rather than formal determinism). Yet a design
language can be quite idiosyncratic and full of the references,
leitmotifs, and particular approaches of an individual designer.
This quality derives from a habitual way of doing things—the use
of "sedimented principles," to return to an earlier discussion—
and is most evident in the work of original and experienced
designers.

Generally, the heuristics designers use in practice are principles
that draw on sources from a number of these categories. For
example, in Shadrach Woods's proposal for the Berlin Free University, where the heuristics at work are fairly well documented
(as shown in figure 35), a number of important organizing concepts, particularly those dealing with overall spatial organization
and qualities of flexibility, clearly derive from both the category
here called typologies and that called environmental relations
(Woods 1964, 1965). In the case of Woods's proposal, the clarity
of the heuristics also derives from the juxtaposition with contras-
tive features that are not to be employed—for example, Woods's
"groundscraper diagrams" versus "high-rise diagrams."

In addition, a heuristic may encompass either a "large idea" or a
"small idea" and may become more developed through repeated

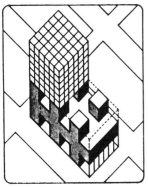

Penthouse/tower
46 units/1BR 2BR

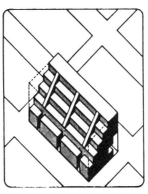

Terrace walk-up
12 units/0BR 1BR 2BR

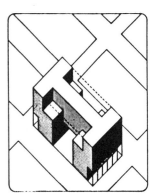

Terrace
16 units/2BR 3BR

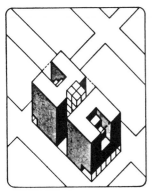

Terrace
20 units/2BR 3BR

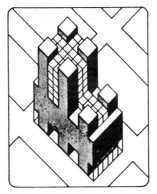

Loft space/flexible living, fixed BR
Number of units unspecified

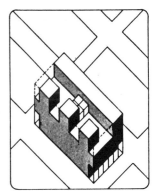

Penthouse/flat
25 units/1BR 2BR 3BR

33
Variations on the New York block typology (part of
the project from the Welfare Island competition,
New York, by O. M. Ungers, 1975).

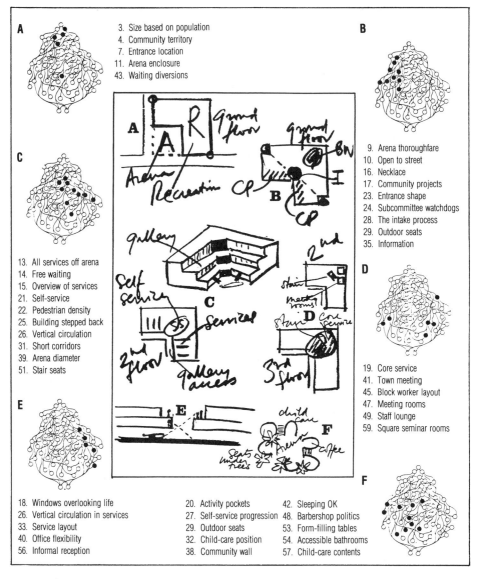

A

3. Size based on population
4. Community territory
7. Entrance location
11. Arena enclosure
43. Waiting diversions

B

C

9. Arena thoroughfare
10. Open to street
16. Necklace
17. Community projects
23. Entrance shape
24. Subcommittee watchdogs
28. The intake process
29. Outdoor seats
35. Information

13. All services off arena
14. Free waiting
15. Overview of services
21. Self-service
22. Pedestrian density
25. Building stepped back
26. Vertical circulation
31. Short corridors
39. Arena diameter
51. Stair seats

D

19. Core service
41. Town meeting
45. Block worker layout
47. Meeting rooms
49. Staff lounge
59. Square seminar rooms

E

18. Windows overlooking life
26. Vertical circulation in services
33. Service layout
40. Office flexibility
56. Informal reception

20. Activity pockets
27. Self-service progression
29. Outdoor seats
32. Child-care position
38. Community wall

42. Sleeping OK
48. Barbershop politics
53. Form-filling tables
54. Accessible bathrooms
57. Child-care contents

F

34

The "pattern language" of Alexander, Ishikawa, and
Silverstein (an application in the San Francisco
area).

application. Using terminology and concepts from Lakatos's writings on the history and philosophy of science, Stanford Anderson presents a convincing analysis of the early work of Le Corbusier in which two large ideas can be seen to emerge (Anderson 1984, Landau 1982). These ideas he calls "programmes"; each has at its core a working hypothesis, or set of related hypotheses, through which Le Corbusier organizes much of his architectural work. The programmes are not mutually exclusive and receive varying degrees of emphasis in different projects. Further, the core working hypotheses can be seen to evolve from relatively vague notions to fixed and clear principles for action.

The programmes Anderson defines are the concepts of *promenade architecturale* and *Maison Domino.* In the *promenade architecturale* Le Corbusier's central concern is with "how we correlate experience and knowledge"; he proposes "an abstract experience of architecture" based on immediate perceptual experience rather than historical association. In the *Maison Domino,* Le Corbusier is seen to be seeking a "rational and economic solution" for the provision of emergency housing. Both programmes come together to influence the later formulation of the "five points," one of which deals with the "free plan" and its possibilities for spatial experience, and another with rationalization of structure using the promise of modern technology (Anderson 1984, p. 3f.).

A final point about the heuristics employed in a design exercise is that they may have an entirely informal quality and a relatively short life span. They may be developed for a particular application and subsequently discarded. Although this is especially true of problem-oriented constraints, it can also happen with an autonomous constraint in the form of a "wild idea" that comes to the fore, is useful for a moment, and is then forgotten.

Aspects of Design Behavior

Equipped with the concept of heuristics and heuristic reasoning, we now can take up the task of identifying and attempting to elucidate the characteristic features of the problem-solving behavior of designers in action. Although a more phenomenological account may at times seem more appropriate to the spirit of design activity, a general adherence to the information-processing paradigm of problem-solving theory will be maintained because of its breadth and precision.

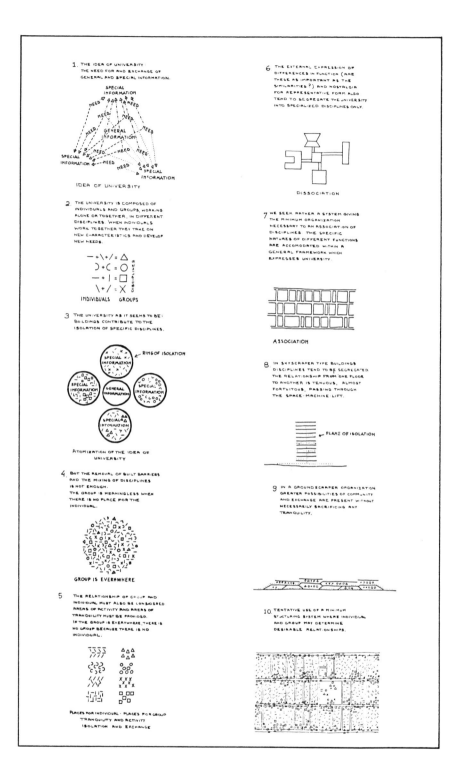

1. THE IDEA OF UNIVERSITY:
THE NEED FOR AND EXCHANGE OF
GENERAL AND SPECIAL INFORMATION.

IDEA OF UNIVERSITY

2. THE UNIVERSITY IS COMPOSED OF
INDIVIDUALS AND GROUPS, WORKING
ALONE OR TOGETHER, IN DIFFERENT
DISCIPLINES. WHEN INDIVIDUALS
WORK TOGETHER THEY TAKE ON
NEW CHARACTERISTICS AND DEVELOP
NEW NEEDS.

INDIVIDUALS   GROUPS

3. THE UNIVERSITY AS IT SEEMS TO BE:
BUILDINGS CONTRIBUTE TO THE
ISOLATION OF SPECIFIC DISCIPLINES.

ATOMIZATION OF THE IDEA OF
UNIVERSITY

4. BUT THE REMOVAL OF BUILT BARRIERS
AND THE MIXING OF DISCIPLINES
IS NOT ENOUGH.
THE GROUP IS MEANINGLESS WHEN
THERE IS NO PLACE FOR THE
INDIVIDUAL.

GROUP IS EVERYWHERE

5. THE RELATIONSHIP OF GROUP AND
INDIVIDUAL MUST ALSO BE CONSIDERED.
AREAS OF ACTIVITY AND AREAS OF
TRANQUILITY MUST BE PROVIDED.
IF THE GROUP IS EVERYWHERE, THERE IS
NO GROUP BECAUSE THERE IS NO
INDIVIDUAL.

PLACES FOR INDIVIDUAL - PLACES FOR GROUP
TRANQUILITY AND ACTIVITY
ISOLATION AND EXCHANGE

6. THE EXTERNAL EXPRESSION OF
DIFFERENCES IN FUNCTION (ARE
THESE AS IMPORTANT AS THE
SIMILARITIES?) AND NOSTALGIA
FOR REPRESENTATIVE FORM ALSO
TEND TO SEGREGATE THE UNIVERSITY
INTO SPECIALIZED DISCIPLINES ONLY.

DISSOCIATION

7. WE SEEK RATHER A SYSTEM GIVING
THE MINIMUM ORGANIZATION
NECESSARY TO AN ASSOCIATION OF
DISCIPLINES. THE SPECIFIC
NATURES OF DIFFERENT FUNCTIONS
ARE ACCOMODATED WITHIN A
GENERAL FRAMEWORK WHICH
EXPRESSES UNIVERSITY.

ASSOCIATION

8. IN SKYSCRAPER TYPE BUILDINGS
DISCIPLINES TEND TO BE SEGREGATED.
THE RELATIONSHIP FROM ONE FLOOR
TO ANOTHER IS TENUOUS, ALMOST
FORTUITOUS, PASSING THROUGH
THE SPACE-MACHINE-LIFT.

FLAME OF ISOLATION

9. IN A GROUNDSCRAPER ORGANIZATION
GREATER POSSIBILITIES OF COMMUNITY
AND EXCHANGE ARE PRESENT WITHOUT
NECESSARILY SACRIFICING ANY
TRANQUILITY.

10. TENTATIVE USE OF A MINIMUM
STRUCTURING SYSTEM WHERE INDIVIDUAL
AND GROUP MAY DETERMINE
DESIRABLE RELATIONSHIPS.

35
Heuristics and model for the Berlin Free University
(Candilis, Josic, and Woods, 1963).

● **The Phenomenon of "Constancy of Appreciation"**
To begin with, it is fairly clear that a given rule, analog, or model will be used in different ways at different times by different practitioners. It follows from this that the clarity and singularity of application of a particular heuristic derive from the moment. Its significance in a design process is thus fixed somehow, at least at a given point in time. Furthermore, at the moment of application, the problem solver's attention is fixed on discrete and specific characteristics embodied in the heuristic that is being employed. This is what Schön refers to as the phenomenon of "constancy of appreciation" (Schön 1983, pp. 272–273).

Although attention may shift, at some other moment, to other characteristics, the use of the heuristic must be discrete, constant, and fixed. Without these conditions a decision could not be made at all. The relevant information provided by the heuristic is regarded by a problem solver as infallible. For example, the designer in the first case study in the preceding chapter had to have been at least momentarily convinced about the efficacy of the principle for shaping urban space in order to have proposed a continuous fabric of building out of which a "place" was cut. This is not to say that once the moment has passed, the decision may not be revoked. However, quite apart from whether it was "correct" or "incorrect," the value of the decision, once made, to further problem-solving activity is that the outcome forms the basis for reflection—for what Schön refers to as "back-talk" between the problem solver and the problem situation (Schön 1983, ch. 3). Thus there ensues an episodic sequence of steps, wherein at different moments attention is fixed exclusively on particular aspects of the problem that seem to warrant consideration.

An interesting question, as yet unresolved, that stems from this phenomenon of constancy of appreciation is whether and to what degree there is congruence in the manner in which designers use particular heuristics. Evidence of very real similarities among examples of architectural and urban design production at certain epochs in history would suggest a reasonable amount of congruence. However, for a more lengthy treatment of this and related issues we must wait until the next chapter.

● **Generation of New Information**
One positive outcome of an appropriate course of heuristic reasoning is that it productively moves the problem into a new light. Consequently, both the scope of the problem (the constraining conditions) and the relative promise of various solution methods

(courses of action) can be reinterpreted. In short, the reasoning process can have the effect of providing valuable new information. For instance, in the second case study the line of reasoning about how to structurally support the building immediately led to a realization about formal design possibilities for the central corridor.

Clearly, it is the testing and comparison procedures inherent in heuristic reasoning that provide this new information. As described before, it is by comparison of the state of a problem space at time t with its state under the rule of an organizing principle at time $t + 1$ that new information is furnished. Logically speaking, this can be accomplished in at least three ways. First, the results of a test can provide information about the conformity of proposed solutions vis-à-vis known constraints. In other words, they can show how close the proposed solution has come to satisfying the constraints. Second, a test can provide information regarding overall progress toward a solution; that is, it can reveal whether the particular line of reasoning appears to be working when evaluated against global constraints. Finally, the application of heuristics can provide new information about other appropriate constraints, not so far considered as being part of the problem. Of course, the validity and import of the new information may not be fully apparent until subsequent steps have been taken making use of the information. As the new information becomes available, it must be provisionally considered useful; otherwise the line of argument through which it was revealed would have to be abandoned. In other words, information about constraint conditions not so far considered may or may not be appropriate, but it will not be until the conclusion of subsequent operations that the value of the information can be fully assessed. For example, again in the second case study, we saw that it was only when the moves associated with compositionally arranging pieces of the building were almost complete that the problem of scale and size became apparent.

Sometimes, through either necessity or a lack of confidence in the outcome portrayed by new information, a line of argument is abandoned. This abandonment can result in the problem solver's backtracking through the problem space to a point that appears to be non-troublesome and promises to allow forward progress. This topic will be taken up a little later in our discussion.

● **Referential Bases of Heuristics**

An interesting aspect of many organizing principles is that, when logically extended, they seem to provide designers with a self-referential rule structure (Eisenman 1979), a rule structure largely governed by the subject matter incorporated within the rule. For example, in the application of an abstract proportional device, such as a 3 × 3 cube, there are many possible implied patterns of orthogonal and diagonal divisions that can be exploited to give rise to a building (as in Eisenman's "Houses"; see figure 36). Furthermore, the full implications or extent of the patterns may not be fully understood by a designer when the proportional device is first employed, owing to the phenomenon of constancy of appreciation. Gradually, however, the latent qualities of the model may become apparent, introducing new information into the designer's problem space. In fact, the device may initially be chosen for a reason that becomes irrelevant as other, underlying qualities are more fully exploited: once the new possibilities inherent in the problem have been revealed, the problem itself is reformulated, sometimes radically.

If this exercise is reduced to a kind of "analog takeover," involving only the willful exploration of the latent properties of the chosen device, then clearly the appropriateness of the exercise can seriously be called into question. A very real issue that attends the dominant use of autonomous constraints is the superficial enrichment of the problem under consideration. It is an enrichment that runs the risk of so distorting the problem that it loses its original meaning and orientation.

● **End Justification**

As defined earlier, the structure of the reasoning process used in applying a heuristic seems to conform to the general argument, "If problem X is encountered, then take action Y under conditions Z." Following from the subsequent discussion of alternative forms of argument, it seems reasonable to propose rewriting the expression as, "If conditions A obtain, then action B is taken for the intention of C," where intention C is clearly bound up with solution of the problem. Thus, we might say that another referential base, or form-giving power, of a heuristic derives from the correspondence that can be realized between a designer's intention, the prevailing conditions of the problem situation, and a formal action.

In many cases, however, an intention and an action are expressed synonymously and may precede the perception of specific conditions. In other words, the intention can be understood

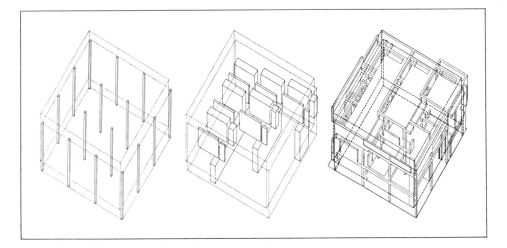

36
Transformations 4, 13, and 16 (House II, by Peter
Eisenman, 1969).

solely by reference to the action; they become so thoroughly
intertwined that we cannot distinguish one from the other. Furthermore, although certain general boundary conditions may be
in view, they lack specificity. For instance, in the second case
study the designer's action of using the model type was indistinguishable from any (separate) intentional orientation that she
may have had at the time.

Clearly, attention has somehow been shifted here, and a trans-
position has occurred in the structure of the argument guiding
the reasoning process. It now becomes, "If action B, implying
intention C, then (specific) conditions A must obtain." The solution of the problem has taken on the character of being "end-
justified." Nevertheless, if we recall the earlier delineation of an
ill-defined problem and remember the underconstrained structure of many design problems, at least at the outset, this seemingly perverse strategy begins to appear plausible, if not
necessary. Taken to extremes, of course, it can force us into a
dilemma similar to that encountered with superficial enrichment
of a problem space—viz., a solution in search of a problem.

● **The Influence of Modes of Representation**
Michael Graves has eloquently described the inevitable reciprocity that occurs in an architectural design process between the
act of drawing and the thinking associated with it—between
"the image" and "the mind" (Graves 1977). The hand moves, the
mind becomes engaged, and vice versa. If we infer from this

statement that what is understood about a problem comes to us via representation of solution images, then the role of media, such as drawings in the case of architectural design and formal mathematical models in some urban planning applications, becomes a very important consideration. We might then ask, what is it about drawing or symbolic modeling that allows us to discover things? Or, conversely, how might the medium of expression actually constrain a design process?

Clearly, in the case of drawings, as Graves goes on to say, different scales and levels of precision reveal different qualities of solutions (see figure 37). Referential sketches, for instance, often have an idiosyncratic, notational quality about them. They are the "marking" of concepts and conceptual developments, rich in meaning to some but meaningless to others. Static standard projections, such as plans, elevations, and sections, may fail to convey certain spatial qualities, such as those time-dependent aspects experienced as one moves through a building; whereas other media—computer graphic displays, for instance—may not be so limited.

On a related note, Kenneth Frampton, commenting on some recent graphic output from contemporary architectural circles, has observed, "The veil that photo-lithography draws over architecture is not neutral. High-speed photographic and reproductive processes are surely not only the political economy of the sign, but also an insidious filter through which our tactile environment tends to lose its responsiveness. . . . When much of modern building is experienced in actuality, its photogenic sculptural quality is denied by the poverty and brutality of its detailing" (Frampton 1980, p. 297). To be sure, these statements are part of Frampton's critique of the modern technological order's debasement of our sense of place, of settlement and lodging. Nevertheless, he is also demonstrating that there is a symbolic value in our choice of media, one that reveals a great deal about what we regard as important and what we don't find so important. Conversely, as has already been suggested, a medium has a way of constraining our choices; and its influence is probably just as marked in the reciprocity between a designer and a drawing in process as it is when the final rendering is given a more public and sober review. What is especially disturbing, however, is that this influence may not involve conscious choice at all.

Ernst Mach once said that a mollusk on a rock at sea could have no knowledge of Euclidean geometry (Ivins 1973, pp. 7–10)— that is, that truths assumed by Euclid to be self-evident, univer-

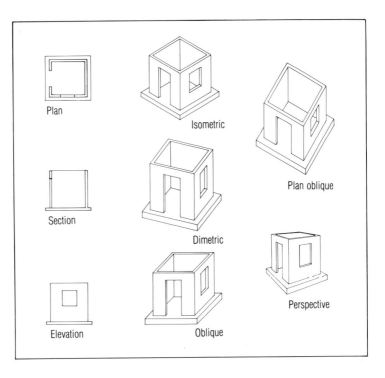

37
Eight projections of a simple cubic object.

sal, and beyond experience could in fact be apprehended only by certain kinds of beings. The mollusk, without fingers or similar movable tactile devices and deprived of, say, a piece of straight timber, could hardly be expected to observe that parallel lines don't converge! It is quite clear from the history of architecture, and the history of ideas for that matter, that developments in representational techniques—such as perspective drawings and the systems of geometry of Pascal and Descartes—have had a profound effect (Ivins 1973, Perez-Gomez 1983). Such developments have altered what we can represent, see, and therefore understand and imagine.

Similar observations can be made in the realm of urban design and planning. Let us take, for instance, recent technical developments in the use of statistical models for predicting the likely choice behavior of individuals in response to a policy, such as increasing the price of gasoline. Here, a lengthy mathematical expression of terms, usually linear, is constructed on the basis of data analyses; each term represents some variable aspect of choice behavior. For example, they may represent the various aspects of a decision about how to make a journey to work, as described in the previous chapter, or the aspects of the choice of a suburban house. Invariably, the validity and very possibility of such mathematical expressions are subject to the availability of data, the kinds of inferences allowed by the particular method of statistical analysis, and even the assumption of independence among variables that a linear expression entails. Consequently, certain variables, or aspects of choice behavior, may be more likely to be incorporated than others about which only qualitative speculations can be made. The upshot is that the proposition and evaluation of policy alternatives can be determined to a significant degree by the technique, or medium, of expression and representation. Furthermore, in the case just outlined, there may also be a tendency to incorporate variables that are statistically relevant, although no really satisfactory nonstatistical explanation can be provided (Ingram 1979). This is tantamount to analog takeover, in that the use of the medium in its own terms far outstrips the message.

As with drawing and other representational media in architecture, unquestionably great strides have been made in urban design and planning circles toward the perfection of technical precision and flexibility. Nevertheless, it is apparent that the planner, in the end, sees and understands only those things for which he or she can provide expression.

● **Transformation of a Problem Space**
This discussion has focused so far on the definition and illustration of organizing principles and other heuristic devices. We have also scrutinized alternative logical structures for the general kinds of argument employed when using these devices and have noted certain observable phenomena in their application, such as self-referential qualities, end justification, and constancy of appreciation. Finally, we have explored the contours of the apparent limits imposed by the media through which heuristics are applied. It is now time to pursue the matter of how such principles are chosen and how switching from one kind of principle to another takes place during a problem-solving process. It is clear that for most design problems of any complexity the thinking comes within the ambit of different rules at different times.

Logic and the Choice of Heuristic Rules and Constraints
Often, the choice of rule and the consequent constraints that are applied in organizing problem-solving activity are regarded as private matters and receive little attention. In other instances,

such rules and constraints are assumed to derive from the problem at hand and are tacitly accepted as such. Nevertheless, it should be apparent from earlier discussions that several general logical forms of inquiry and argument can be seen at work in the choice or devising of a particular rule, and therefore the method by which constraints are introduced into a problem space. This section will outline three species of logic—*deduction, induction, and abduction*—and the types of design situation to which each is most likely to apply.

In the application of a rule of the form "If problem X is encountered under conditions Z, then make use of action Y," deduction is at work when action Y belongs to X and includes conditions Z. Here the relationship between problem X and action Y acts as a rule, while conditions Z bound the problem by providing certain specific parameters to be addressed through action Y. For example, a problem of building a structure with a minimum amount of deflection in its members would probably be addressed through an empirical determination of the size and composition of the members, using some general mathematical expression about loads, spans, and so on, subject to specific requirements for the problem at hand. The same might be said for the application of other well-known environmental relations that address specific classes of problems while admitting variation in the conditions over which the relation can obtain. Logical deduction appears to be most valid in well-defined problem situations, where problem X is taken as a bona fide given, with a clear expression of ends, and where one deduces the appropriate means by using available rules and principles.

It is apparent from another form of argument presented earlier in connection with heuristic reasoning that induction, too, is a plausible direction of inquiry. For example, the expression "If conditions Z are encountered, then problem X becomes defined" can be seen to lend itself to an inductive reasoning process, where one moves from the particularities of a situation to a more comprehensive conclusion. During architectural design this is often the case, as when the observation of particular user needs precipitates formulation of a more general problem and the actions that stem from it. In the activity analysis described by Sanoff, for example, building users formulate their own design problems with the help of game-playing techniques. During the course of attending to detailed arrangements, the users and designers often perceive larger issues (Sanoff 1977, ch. 4).

A third form of logical inquiry and argumentation is to be seen at work in the cases of end justification described in a previous section. As we have seen, in such cases the action and the problem definition become intertwined. To all intents and purposes, the problem becomes defined simultaneously with the proposal of a solution. It is adduced, in much the same manner as a law is adduced in the service of explaining natural phenomena (Hempel and Oppenheim 1948). This is clearly not a case of deduction, as there are not sufficient grounds for the erection of a deductive logical system. Nor is it a case of induction, as the reasoning process does not necessarily involve systematic argumentation from particulars to some generality. Rather, it is an appropriation from outside the immediate context of the problem space, used for its promise of providing a higher level of organization. For instance, a designer at the outset of tackling a problem in housing may decide to make use of a particular type of configuration. Furthermore, that type becomes the model through which the problem is essentially understood and construed.

This form of inquiry is closely akin to what Peirce refers to, in his treatment of the logic of scientific inquiry, as "abduction" (Fann 1970). He describes the principle as follows: "A surprising fact, C, is observed. But if a proposition, A, were true, C would be a matter of course. Hence, there is reason to suspect that A is true" (Peirce 1965, p. 374). He goes on to distinguish abduction from deduction and induction on the basis of the fact that abduction includes the case where A and C are distinct from one another and only become related through the existence of some appropriated scheme, or "view of the world," that has meaning for both A and C (Peirce 1965, p. 374f.; see figure 38).

A simple abstract example will serve to illustrate this mode of reasoning (Handa 1983). Suppose we wish to relate two propositions, A and C, that appear to belong to two different and distinct realms, X and Y respectively. Here deduction or induction by means of a third linking proposition B must be ruled out, as B must belong to either realm X or realm Y, and both are distinct. In order to relate A and C, we must extend the two distinct realms and appropriate an alternative view in which they are no longer distinct, so that B belongs to both the X part and the Y part. For instance, let us say that A, B, and C are two-dimensional areas on a plane surface (see figure 39). If A is a subset of X and C is a subset of Y, then X and Y are different planes floating in three-dimensional space, so to speak, such that $A \subset B$

	Premise	General case	Special case
Deduction	$A \subset B$ and $B \subset C$	$A \subset C$	[diagram] $A \subset C$
Induction	$A \supset B$ and $B \subset C$	$A \cap C \neq \emptyset$	[diagram] $A \subset C$ [diagram] $A \supset C$ [diagram] $A \cap C \neq \emptyset$, $\neq A$, $\neq C$
Abduction	$A \subset B$ and $B \supset C$	$A \cap C \neq \emptyset$, $A \cap C = \emptyset$	[diagram] $A \subset C$ [diagram] $A \supset C$ [diagram] $A \cap C \neq \emptyset$, $\neq A$, $\neq C$ [diagram] $A \cap C \neq \emptyset$

38
A comparison of deduction, induction, and abduction.

and $C \subset B$ cannot exist on a specific two-dimensional plane. If we allow inclusion of a curved three-dimensional space, however, another area, shown by B, may exist.

Abduction (or adduction) is not a random process. The appropriation that is made must show promise in facilitating problem-solving activity. Returning to our example, presumably it would be possible to provide a three-dimensional world D that linked A and C but had no meaning for our investigation. In that world the means B for providing a satisfactory relationship between A and C would have no status.

As we have seen from the case studies and other instances, this mode of inquiry is very common in design. We often employ heuristics that allow us to import autonomous constraints into our problem spaces in order to facilitate further activity. In fact, in the case of ill-defined and wicked problems abduction is the rule rather than the exception.

Switching of Rules and Constraints
It becomes evident when one examines the structure of problem solving in architectural design that the distinction of problem definition, solution generation, and solution evaluation as independent stages does not entirely obtain. Often, the provisional rules that are employed at once define the problem, incorporate

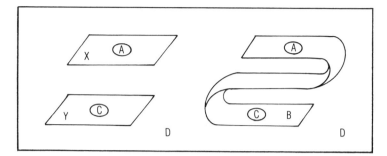

39
Concepts *A* and *C* and their worlds *X, Y, B,*
and *D.*

solutions, and prescribe means for performing evaluations. To put it another way, success in applying a rule, particularly when measured in terms of the solution properties of the rule, is largely guaranteed. For instance, once a housing problem is construed as one of elaborating a particular typology, then evaluation becomes similarly directed and the likelihood of reaching a solution is relatively high. Nevertheless, in actual practice, judgments are made outside this self-referential framework. Particular approaches and organizing principles are abandoned and backtracking does occur. Clearly, for these changes in direction to take place, some form of evaluation must occur outside the immediate context of exercising a particular organizing principle and therefore beyond the realm of a strict constancy of appreciation. Setting aside criticism from some other agent, what might be the mechanism for such switching? How does one organizing principle relinquish control in favor of another?

In response to these questions several models might be proposed.[12] Let us first consider the case of a (reasonably) well-defined problem, in which an organizing principle is selected and applied under conditions of constancy of appreciation, a solution is proposed, and then the latter is evaluated in the light of known solution properties. Evaluation reveals discrepancies, if any, between characteristics of the proposed solution and the properties required for solution. This information forms the basis for a means-ends analysis by which another rule is selected or formulated, and so the problem-solving activity proceeds. Even under the circumstances of a relatively ill-defined problem, if certain properties of the required solution are known or are assumed to hold, a similar process can take place and a switch be made from one heuristic to another.

In a more extreme case of an ill-defined problem, however, where the required properties of a solution are undefined, extremely uncertain, or so vague that evaluation cannot adequately be sustained, the model begins to break down; the process becomes a matter of trial-and-error. The "dialogue" between problem solver and problem situation (Schön 1983, ch. 3) cannot be productively continued, as evaluation can only be performed self-referentially—within the frame of reference presented by the rule itself—and therefore no discrepancies are likely to be found. Strictly speaking, problem solving cannot continue other than by simply starting again.

This extreme case becomes less problematic if we admit "selective inattention" in the constancy of appreciation that takes place during the dialogue between a problem solver and a problem situation. Selective inattention involves calling to mind other organizing principles in the process of applying one in particular. It is a speculative aspect of the dialogue, by means of which a note is made to oneself of the kind, "Gee! I recognize a particular problem here because of other criteria that I have so far ignored, but I shall press on for now!" In other words, for an extreme case where conventional means-ends analysis or like strategies for making a transition must be eliminated, the switching model might be expressed by the recognition of a new principle that is related in some way to the old.

With this formulation as a plausible explanation of the lines along which switching occurs, the issue now becomes what might determine the selection of successive organizing principles. What lies behind selectivity of inattention? Is it a case of parallel streams of argument, vying with each other in some way? Or is it just a matter of random association?

To the extent that it can be observed, the selection of successive organizing principles may appear in a given instance to be quite idiosyncratic. It is unlikely to be random, however. For if it were, convergence on a solution of any kind would not happen with the consistency that is apparent from observation. As we saw in the case studies in chapter 1, the designers proceeded more or less directly toward solutions after some adjustment and reorientation.

The parallel-stream concept might appear to be supported by frequent remarks on the part of problem solvers in action, of the type, "Now, I can see two possible alternatives," or "I can think of several ways to go." Yet under the constancy of appreciation that is required when one pursues a particular strategy and line of reasoning, even with sufficient selective inattention to note other possibilities, "parallel processing" is probably not occurring. Instead, problem-solving behavior would seem to be serial, moving in sequence from one line of argument to another, with a second line of argument perhaps noted during pursuit of the first. This claim is supported by substantial experimental evidence. In effect, observations on the part of problem solvers such as "I can see two alternatives" are better explained as taking place at the moment of switching organizing principles or of considering such an action, than as signifying the pursuit of two directions at once.

Another rationale for switching from one principle to another might be found within the information contained in an initial line or argument, without resort to selective inattention or some other similar mechanism. By simply adopting the opposite, or "not," properties to those rendered by one (failing) line of reasoning, the solver could formulate a plausible alternative strategy. For instance, when difficulties are encountered with the use of symmetry in making a composition, then we might change to the use of asymmetry. In other words, the very proposition of certain specific properties through an organizing principle may imply the meaningful existence of opposite properties within the context of essentially the same rule. This strictly dichotomous mode does not, however, account for the attention that is seen to be paid toward other, nonoppositional properties, even during moments of applying a particular rule. We have seen an instance of this in the designer in the first chapter who shifted from an organizing principle about engineering structure to one about circulation.

Yet another explanation for the switching that occurs might be proffered, one that is perhaps closer to the mark. If selective inattention when applying a particular rule means calling to mind other procedures, possibilities, or solution images, we may usefully regard such organizing principles and heuristic devices as having properties that allow relations to be struck with other principles and devices. Here a sufficient overlap of properties among otherwise distinct organizing principles would allow such connections to be established in the mind's eye of a problem solver. For example, in the second case study described in chapter 1, the designer began by referring to a specific building type as a model for the overall organization of a program of activities and for the manner in which they might be architecturally expressed and resolved. This led, perhaps naturally enough, to more general speculation about the very idea of combining parts of a building, thence to consideration of other ways of addressing the issue of "combining of parts," and finally to a thoroughgoing functional analysis of basic programmatic considerations. What might have appeared to be a fairly radical jump in procedure—from exploration of the formal architectural features of a building type to a "first-principles" examination of adjacency requirements among the areas of activity to be accommodated in the building—was "in the cards" from the outset. In this particular instance the switch was occasioned by a realization on the part of the designer that the building program and its parts were too cumbersome to be resolved in the formal architectural terms inherent in the building type that had been originally adopted. This realization, in turn, gave rise to a generalization of the dilemma to one of "parts and their combination," and hence to a functional analysis of required spaces and desirable adjacencies between them. Thus, the perception of common underlying dimensions of organizing principles may well account for the lines along which switches from one heuristic to another take place, particularly in cases where the general thrust of the original organizing principles seems appropriate but the particular procedure itself is found to be practically inadequate.

Switching among organizing principles appears to occur not only when difficulty is encountered but also more casually under successful pursuit of a particular procedure. Here the purpose, or result, is the enrichment of a problem space and the supply of useful additional information. In the protocol analysis just mentioned, the designer, having reached the realization of the general issue of combining parts, noted that this also meant something both about the structural support of the building and about the functional and social purposes to which it would be put.

● Order of Application of Rules and Backtracking
When tackling complex problems, designers seem to switch among heuristic devices as the occasion dictates. Rarely, if ever, does one organizing principle suffice and provide all the information necessary to resolve a problem. It may be seen, however, from protocol analyses of designers in action, such as those presented in the first chapter, that the order in which heuristic devices are applied significantly affects the final outcome of the proposals that are made. Generally, it is the early attempts at

organizing the problem space that have a prevailing influence on subsequent directions, regardless of difficulties that might be encountered later on (Simon 1970, p. 7).

In light of the foregoing account of problem-solving behavior, this tendency is quite understandable. The initial structuring of a problem is the basis on which that problem becomes understood, and thus it is the vantage point from which fruitful avenues toward solution are sought. Experimental evidence suggests that the guidance provided by early ordering of a problem space is relatively long lasting and difficult to abandon (Simon 1970). This phenomenon was particularly noticeable in our third case study, as the persistent recurrence of the two major organizational themes.

Subsequent lines of inquiry are more likely to be abandoned as unfruitful (that is, not relevant) or intractable. Usually the acknowledgment of their failure triggers a backward pass through the problem space to a more propitious orientation with a higher perceived chance of success. This is the phenomenon known as backtracking, with which we have already become somewhat acquainted (Newell, Shaw, and Simon 1967, p. 72).

Backtracking is most clearly illustrated in relation to a decision tree, as shown in figure 40. (In most reasonably complex design problems, of course, a complete representation of the problem space as a decision tree would be very extensive and well beyond casual enumeration of the possibilities by the problem solver, to whom many of the branches and nodes might be invisible.) Here, the initial pass through the problem space is given by the link-node sequence a_1, b_1, c_2, d_3, e_1, and difficulty is encountered at node e_1. Backtracking occurs to the point c_2 before a forward pass is made through nodes d_4 and e_5.

The essential difference between backtracking and the kind of switching discussed in the preceding section is one of direction: in switching there is forward motion through the problem space during successive attempts to restructure the space toward a solution, whereas in backtracking—which may be regarded as a particular case of switching—there is a retreat to an earlier understanding or construal of the problem. Backtracking may not involve switching entirely from one organizational device to another. Instead, a particular line of reasoning may have choice points embedded within it, among which there might be movement in search of better opportunities, but without necessarily suspending the overriding organizational concept that is being applied. Indeed, backtracking rarely involves a radical re-

40
A diagram illustrating backtracking through a
problem space.

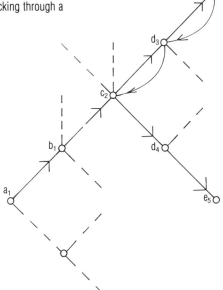

thinking of a problem, other than in the exceptional case where
difficulties are encountered early on in the process, say at
choice point b_1 in figure 40. Clearly, here reappraisal will lead to
a different trajectory through the problem space. Another interpretation of this kind of behavior, however, is that it is quite
characteristic of an initial reckoning with a problem, when various points of attack, each valued more or less equally, are tested
before a commitment is made to sustain one in particular. Early
skirmishes with a problem during which various lines of attack
are very provisionally assayed are quite familiar among
designers.

● **A Concept of Style**
Finally, as noted by Simon and others, this kind of theoretical
appraisal of design offers the prospect of a concept of style (Simon 1970, pp. 9–10; Gombrich 1965). It is a concept based not
on the classification of various physical features of architecture
and urban design but on the problem-solving process itself.

We have seen that the final outcome of a design process is
strongly determined by at least three aspects of that process: the
subject matter of the organizing principles that are adopted, the
manner in which these principles are interpreted and reinterpreted in the context of the problem at hand, and the sequence
of applying such organizing principles. Consistency in style

among the output of designers can thus be understood as a habitual way of doing things, of solving problems. The tendency for this consistency to be most pronounced during particular times in a designer's career, say toward the end of "stylistic" episodes, is also understandable. A fluency in a particular way of designing, and the consistency that comes with it, can only be reached through experience and constant development. It also seems to coincide with conditions under which Merleau-Ponty's "sedimented principles" lead to enhanced know-how. At such moments the potential of certain preferred organizing principles and enabling prejudices has been more fully realized, and they become something of a personal form of architectural expression. For example, Stirling, like many other great architects, has developed a distinctive repertoire of techniques for dealing with, say, interior spaces. In his work we see the use of "porthole" windows to provide visual access without overly interrupting wall planes, the use of "pullman-car" cone lighting, and so on. By extension, style in the broader community sense may be regarded as congruent with the collective adoption of certain organizing principles and practices—that is, with forms of heuristic reasoning. When dominant principles and forms no longer prove productive, they are replaced, and shifts in style— in habitual ways of doing things on the part of the design community—can be observed.

Limitations of a Procedural View

As Bruner notes in a discussion about creative problem solving, there is a certain "shrillness to our contemporary concern with creativity" (Bruner 1967, p. 26)—a shrillness, or heartfelt need, that he believes stems from our search for sources of dignity in what we do. "In an age where dominant values are pragmatic and whose achievement is an intricate technological order . . . it is not sufficient to be merely useful. . . . Creativity seems to imbue acts with dignity" (Bruner 1967, p. 2).

In architectural circles during the 1960s and early 1970s, the shrillness of the concern for the creative problem-solving process that Bruner refers to became very apparent, although toward somewhat different ends. Armed with the emerging information processing theory of problem solving and earlier rigid-state models, the design disciplines sought to describe and exemplify *the* design process (Thornley 1963, Gregory 1966, Broadbent and Ward 1969, Jones 1970, Broadbent 1973, Wade

1977). As Mitchell describes their chronology, these efforts were less the result of theoretical developments in the field of problem solving than a reaction to the apparent disintegration of existing techniques and orthodoxies, coupled with a rise in pressure for higher degrees of user participation (Mitchell 1970). In this latter regard, what seemed necessary was a clear and logical procedure for producing designs and plans that could be understood and participated in by all those involved. With respect to the former point, what seemed necessary was a far greater understanding of design processes, in order that procedures could be improved. In spite of the very real contributions that were made, at least to our understanding of these processes, in almost all cases the step beyond description into a normative realm in which process became pursued as an end in itself resulted in abject failure. Attempts to devise *the* process became exercises in inanity when compared to the great subtlety and profundity of observed problem-solving behavior. This movement, in the view of many, eventually resulted in a form of "methodolatory" (Colquhoun 1967); it is currently experiencing a relative hiatus, with the possible exception of developments in the field of computer-aided design, mentioned earlier.

Quite apart from the prescriptive orientation of the design methodologists, the program of converting description into explanatory theory about what designers do can be seen to founder in another way. So far, what we have discussed about design could probably just as well be said, at least in large measure, of some other realm of inquiry. In fact, most adherents of the information processing theory of problem solving would make such a claim for this kind of speculation. It is intended to be general and, as such, applicable to many different fields of inquiry. There is no reason to believe that architects and urban designers attack problems in fundamentally different ways from, say, scientists and mathematicians, at least at this level of theorizing. Common kinds of means-ends analysis, heuristic search, problem-space planning, and other procedures can be seen at work across disciplinary boundaries (Perkins 1981, Ghiselin 1952, Polya 1954, Simon 1973). The fact remains, however, that we don't have much difficulty distinguishing what architects do from the activities of psychologists or doctors, and have only a little more difficulty with distinctions between, say, architects and painters or between architects and planners. Similarly, how these various fields actually conduct their inquiries may be less well known, but discrimination is still possible. It would seem, therefore, that such distinctions can be drawn, but as much through the subject matter embodied in the principles of practice as through the structure of inquiry. Furthermore, these are principles that derive not only from the kinds of problems being worked on at the time but also from the frames of reference, attitudes, and perspectives that are more generally adopted. In short, they come from another realm of theoretical speculation.

At this juncture we might say that design, like other disciplines, involves a kind of procedural knowledge—that is, both tactical understanding and know-how—and a kind of substantive knowledge outside the procedures themselves (Schön 1983, Ryle 1949). Clearly the two kinds are related; indeed, they are inextricably intertwined. A carpenter, for instance, not only has a "knowing-how" understanding of procedures such as sawing, nailing, and routing but also has a "knowing-that" understanding of the circumstances under which such procedures should be applied. Through the reflection of the moment, that know-how and knowledge of criteria are applied at once, constituting a judgmental action (Schön 1983, pp. 50–69).

With this definition of its constitutive elements, we are brought more squarely on the question of where next to turn in rendering an account of practical inquiry in architecture and urban design. Both an explicit and an implicit part of our discussion so far has been the idea that structural aspects of a problem-solving process, of which we have enumerated nine or ten, significantly determine the outcome. Let us assume, however, that we are given an elaborate protocol analysis of several problem solvers in action, each in the same problem situation. From what has been said, how might we go about commenting upon the relative appropriateness of each outcome? In other words, how might we address the issue of adjudicating merit?

First, we could use the protocol analyses, in conjunction with the structural considerations that have been discussed, in order to comment upon the comparative technical skill and logical qualities with which the problem solvers have addressed the problem situation. With very little extrapolation we should be able to discern whether the self-referential qualities of various organizing devices have been fully realized. We could make comment on the relative efficiency of one approach over another, by reference to episodes of backtracking and other kinds of switches among the principles employed. We could also probably detect patterns of more or less logical reasoning and discuss the extent to which this appears to have influenced outcomes.

Second, we could measure the extent to which each proposed solution appears to satisfy the solution properties of the problem as given. Here, connections might be drawn between the various aspects of the problem as stated and the manner in which they were addressed in the proposed solutions. From this a critical evaluation could be rendered with respect to the comprehensiveness and logical precision of the solution.

Third, we could compare the manner in which the problem has been construed by each problem solver with the manner in which it was given. We might ask whether the proposed solution seems overly end-justified, so that it is a response but not necessarily to the stated problem. On the other hand, we might be in a position to discriminate instances in which the constraints that were autonomously supplied to the problem space were never fully realized and exploited, thus raising questions of redundancy and superficial enrichment of the problem space.

Beyond these general points, however, little can be said without venturing into comparisons of the appropriateness of the organizing principles or heuristics themselves. This would become particularly apparent in the case of those principles that are independently supplied to the situation, where differences among problem solvers are apt to be greater than in instances of stricter problem definition. To achieve an adjudication of merit that transcends personal likes and dislikes would also seem to require inspection, discussion, and debate about the perspectives through which organizing principles and constraints are supplied. Otherwise, important issues of applicability, appropriateness, opportunity, and real enhancement of a problem cannot very well be broached. Clearly this is in large measure a normative terrain concerned with values and aspirations. Therefore it is to the normative perspectives that supply and shape organizing principles that we should turn in order to develop a more thoroughgoing account of practical inquiry in architecture and urban design. This will be the task of the following chapters.

Normative Positions That Guide Design Thinking

3

For architects and urban designers, a major source for the perspectives that guide the choice of organizing principles and constraints is the realm of theoretical discourse. Theory is assumed to be about general principles with applicability beyond specific cases, and, whether it comes by way of systematic speculation and codification or by way of more indirect experience, to be well substantiated. To the extent that it has a community of subscribers, theory represents a corpus of principles that are agreed upon and therefore worthy of emulation.

Normative Positions

A quick perusal of published compendia of various theoretical positions in architecture will attest a rhetoric that is usually censorious and acerbic, and ineluctably concerned with "what ought to be" (Conrads 1964). Such writings contain essential statements of values and thus of priorities among concerns pertaining to architecture. The thrust of the messages is about the location and merit of norms to be categorically valued and aspired toward in the practice of architectural design. Furthermore, most positions can be said to address in some way the ontological question "What is architecture versus something else?"—or, "What constitutes proper architecture?"

Sir Nikolaus Pevsner's response to this question is the celebrated statement in the introduction to *An Outline of European Architecture*: "A bicycle shed is a building; Lincoln Cathedral is a piece of Architecture." A rationale follows: "Nearly everything that encloses space on a scale sufficient for a human being to move in is a building. The term architecture only applies to buildings with a view to aesthetic appeal" (Pevsner 1961, p. 1).

This definition has its limitations, of course. In it architecture is portrayed as a subset of building, and therefore built objects that don't enclose space sufficient for human activity—facades, some bridges, and so on—are erased. More important, aesthetic appeal and not, say, utilitarian considerations is the essential and sufficient criterion for architecture. The point here, however, is not to take issue with Pevsner's definition, but rather to indicate the kind of direction we shall be looking in for a reasonably consistent idea of theory among competing normative positions.

In this examination we shall follow a similar method to that pursued with regard to problem-solving behavior. Classes of positions rather than individual positions will be defined, and their implications for design assessed. These classes of theoretical positions will be examined for their qualities of logical coherence and for the substantiation on which they base their claims to legitimacy.

Surface Features and Broad Inclinations

Statements of normative positions can generally be found to include the following elements: (1) the location and identification of a problem or of pertinent issues under contention, (2) an unfavorable assessment of prevailing practice and an enumeration of untapped opportunities, and (3) a counterproposal with its rationale. Further, the proposal and rationale are typically founded in the distinctions made between the prevailing practices and the latent opportunities. For example, Hannes Meyer, addressing the Bauhaus in February 1928, outlined his thesis on "building" in the following manner:

all things in this world are a product of the formula: (function times economy)
all these things are, therefore, not works of art:
all art is composition, hence unsuited to achieve goals.
all life is function and therefore unartistic.
the idea of the "composition of a harbor" is hilarious!
but how is a town plan designed? or a plan of a dwelling? composition or function? art or life?????
(Meyer 1928, Wingler 1969, p. 153)

This stanza contains a critique of what was perceived to be prevailing practice—namely, architecture as art, art as impractical and not of this world. It also contains statements concerning the opportunities for otherwise addressing the issue of building and architecture—that is, by way of function. Furthermore, the statements locate the problem as being a fundamental question about how to design and build.

Meyer goes on to elaborate a counterproposal by presenting building as a "biological process" and calling for the organization of new building materials "into a constructive whole based on economic principles." Completing the biological analogy, he asserts, "the individual shape, the body of the structure, . . . evolve by themselves and are determined by life" (Meyer 1928; see figure 41). His position is presented in an almost syllogistic form. The argument links the location of the problem, through a critical assessment of existing approaches and a survey of other

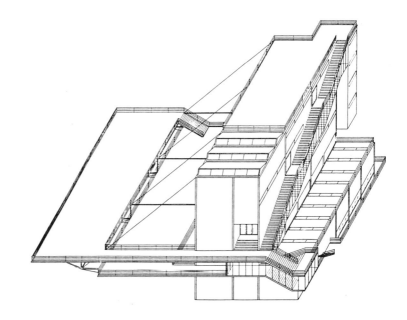

41
Project for the Peters School (Petersschule) in
Basle, by Hannes Meyer (1926).

opportunities, to a counterproposal. Whether or not we agree
with it, the thesis has a compelling logical structure.

In Le Corbusier's "Five Points towards a New Architecture," to
use another well-known example, the line of argument is not
quite so clearly set out. Nevertheless, the opening paragraph
provides a summary of its general tenor, as well as an indication
of the perceived problem. "The following points," announces Le
Corbusier, "in no way relate to aesthetic fantasies or a striving
for fashionable effects, but concern architectural facts that imply
an entirely new kind of building" (Le Corbusier and Jeanneret
1926; Conrads 1964, p. 99). Here, a negative judgment is implicit
in the phrases "aesthetic fantasies" and "fashionable effects."
Elaboration of the five points follows, largely aimed at justifying
their autonomy and viability on technological and functional
grounds. The five points are (1) supports, (2) roof gardens,
(3) free design of the ground plane, (4) horizontal windows, and
(5) free design of the facade; held to be the necessary ingredients
of "proper" architecture, they are presented as inherently new
opportunities for building and ones that are more intrinsically
appropriate to the conditions of the time (see figure 42).

42
The Villa Stein–De Monzie (Maison Stein) in
Garches, by Le Corbusier and Pierre Jeanneret
(1927).

Le Corbusier concludes the argument by asserting that "the
essential points . . . represent a fundamentally new aesthetic.
Nothing is left to us of the architecture of past epochs" (Conrads
1964, p. 100). Although he omits several steps linking the
counterproposal of the five points, and their rationale, to the perceived problem of socially disconnected, historicist "aesthetic
fantasies," the syllogism can be readily filled in by implication.

A more vexing subject for this kind of analysis and framework is
the credo or the aphorism, sometimes drawn from architecture's
oral tradition. For example, there are Van der Velde's "Credo"
(Van der Velde 1907), Kahn's poetic invocation "Order is . . ."
(Kahn 1961), and Mies van der Rohe's oft-misquoted "beinahe
nichts"—"almost nothing" (Mies van der Rohe 1923).[1] Despite
their idiosyncratic use of language, the same kind of argumentation can still be discovered in these statements, if one is willing
to place them in context and engage in some interpretation.
Their effectual status as expressions of normative positions is
attested by the reverberations they have caused in architectural
circles.

On a more prosaic level, a considerable body of commentary has been developed around the central question posed by "form follows function."[2] This commentary moves beyond the emblematic qualities of the aphorism and stands at the center of a long-standing debate regarding these two architectural categories.

The import of vague or brief statements can be just as rigorous and compelling as that of more complete dissertations. For our purposes, therefore, any serious statement of a normative position, regardless of its surface qualities, should be admitted for further scrutiny. It will be useful, however, to differentiate among these positions according to one of their surface qualities: their location on a continuum that ranges from what will be called, after Attoe, *doctrinaire positions* at one extreme to what will be called *categorical systems* at the other (Attoe 1978).

● **Doctrinaire Positions versus Categorical Systems**
In the extreme case doctrinaire positions will coincide with the assertion of a singular point of view, attitude, and approach that is of primary if not sole importance for defining "proper" architecture and for guiding production. Such positions may take several forms, as can be seen from the foregoing discussion. They may involve a general invocation of a guiding principle, aimed at influencing the attitudes of designers. For example, there are the positions closely aligned with certain construals of aphorisms such as "less is more," "form follows function," and so on. They may also involve a prescription of those architectural elements that should be given primacy. Le Corbusier's "Five Points" exhibits this characteristic, as does Hannes Meyer's proposal in its entirety.

By contrast, categorical systems may appear on the surface to be less definitional and prescriptive regarding their requirements for proper architecture. Nevertheless, they are frameworks necessary for answering what proper architecture is, versus something else. They are ostensibly less singular in viewpoint than doctrinaire positions. They also have the distinguishing feature of possessing some explicit external model that elaborates, connects, and sustains norms and categories for distinguishing what counts from what does not count. The model is external in the sense that it has a coherent existence ouside the environment under immediate scrutiny. In practical inquiry the model provides the basis for assessment and guidance (Norberg-Schulz 1965).

Categorical systems have a long and noble tradition. They can be traced through the theoretical proposals of such luminaries as Vitruvius and Alberti to the more contemporary efforts of scholars such as Norberg-Schulz (Vitruvius 1940, Alberti 1955 [1726], Norberg-Schulz 1965). Even if these works do not entirely live up to the foregoing definition, they certainly seem to lean in a systematic rather than doctrinaire direction.

The major features of a categorical system are illustrated by the early theory construction of Norberg-Schulz—specifically, by his "integrated theory of architecture," as propounded in *Intentions in Architecture*. An "architectural totality," as he calls it, is completely described by definitions in three categories, or dimensions. These are the "building task," "form," and "technics." A particular architectural totality at time *t* is regarded as an "architectural system," its style corresponding to the mode of formal organization. Independence is claimed for these broad categorical distinctions: as Norberg-Schulz puts it, "The totality of a building task is realized technically within a style" (Norberg-Schulz 1965, p. 87). The three dimensions, then, serve as useful abstractions for thinking about architecture and for distinguishing it from something else.

The definition of the building task roughly follows Paulsson's distinction between physical and symbolic aspects of the built environment. It is assumed that the building task is equivalent to the provision of shelter and physical control on the one hand and the provision of a "frame for actions and social structures" on the other (Norberg-Schulz 1965, pp. 109-130).

The dimension of form is essentially concerned with the depiction of "elements" and "relations" (Norberg-Schulz 1965, pp. 131–160). Here, elements are the characteristic units that make up an architectural form. Norberg-Schulz tends to regard them in terms of "space cells," "mass forms," and "boundary surfaces" (p. 97).[3] Relations, on the other hand, are tridimensional, or spatial, and represent a "lawful" way of distributing elements. Thus, "formal structures" and "style" denote various types or groupings of elements and relations, as well as the rules and lawful procedures. In other words, formal arrangements constitute a formal language, out of which emerges the style of the architectural production.

The dimension of technics is concerned with how technical components are made from materials and organized into "technical systems" (p. 161f.). Furthermore, the "capacity" of such systems is open to scrutiny—that is, the ability, technically speaking, to realize a building task. A technical system is not a symbol system; the relationship between building task, form, and technics is that the form always mediates between the task and its technical realization, or the means that are brought to bear.

What Norberg-Schulz presents us with is an almost Vitruvian tripartite schema of related yet independent dimensions and categories of proper architecture. The framework is ostensibly analytical and concerned with the definition of appropriate categories and their relations; it is, then, a categorical system. It is *ostensibly* analytical because in the selection of sub-categories, such as formal elements, the definitions border on prescription of certain features at the expense of others. For example, mass forms are accorded a relatively special status (p. 133f.). Nevertheless, the scheme is a far cry from the definitive, prescriptive pronouncements of true doctrinaire positions.

The differences between doctrinaire positions and categorical systems are by now, it is hoped, clear. The principal dimensions along which distinctions can be made are (1) the singularity of viewpoint; (2) the explicit nature of the external model of norms at work in promulgating the position; (3) the systematic level of explication, a corollary of (2); and (4) the scope of the rationale provided for the theoretical propositions. In connection with this last point, it should be noted that Norberg-Schulz provides extensive and well-argued support for his categorical system, building on prior works of a similar kind. This is particularly evident in earlier sections of the work, where background material is presented and a conceptual framework is established.

All positions, of course, can be seen as ideological or biased to some degree. They clearly favor one set of circumstances over others. If they are to be coherent, all must contain some line of argument. And if they are to hold designers' attention, all are required to sustain claims of legitimacy and centrality. This statement of the obvious has the intended function of holding at bay the probable judgment that categorical systems are preferable to doctrinaire positions on the grounds that the former are more overtly comprehensive and well organized. For, as the examples of Meyer, Le Corbusier, and others have shown, a sense of explicitly defined comprehensiveness and organization is not necessarily the sine qua non for rendering such judgments.

● **Normative Positions and Architectural Categories**
The assertion that normative positions, as so far described, provide much of the basis for architectural design requires little

defense. Leading practitioners, educators, and critics each espouse normative positions of some sort. To deny the connection would be perverse in the extreme, as it would amount to saying that what these people profess and what they do in architecture are entirely unrelated.

Even theoretical positions that may appear to be otherwise inclined are really of the same stripe. For example, Hillier, Musgrove, and O'Sullivan's propositions revolving around a building acting as a "climate modifier," a "behavior modifier," a "resource modifier," and so on, may incorporate different kinds of norms and architectural categories from those discussed, but they are norms and categories nonetheless (Hillier, Musgrove, and O'Sullivan 1972). Alexander's opus, ranging from *Notes on the Synthesis of Form* to *The Linz Cafe,* although it may take on the guise of "scientific" explanatory theory, fundamentally espouses a consistent set of norms and categories (Alexander 1964, 1981). They are norms founded in a strong sense of behavioral determinism and a popular or consensus view of what is proper. Throughout Alexander's work there is also a very definite orientation toward practical guidance and a strong conviction of the possibility of defining immutable and foundational categories.

Even ostensibly mundane building codes and occupancy standards must be included. Such texts are also normative and set squarely in the realm of practice. Clearly, examples other than those used might have been discussed in a similar manner; the range of surface features and the essential nature of the inherent structure of argumentation could have been shown to conform sufficiently to the scheme that has been advanced.

Further Differentiating Features

Beyond the doctrinaire or categorical inclinations and other surface features of normative architectural positions, a number of other differentiating characteristics can be observed. For instance, there is the general orientation, or program of investigation. As we saw in the last chapter, Anderson describes the early work of Le Corbusier in terms of several instrumental ideas, or "programmes," in which the implications of various related design concepts were explored and refined over time. There is also the matter of preferred spatial concepts, to the extent that they can be discerned independent of orientation. For example, the use of a formal type as a guiding idea, or ideal, may involve a quite different spatial concept from one predicated on a relational model of functional requirements. In addition, there is the degree of emphasis accorded to the context outside matters of purely architectural expression (such as the long-term use and institutional sponsorship of a building). Finally, most well-developed architectural positions exhibit a multiplicity of these characteristics. Designers are at once concerned with exploring influential programs, favoring particular spatial concepts in the expression of their ideas, and addressing the general social context and the object quality of the work. This last aspect will be developed further in the next chapter.

● **An Analytical Framework**

For the purpose of discussing these characteristics of architectural positions, let us imagine a simple taxonomic construct that allows aspects of various candidate positions to be commonly portrayed. The aspects in question are *production, architectural devices,* and *orientation. Production* shall refer to visible works under some commonly expressed or descriptive term that identifies the kind of architectural output of the position—in other words, a "label," stylistic or otherwise, that is or might be used to identify the group of practitioners and theorists ("Brutalists," for example). *Architectural devices* will refer to kinds of architectonic elements favored or prescribed by the position, as well as the use of other less tangible leitmotifs that operationally describe the position's production. For example, Le Corbusier's five points are clearly architectonic elements or devices, and ones that are just as clearly prescribed for the production of proper architecture. Finally, *orientation* will cover the critical stance and larger (social) purpose of the position, or one that might legitimately be imputed to that position.

In addition to incorporating these three types of information, let us further enrich the construct by regarding it roughly as a line of argument in which statements about orientation support prescriptive devices, and so on:

Orientation → Architectural Devices → Production.

Generally, among the practitioners who may be categorized as ` more or less belonging to a particular position, a reasonable amount of agreement is likely to be found on matters of orientation. Considerable variation, however, is likely to be seen in the choice of architectural devices, and a very real contrast is often evident in the conformation of the actual work. With these observations in mind, we are now in a position to fill in the analytical construct with specific information from some normative positions.

● Application of the Framework

Four positions, or classes of positions, have been chosen, but only for purposes of illustration. This is certainly not an attempt to conduct a comprehensive survey, or a survey of any kind for that matter. The choice of positions reflects four strains of architectural thinking that are highly visible in contemporary theory and practice; but they have existed in the past, too, and will no doubt exist in the future. Further, when examining each position, it is not proposed to conduct a critique of specific examples, although how at least one kind of critique might be performed will probably be clear from the application of the analytical framework just described. Finally, a certain amount of caricature and overlap is probably unavoidable in this kind of contracted analysis. Nevertheless, a sense of the broad orientations of the positions in question can be maintained in a reasonably defensible fashion, or at least the strains can be seen to appear and sometimes commingle in much of contemporary production.

The four positions that will be briefly examined are as follows. First, there is a *functionalist* position, distinguished by an emphasis on the accommodation ot activities and the influence of building technology. Second, there is a *populist* position, characterized by an acknowledgment and interpretation of contemporary commonplace building practices and user preferences. Third, there is a *conventionist* position, using an architecture of largely historical reference; and finally, a *formalist* position, using an architecture of formal possibilities for their own sake.

The orientation of the functionalist position may be described in the following way. Architecture is a matter of accommodating the functions that are prescribed for it and of functioning in a manner that is consistent with its material composition and construction. "Form follows function" is the guiding doctrine on both matters of use and building technology. Architecture must be made of the "right stuff" and in the "right way" without superfluous ornament or artifice. It must also work efficiently, in the sense of directly conforming to some ideal of use requirements; it must, as Le Corbusier put it, be a "machine to live in," with all the parsimonious aspects of machine design (Le Corbusier 1959, p. 263f.; 1967, p. 204).

The specific architectural devices of the position are numerous and varied. Often, however, explicit expression of a building's essential structure and process of fabrication are hallmarks. Spatial organization invariably grows out of the program of uses, in a straightforward manner (Herdeg 1983). Ulrich Franzen's Alley Theater of 1965, for instance, presents use with a diagram of functional organization, boldly clad in "off-form" concrete. The outlines of both major spaces and circulation elements (such as stairways) are clearly visible (see figure 43). Frequently there is an underlying concern with standardization and systematic organization on a number of counts. First, a building is seen to be made up of an assemblage of parts, each under the discipline of rational (that is, functionally systematic) organizing principles. Consequently, the parts themselves tend to become standardized, their variation minimized, and their assemblage conceived as a "building system" (Dietz and Cutler 1971). Second, "use standards," representing so-called optimal spatial configurations for accommodating human activities, are employed. Frequently these standards are ergonometrically determined, and in some settings (such as mass housing) there is an effort to hold to minimum standards.[4] Circulation within a building or building complex is often seen as a matter of maximizing the proximity of use functions and minimizing travel distances. Third, there is a concern for a clear hierarchy of uses and elements of buildings. Consequently, categorical distinctions are made between prominent and subordinate areas of activity and between the modes in which they are expressed.

Functionalist production is perhaps epitomized by the so-called International Style, with its ubiquitous array of steel, concrete, and glass commercial buildings, each consistent in basic format, regardless of location and resulting differences in cultural setting. The position can also be seen at work in the spatial organization of many postwar urban and suburban areas, with their adherence to concepts of transportation efficiency and an economically determined distribution of land uses.

The orientation of the populist position might be characterized thus: Architecture has drifted too far from popular conceptions, needs, and aspirations with regard to building. Therefore, an inclusive interpretation of the prevailing sociocultural climate, and especially its commonplace physical and symbolic qualities, is required as a source for architectural expression. Very much at issue are understanding the popular consensus in matters of building and the use of popular preferences as a legitimate source of guidance for architectural production.

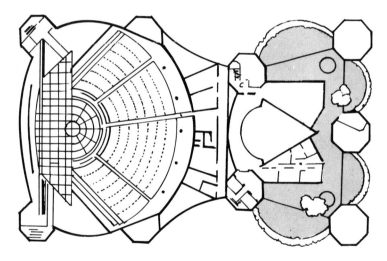

43
Plan and general view of the Alley Theater in
Houston, by Ulrich Franzen (1965–1968).

The architectural devices of the position can be seen to range widely in the use and rearticulation of commonplace elements of the contemporary built landscape (see figure 44). For example, the architecture of the commercial strip and the franchise are elevated, by some, to the level of serious discussion and development (Venturi and Scott Brown 1968, 1971; Venturi, Scott Brown, and Izenour 1972). They become a basis for appropriating formal organizing principles. Similarly the eclecticism with which otherwise functionally rational suburban apartment and housing complexes are adorned is given serious attention. In short, the symbolic qualities of popular forms of architectural expression are acknowledged and interpreted (Rowe 1972). There is another strain, or orientation, at work within this general position, although relatively separate from a direct concern with formal devices of the above kind. Here user needs and preferences are often regarded as both necessary and largely sufficient determinants of form. In the work of Alexander and his followers, for example, on reusable "patterns" of building strong populist arguments are made, alongside the practice of a fairly high degree of behavioral determinism. More broadly, the relationship between behavioral and building environments and the effect the latter has on the former are given undeniable status (Alexander et al. 1977).

It might be argued that this is the same concern that we saw in the functionalist position's expression of use program. If anything, however, the populist position represents a reaction to that kind of determinism as being biased and preordained by "elite" institutions, while the actual users have little or nothing to say. By contrast, the programming of facilities is aimed at revealing those hidden biases and at democratically satisfying the environmental requirements of a building or building complex. Consequently, the procedural devices of data collection and analysis of user needs take on a dominant role.

The work of Venturi and Rauch is probably most directly associated with the appropriation of popular signs and symbols (Scott Brown 1977). In a recent residential development in the Houston area, a skillful layout of housing units was adorned with "classical elements" in the form of a direct appliqué to the building facades (figure 45; Kaliski 1983). The message was clear. These are the residences of people of substance and status. As a newspaper advertisement for the project put it, "Park Regency, you've got great deals and lotsa class." In the end the devices have much in common with surrounding signs and symbols, while at the same time clarifying the general proposition of such symbol-

44
Signs on the commercial strip (Houston).

45
The Park Regency Terrace residences in Houston, by
Venturi, Rauch, and Scott Brown (1981–1983).

ism. After all, this is an area in which apartment and condo-
minium complexes, constructed on relatively low budgets,
strive through decoration and other surface accessories to set
the "right tone." Ersatz Regency competes with mock Tudor, as
the marketplace takes a distinct turn toward Vanity Fair. The
Venturis' unabashed use of applied decoration, which borders
on caricature, makes the symbolic statement but at the same
time almost disengages the signs themselves from the buildings.

Closely akin to the populist orientation is that of conventionism,
expressed in the following statements. First, architecture must
engage and be appealing to its audience—both its users and
those who only look at it. (There is a concomitant criticism involved here, that such engagement is somehow lacking in the
contemporary setting.) Second, certain widely held conventions
have developed in architecture over the centuries. These conventions rather literally frame sociocultural expectations regarding the selection and conformation of architectonic elements.
Therefore, the body of historical references, conventions, devices, and types is an essential source for appealing architecture. At issue within the position are matters of selection and
reinterpretation of elements.

Typical architectural devices of the position include the use of building types, as much for their iconography as for their overall organizational principles. But perhaps most important, a reliance is placed on historical and historicist references, conventions, and rule structures for the palette of architectural expression. For example, classical orders and iconography are often used as a point of departure for architectural renderings. In various hands these renderings may be quite literal or quite abstract. In the work of Thomas Gordon Smith, for instance (House in Mathew Street, 1978), the references are quite literal, whereas those in the recent work of Stern are less so (Jencks 1980).

Much of the work presented in Jencks's recent *Post-Modern Classicism,* among other texts, serves to illustrate this position (Jencks 1980, Portoghesi 1982). For instance, the Laurentian House, in Livermore, California, by Thomas Gordon Smith, clearly draws upon historical references for both its figurative expression and its organization. The Municipal Control Building for Quail Valley in Missouri City, by Taft Architects (shown in figure 46), evokes a strong memory of similar buildings built during the 1920s and 1930s (Papademetriou 1980). Finally, Moore's celebrated scheme for the Piazza d'Italia in New Orleans (1978–1979), commissioned in celebration of the Italian community in that city, makes direct figural and formal references to Italian classicism and the tradition of fountain design and plaza making (figure 47). More specifically, as Jencks notes in his photographic juxtaposition of images, the likeness to Salvi's Trevi Fountain in Rome (c. 1732) is unmistakable (Jencks 1980, p. 21).

As for the formalist position, its orientation might be summed up in this way. Architecture is largely an autonomous realm of expression. It has been and will continue to be so. Therefore, the program for development in architecture must be located strictly in the realm of architectural possibilities. Here we find an overriding concern with autonomous "languages" of architecture, their compositional qualities, and their inherent and possible meanings. At issue are formal and figural possibilities made legible by the use of conventions that are agreed upon and promulgated by a community of peers.[5]

This description would seem to fit the conventionist position as well. After all, the use of recognizable architectural conventions is a form of expression that is essentially autonomous to architecture. The important distinction here is the insistence on exploring new formal and figural possibilities, and on reinter-

46
The Municipal Control Building of the Quail Valley
utility district in Missouri City, by Taft Architects
(1978–1980).

preting traditional architectural conventions, which goes well
beyond borrowing. For this reason production is apt to incorporate much more from the private languages of architectural
expression.

The architectural devices of formalism, as one might imagine,
are apt to be quite diverse. They include exploitation and transformation of the formal qualities of regular solids, as seen in
Eisenman's "Houses," with all their linguistic, syntactic meta-
references (see figure 48). By contrast, in the later work of
Graves one sees figural explorations and inventions, based upon
"the myths and rituals of a society" (Graves 1984). Formalist devices might also include Hollein's more geomorphic constructions, about which he observes, "The shape of a building does
not evolve out of the material conditions of a purpose. . . . A
building is itself. . . . Architecture is purposeless [and] what we
build will find its utilization" (Conrads 1964, p. 181). Finally, the
rationalist doctrines of Rossi, Krier, Huet, and others attach
great importance to the reinterpretation of artifacts within the
urban landscape such as monuments, streets, squares, and
quarters (Rossi 1982, Krier 1978, Huet 1978).

Other positions might also have been discussed. For instance,
use of the "vernacular" and the "situational context" are both
common sources of organizing principles in contemporary ar-

47

Piazza d'Italia in New Orleans, by Charles Moore,
Perez Associates, and Ron Filson (1978–1979).

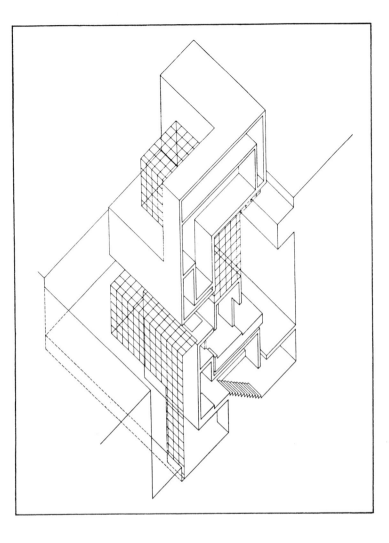

48
House 11a in Palo Alto, by Peter Eisenman (1979).

chitectural production.[6] In our scheme both might be regarded as combining elements of the populist and conventionist doctrines. Vernacular and contextual urban architectural expressions are certainly populist with respect to their incorporation and celebration of commonplace elements, and they can also be said to involve rule structures of a conventionist kind that lend them coherence and meaning. They do have an independent aspect, however, particularly as expressions of the phenomenon of place, or genius loci (Norberg-Schulz 1980a). In this connection, Frampton views contemporary works of Siza, Utzon, Barragan, and others as deriving their importance and special meaning from an acute sense of place, sociocultural milieu, and local building practices; his concept of regionalism defines architecture largely from this standpoint (Frampton 1982, 1983).

Problems of Substantiation

With this general idea of theory in mind, we must now pursue more fundamental questions concerning the substantiation and legitimation of normative positions in architecture. This analysis will begin with questions of logical coherence and will proceed to a discussion of two alternative frames of reference from which interpretations and evaluations of normative positions might be rendered. The first of these frames of reference assumes that claims to legitimacy are predicated on fundamental conceptions of the human condition and must be judged in terms of the validity of those conceptions; the second considers architectural positions from the point of view of the relative appropriateness of the means employed, under the assumption that the ends are more or less commonly agreed upon. This discussion will be followed by an attempt to address the problem of assigning priorities among architectural principles, once those principles have been judged to have merit.

● Logical Coherence

Let us begin examining the issue of logical coherence from the vantage point of an abstract model of the basic structure of the theoretical positions, as identified during the earlier discussion of surface features. This model may be described as a critique of existing practices (C), implying the location of a problem and alternative opportunities (P), implying counterpropositions and their rationale (CPR). Symbolically the relationship may be expressed as $C \rightarrow P$ and $P \rightarrow CPR$. The model should be regarded less as a three-step process for theory construction than as a constellation of statements with logical connections. It is also an abstract representation of how architectural positions might be seen to change and shift over time, building upon prior positions as points of departure. Further, it might be seen in a more temporary light, as a model for the selection of an organizing principle during a particular design project. Thus it may also be written more simply in the form of a single relationship: location of a problem (P), implying a proposition (Pr), or, $P \rightarrow Pr$.

Clearly in this reformulation an assumption has been made that the problem definition P and the proposition Pr are clear declarative statements of the kind we saw earlier in Le Corbusier's and Meyer's proposals, or that they can be faithfully contracted to form such statements. The earlier subdivisions of critique, identification of alternative opportunities, and rationale for the propositions can be understood as auxiliary statements involving modes of argumentation linking the problem statement P with the proposition Pr. For instance, the critique may be made in the light of the potential offered by alternative opportunities (for example, technology) and may develop a rationale that is contingent upon these opportunities (such as, that new technologies should be embraced because of their efficiency). This reformulation also squares better with the idea of an external model mentioned earlier in connection with categorical systems and the work of Norberg-Schulz. In other words, the relation between P and Pr is defined and orchestrated by the external model M containing information about what constitutes proper architecture and the underlying rationale for such an assertion.

In more extensive form, the idealized structure of a position can be expressed in the following manner. If problem P is located, then proposition Pr follows. Furthermore, if P is true, then Pr also holds, subject to auxiliary arguments. That is, in the presence of the external model M (for instance, a matter of "technics"), the problem P is located (for instance, ignorance of modern technology), and if M is true, then P also holds. In addition, in the presence of the same external model M the proposition or counterproposal Pr (say, the use of modern technology) also holds, and again, if M is true, then so is Pr. In summary, $P \rightarrow Pr$ subject to $M \rightarrow P$ and $M \rightarrow Pr$. Thus, the claim for legitimacy, or the process of substantiation, rests on the extent to which the external model or its implied surrogate can be sustained and proved for both the problem statement P and the proposition Pr. Moreover, if we allow that M is in fact robust enough to allow explication of P and Pr in complementary fashion so that they are "connected," at least in rough content (that is, provisionally

$P \to Pr$), then the strategies or types of argumentation at work in making the connection become important. Otherwise Pr would be entirely independent, an issue we shall take up a little later on.

For the sake of further clarity in exposition, let us also assume that Prp constitutes a set of principles under contention in the perception of the extant problem P (that is, $P \to Prp$). As we saw earlier, both Le Corbusier and Meyer were essentially arguing against a set of existing principles and practices when they promulgated their theoretical positions.

General Strategies

In principle, at least three kinds of strategies can be employed in making the connection between a perceived problem P, or problematic set of principles Prp, and a proposition or counterproposal Pr. First, there is the type of approach that involves modification of troublesome yet reparable features of an existing position without entirely undermining that position—that is, $Prp \to Pr$, where $Prp \cap Pr$ and $M \to \overline{Prp}$. In other words, in making the counterproposal the troublesome subset of principles Prp is excluded in the presence of the external model M. In practice, this strategy would correspond to the general adoption of a particular orthodoxy or architectural position, with the absence of certain of its features. Here the exclusion of features may arise not only through disagreement but because they are considered irrelevant to a particular realm of application or speculation.

A second strategy is that of extending existing positions to take into account other contingencies or possibilities that have so far been ignored—that is, $Prp \to Pr$, where $Prp \cup Pr$ and $M \to \overline{Prp}$. In making a new proposition, a set of existing principles is accepted as appropriate with either an elaboration or the addition of consistent principles furnished through the external model. This is a common practice in the normal development of architectural positions and often coincides with their rise to prominence and acceptance from relatively tentative beginnings. In effect, the general thrust of a position, articulated by certain key principles, becomes elaborated and extended in a coherent and complementary manner. Episodes in the development of "modern movements" are cases in point.

Third, there is the strategy of replacing an existing position entirely. This should not be construed as a willful act for the sake of being contrary. Rather, in the course of the development of architectural positions the systematic questioning of certain basic premises can result in what turn out to be new positions. Here several variations can be distinguished.

To begin with, there is what we might call an oppositional or even an iconoclastic approach. If a position currently at work is seen to be problematic in some way, then something close to a diametrically opposed counterproposal is made: $Prp \rightarrow Pr$, where $Pr = \overline{Prp}$. The positive effects of this strategy can be seen in the use of paradox as a point of departure. In certain regards, the doctrine Venturi expresses in *Complexity and Contradiction in Architecture* can be seen to represent such a shift within a modernist position (Venturi 1966). Here, we are confronted with a well-argued case for replacing a generally accepted rational and systematic ordering of architectural elements and design principles with another view that stands many of the accepted principles of modernism on their heads. In addition to the use of historical references, the work calls for celebration of certain ambiguities in architectural expression in contradistinction to their unambiguous resolution. To quote from Venturi's introduction, "Everything is said in the context of architecture and consequently certain targets are attacked—in general, the limitations of orthodox modern architecture and city planning, in particular, the platitudinous architects who invoke integrity, technology, or electronic programming as ends in architecture . . . and suppress those complexities and contradictions inherent in art and experience" (Venturi 1966, p. 21).

There is also what might be called a comparative approach, whereby new propositions are based on an enumeration of and comparison among alternative principles of the same general kind as the extant set *Prp*. Symbolically

$Prp \rightarrow Pr$, where
$M \rightarrow (Pr_1, Pr_2, \ldots, Pr_n)$ and
$|(Pr_1, Pr_2, \ldots, Pr_n)| \rightarrow Pr$, as well as
$(Pr_1, Pr_2, \ldots, Pr_n) \rightarrow \overline{Prp}$.

Here the concept of "principles of the same general kind" may be subject to several constructions. It may suggest that there is a difference with regard to means, while the principles involved follow the general direction of the extant set *Prp*. For example, although the broad goals of an architectural position may be maintained, the strategies for achieving those goals are replaced by others deemed superior. Or it may mean that the issues of central concern in an architectural position are accepted, but entirely different propositions about those issues are offered. In the "form follows function" debate, for example, the aphorism, and all that it intends, might be reversed so that "function follows form," thus shifting the emphasis of architectural production, although still around the same central issue.

It could be argued that this last example is more closely aligned with the oppositional approach described earlier, or, conversely, that Venturi's argument in *Complexity and Contradiction* is a case of the comparative approach. Such distinctions are largely a matter of degree. It should also be noted that it is possible to combine the modification and extension of an existing position; indeed, such a combination frequently occurs. If anything, Venturi's position most closely fits the latter mold in that it broadens the realm of modern architectural concerns. Clearly, in practice less-than-perfect examples of these "in principle" strategies are likely to be found.

Finally, there are what we might call independent strategies, in which a set of principles constituting an architectural position emerges largely independently of any perception of an initial set *Prp*. In fact, the position might arise without the explicit existence of some set of norms that poses difficulties. This is clearly a case of manufacturing a position out of whole cloth—of proposing a direction that is both complementary to and independent of existing positions. The work of Cedric Price in the days of the "Potteries Thinkbelt" (Price 1965, 1966a, 1966b) and other similar excursions into the realm of infrastructural reuse and interpretation by the likes of Archigram represent this kind of approach (figure 49).

Pitfalls

In all cases save the last, the strategies have a distinct referential character. They in some way involve a prior set of propositions and positions, whether in the form of acceptance, indifference, or rejection. This can pose a severe problem for sustaining claims of legitimacy, on at least two counts. First, the interdependence between the proposed position and prior positions may be so overdrawn as to amount to a circularity of argument. It is a circularity that may increase understanding but that makes the proposal neither more nor less legitimate than its predecessor. For example, in the oppositional strategy outlined earlier, the prior proposal Prp and the counterproposal $\overline{Prp}$, logically speaking, have the same status. They rest on the same foundation, even if one is the "not" side of the other. Thus, "less is more" and "less is a bore" have equal force, more or less, depending on who's using them (Norberg-Schulz 1968). Further

49
Walking City, by Ron J. Herron (1964).

substantiation of one at the expense of the other is lacking at the level implied by the rhetoric.

Other, less clear-cut cases may suffer from the same kind of impediment, albeit at lower intensities. Definition of a problem solely by way of an alternative position may raise questions regarding the substantiation of the problem statement in the first place. Hannes Meyer's thesis on building can be seen to come perilously close to this position, through the strictly oppositional use of "function" and "aesthetics" in relationship to "life" and the "process of building." It is tantamount to an argument by assertion.

The second kind of difficulty arises when the position being proposed uses prior propositions as building blocks and tacitly or uncritically assumes their legitimacy. Clearly, the strategies of extension and even replacement have this characteristic. Whether this is done unwittingly or not is beside the point. For example, if one were to develop a theoretical position in design tacitly using the notion of "type," one might run the risk of subverting the proposal by claiming a relevance that cannot, in fact, be supported. Similarly, embracing "traditional" and historical principles per se, without regard to their sociocultural import in a contemporary setting, can also be disastrous.

We have seen that normative positions consist of finite sets of categories that are, or can be, used to distinguish one position from another. They are at once the core of the definition of what proper architecture is, versus what it is not, and the principles that provide guidance for practical inquiry. It would seem, therefore, that adjudication of the claims of competing positions, unless it can be clearly decided on the basis of logical coherence within the realm of accepted architectural categories, should proceed in another direction.

● Architectural Positions as Doctrines about Ends

But what is this direction? How might we further substantiate claims for legitimacy for the architectural categories presented by competing or coexisting positions? Here, it is apparent that we need to move outside the realm in which architecture can claim exclusive knowledge or expertise. Substantiation for categories, and hence positions, must come through linking the subject of speculation, namely the concept of architecture, to a broader frame of reference. Furthermore, the frame of reference must not only represent a touchstone for architectural experience but also have certain inert or stable qualities; otherwise, the dilemma of making distinctions among positions will remain unresolvable. Such a link is clearly assumed in statements like the following, by Vincent Scully: "Architecture, like all art, . . . has revealed some of the basic truths of the human condition and, again like all art, has played a part in changing and reforming that condition itself" (Scully 1979, p. 10).

A useful way of illustrating and exploring this point is by inquiring what is held to be the basis for the claim to legitimacy of each of the architectural positions outlined earlier in the chapter. Briefly, the functionalist position would seem to be founded on the belief that man's choice behavior can be analytically typified and idealized and that an unadorned, efficient reckoning with building can provide an appropriate form of architectural expression. There is no need for self-conscious references to be made to the past; the present circumstances are what count. A "science of man" is possible and, in combination with technical achievements from natural science, will provide a firm basis for architecture. By contrast, the apparent basis of the claim for legitimacy of the populist position is the existence of commonly held preferences and needs vis à vis the built environment. Although these preferences and needs are usually latent or unconscious, they can nonetheless be approached, understood, and appropriated through outward building practices. Substantiation also seems to hinge on a belief that a consensus struck in the "popular marketplace" is reasonable and good, at least for the purpose of guiding architectural production.

For the conventionist position the apparent basis of the claim to legitimacy is that commonly held expectations exist vis à vis the formal qualities of architecture, as can be demonstrated by the endurance of past forms of composition, organization, and expression. Such a claim hinges on the conviction that variations in the expectations within a sociocultural milieu are continuous and small. In other words, conditions of the past can be sustained into the future without undue or disabling distortions. In contrast, claims of legitimacy by the formalist or elitist position seem to be predicated on the possibility that intersubjective conventions can be broadly developed, based on common human experience, or more particularly, common human rationality. Non-alienation from an "autonomous architecture" would, therefore, seem to hinge on both broad societal acceptance and inculcation of these conventions.

From this admittedly sketchy account several interesting observations emerge. In all cases it seems possible to erect an appeal for substantiation that is based on a conviction involving a widely held view of man and his world. At least there is the common belief in the possibility of human engagement with architecture beyond matters of shelter and mundane function. At the heart of this conviction would seem to be a faith in a common rationality and a common thread of experience. If this were not the case, then the idea of a consensus of peers and its broader influence, implicit in the elitist position, could not have been established. The habitual proclivities of laymen would not result in the necessary foundations for populist programs. And the idea of aesthetic conventions as social rule structures, needed to advance the conventionist position, could not be sustained. Moreover, it is a belief about man's being and aspirations that goes beyond surface conduct.

Within this general conviction, however, two ideas would seem to be competing for attention. To use Bernstein's terms, they are a "foundational" view of man and his world and a "relativist" view (Bernstein 1983, p. 8f.). According to the foundational view, man's experience can be reduced to certain "common denominators" through some ahistorical and aspatial matrix or framework. Hence, the postulated common human rationality spoken of earlier can be located and, once located, will remain invariant. By contrast, the relativist view claims that no matter to what extreme one moves within a foundationalist program, the observations one can make about rationality and experience can never escape the influence of particular traditions, cultural frameworks, or "forms of life."

It might be argued in the case of an elitist position that man's basic perceptual equipment, with sufficient guidance, should allow engagement with architecture of a foundational kind. It can also be argued, however, that such engagement must make use of a certain knowledge about the architectural conventions that are inevitably associated with a particular tradition or form of life.

Similarly, a populist position would seem to be quite relativistic in embracing the prevailing preferences of a specific time and place, yet the position must also assume that these popular manifestations are foundational, at least for that specific time and place. The problem with such a view is that popular manifestations need not be foundational, particularly in cases where the range of available models is narrowed by notions that people have been taught to have about what is appropriate to their economic or social circumstances. This point is central to the position of Alexander and his followers, who seek to subvert the "tyranny of hidden programs" and replace what people think might be expected of them with what they themselves hold "near and dear" (Silverstein and Jacobson 1978). Yet what is held near and dear by a group may reveal a narrow preference for certain environmental elements through an ignorance of other possibilities. Under these circumstances a popular consensus view may prevail where better and even more acceptable solutions could have been found.

The functionalist position is clearly foundational in almost all respects. As pointed out, this inclination can produce an unrelenting sameness in the built environment that disregards special local circumstances. Hence, the presumed universality of the position tends to become more and more narrowly defined.

The foundational aspect is apparent in the conventionist position's (implicit) belief that certain forms of architectural expression found in the historical record are worthy of emulation because they represent touchstones of human experience with architecture. Nevertheless, it is also clear that the history of architecture is inextricably linked to history in general—that a particular form of expression is linked to the culture and traditions of the moment in history when it was devised. It is possible that that form of architectural expression will take on a meaningful aspect in the absence of other conditions of shared thought and experience, but it is hardly self-evident.

Finally, an inherent weakness of the type of theory under discussion is that even though foundations in a larger frame of reference might be provided, discourse often fails to turn sufficiently in that direction in order to substantiate merit. Without this turn it is all too evident that the locus of these normative positions in architecture remains very much at the level of production, architectural devices, and general outlines of orientation. What then appears lacking is a more profound basis from which the question of the efficacy of the proposed categories might be approached. Whether this is a serious weakness for design thinking is an issue to which we shall return.

● Architectural Positions as Doctrines about Means

There is another way of looking at architectural positions and their substantiation that makes many of the same points, but with some important differences. Instead of regarding architectural positions as arguments with proposals linked solely to some deep-seated view of man and his world, we can regard them as essentially teleological doctrines, or doctrines about means.

Teleological doctrines, after Frankena's definition, are those in which the concept of "good" is defined independently from the concept of "right" (Frankena 1963, p. 13). To paraphrase Rawls, the right is then defined as that which maximizes the good. For example, institutions and acts are right that of the available alternatives produce the most good (Rawls 1971, p. 24f.). Or, in our case, architectural positions are right that maximize their concept of good. Those that are right are also presumably preferable. The necessity for the independence between good and right is fairly clear. It avoids the problem of defining good in terms of what's right and vice versa.

One might well ask what is the pertinence of seeing architectural positions in this way. First, in the four cases just described an inherent concept of good can be seen to be roughly congruent, or shared. It is a concept of good that says, among other things, that all architecture must engage its audience. It must foster understanding and be intelligible. This is clearly not the only concept necessarily at work, but it is one that would have broad adherence, even beyond the four positions mentioned.

Second, on the issue of right seen independently of good, four rather different interpretations, or means toward maximization of the good, would seem to be at work. Certainly, as we have seen, the general orientations and architectural devices of the four positions are distinctive and different. The question then becomes, Which position might be right, seen in terms of maximizing, for instance, the concept of engagement? Or, conversely, under what circumstances can an architectural production, in these same terms of engagement, be called arbitrary?

In Hubbard's defense of an "architecture of convention," which is close to our conventionist position, he asserts primacy for "immediate appeal" on the engagement issue (Hubbard 1981). By this he means the mustering together of those sensations and concepts that facilitate immediate understanding, comprehension, liking, and gratification. A proponent of a populist position would presumably go along with the general thrust of this criterion but would assert primacy for production coming out of the realm of commonplace artifacts. To the extent that the same conventions and rules are at work in the locale of interest, the populist and conventionist positions would seem to be congruent. Both positions would also seem to be at odds with the elitist position, and proponents of each position tend, in fact, to be overtly critical of the elitist position for its alleged formal arbitrariness.[7] At this point we might be inclined to conclude that the conventionist and populist positions are right and the elitist not, in spite of all three's shared conviction about what is good. In a similar vein, production from the functionalist position would seem to straddle the fence, appearing to some as what it is and what it is made from, while appearing to others as aloof and abstract.

We might, however, supplant the largely consensus-based idea of "appeal" as the criterion for non-arbitrariness with one that is a little more even handed—in other words, not use an obvious strength of one position at the expense of others. Here we might go on to say that a work of architecture is arbitrary when it transgresses the limit of its (architectural) possibilities without also providing a framework for extending the level of reflection, so that the transgression might be understood.

Under this criterion the elitist and functionalist positions might have just as legitimate a claim to being right as the others, at least to the extent that the framework for extending the level of reflection is manifest. For example, a work based upon the geometric possibilities of regular solids may be very abstract but certainly approachable through the rules of geometry. Adherents of an elitist position might also argue, and do, that that extension of inherent formal possibilities in architecture is a good in itself and therefore a social responsibility.[8] It should also be pointed out that both the populist and the conventionist position are fundamentally engaged in interpretation, and hence in extension of this kind.

The overall effect of this line of discussion is that it raises not only the issue of a good itself as requiring substantiation but also the question of right and proper architecture, given some reasonably common agreement about good. Without attempting to resolve this issue among the positions just presented, the discussion does point up the need for theoretical frameworks that go beyond a parochial form of discourse about certain categories, in search of better bases for substantiation.

Besides the admittedly somewhat vague matter of engagement, we might speak more directly of other qualities of architecture, such as its "thingness" (Bachelard 1979, pp. 201–206) and tectonic aspect, or its "placedness" as a part of a locale or collective enterprise. As to the former quality, the functionalist position might rise to the fore with its program and orientation toward material integrity. In the latter case, the populist position, at least for the present, could lay a strong claim to our attention; although if continuity is a valued dimension of the quality of placedness, then the conventionist and elitist positions could both press their claims. First and foremost, however, there must be engagement for us to have knowledge of these qualities. As a corollary, it is through these kinds of qualities that we are engaged and can therefore participate.

● **Assignment of Priority to Categorical Claims**

At least in practice, one of the pressing problems involved with architectural categories, once they have been defined, is the assignment of priorities among the aspects that are to be considered good and proper. For example, suppose one had to choose between "imageability," functional conformance, and structural innovation; how might one assign the priorities among these three categories in designing a building? An essential feature of theory that purports to guide practical action is the provision of some basis for assigning such categorical priorities.

Following Rawls's analysis, we can distinguish five methods or procedures for assigning priorities (Rawls 1971, pp. 40–45). First, there is the use of intuition, or more precisely, the balancing of prima facie principles (implying categories) on the basis of individual experience, insight, and discretion. This is certainly not necessarily a systematic approach, but it is also by no means necessarily irrational. For instance, experience may have shown us that by first attending to functional conformance we can then produce a technically sound building with a pleasing appearance.

Second, there is the use of some single-principle doctrine whereby all candidate considerations are conflated to one overriding set of categories or principles. This procedure is explicit in the so-called doctrinaire positions described earlier, at least to the extent that they require such considerations to be made. It is certainly systematic, although it can become troublesome when the otherwise highly valued principles or goods involved are too disparate to warrant such aggregation. This may occur, for example, under circumstances when a striving toward structural innovation severely compromises performance with regard to functional organization.

The third procedure, in principle anyway, is the ordering of a true multiplicity of principles, or goods, through a categorical system that explicitly identifies architectural categories and their most appropriate interrelationships. Embedded in Norberg-Schulz's theory, discussed earlier, is an example of this kind of approach: "The totality of a building task is realized technically within a style" (Norberg-Schulz 1965, p. 87). In general, however, explicit guidance as to how to approach the ordering problem is not fully provided by systems of this type. The preference for certain forms of expression over others invariably clouds the issue, reducing the ordering to something closer to an intuitive or single-principle process.

The use of what Rawls calls "prudential judgment" is a fourth kind of procedure that is evident in theoretical development of normative architectural positions (Rawls 1971, p. 44). This is where decisions about the relative priorities and underlying ordering of principles are made from the standpoint of specific "settings," or contextual viewpoints. For example, in architecture there is a reasonably extensive tradition of adjudication through the use of concepts such as genius loci, social domain, and sense of place. This can be contrasted with various brands of "universalism" that deal with organizing principles and categories independent of time and place, such as the so-called universal principles about building technology that are embraced by the functionalist position. One of the advantages of this type of procedure is that it can, or should, provide systematic speculation regarding the circumstances under which the particular concept of setting becomes uncoupled or disengaged from the principles, categories, and goods at hand. For instance, the cultural setting for a design may be such that imported references from another tradition are anachronistic, in spite of a designer's opinion on the matter. In other words, the presence of a bounding critical perspective is required. In practice, however, such a perspective may not actually be provided.

The final procedure involves a process Rawls terms "lexical ordering" (Rawls 1971, p. 44). This approach entails identifying, from among all candidates, the principle or concept of good that would have to be satisfied in the first instance, followed by the next principle or good for the second instance, and so on. Rather than being merely an intuitive rank ordering of principles, it is systematic, at least to the extent that superordinate and subordinate connections and relations among principles are made explicit. It certainly moves beyond both the single-principle and categorically systematic methods, in that more than one kind of concept of good is involved, and a basis for substantiating an ordering is explicitly provided beyond an individual designer's opinion.

An example of this approach, albeit outside the realm of architecture, would be the ordering of the two principles "equality for all" and "equal distribution of wealth." Here it might be argued that equality is the greater good, for it sets up certain indispensable preconditions or rules about questions of wealth distribution, and not vice versa (Rawls 1971, p. 41). In the realm of architecture, it was argued earlier that meeting the criterion "architecture must engage its audience" was an indispensable precondition for achieving other goals. Without such engagement there can be no further understanding of a work.

In summary, whether we take an ontologically inclined or a teleologically inclined view of architectural categories and their substantiation, the underlying principles employed in the ordering process, once valuations of merit have been made, should be of interest. There are, in fact, a number of such procedures already at work in architectural discourse and others that are less widely used but just as plausible.

● **Theory and the Implied "Urcorpus"**
Before concluding this discussion of normative theory in architecture, it will be useful to return to two issues raised in earlier portions of the account. They are (1) the *centrality* of a position to the realm of contemporary architecture and (2) the *comprehensiveness* of a position in the same realm. It is safe to say that the most compelling positions, at a given moment, are the ones that seem to address the important issues of that moment. For example, in early modernism, the opportunities presented by a new technology and, at least in Europe, a new set of social and political conditions were important and central issues of the

time. We would also probably agree that architectural theory should attempt to comprehensively address and define the realm of architecture. This is a question of both determining what architecture is, versus what it is not, and filling in between the bounds thus demarcated.

In examining many normative positions, however, and following the contours of theoretical discourse more generally, one finds much that remains unsaid. Certain dimensions in the realm of architecture are implicitly assumed and embraced by otherwise distinct architectural positions. That such incompleteness should be the case is understandable. The focus of good theory is usually on those aspects of interest or those that command speculation at a point in time. More mundane aspects are often only cursorily dealt with, if they are dealt with at all. During these moments the theorist appears to be drawing on what one might call, after Levi (1980), an "urcorpus" of knowledge that is considered to be "incorrigible" and infallible.[9] There are certain aspects of architecture, at least at certain moments, about which there appears to be unanimity. Theory then, it would seem, is mainly concerned with that which lies outside the urcorpus of knowledge.

A significant problem can develop over time, however, when theoretical discourse in the controversial realm outside the urcorpus begins to demonstrate considerable variation and differences in direction—when the locus of debate shifts from one set of dimensions or issues to others. For instance, it might be argued that the attack on modernism, on the grounds of its contemporary failure in the realm of popular visual appeal, ignores the sociopolitical conditions of dwelling that were being addressed at the time of modernism's evolution. Here the problem is that such shifts may call into question the very contents of the urcorpus. For when dimensions of architecture in one position or at one time are ignored in other positions or at other times, the qualities of the stand taken by the positions that choose to ignore those dimensions come into question. The upshot is that the urcorpus appears to be subject to correction and change. Thus, failure to define the boundaries of the urcorpus, when engaging in debate outside its precincts, raises questions of ambiguity in normative positions and weakens their claims to substantiation. When a challenge is made to a position, retorts like "Of course we consider those things, but what architecture is really about is ———" become suspect.

If we accept that many otherwise competing, complementary, or simply different architectural positions embody similar notions of good, then their competing claims to legitimacy and centrality might be seen as essentially of the moment. Proponents are dealing each in his own way with what they see as the valid hierarchy or priority of needs and aspirations during their time. They are also each attempting to maximize those goods in the manner that is most appropriate to this supposed hierarchy and to the resources available at the time. Substantiation is thus a question of goods, their priority, and the right means for bringing them about.

On the other hand, there is at least a tacit assumption of intertemporal transcendence in most positions. They attempt to stand for concepts of proper architecture regardless of the moment. Therefore, adequate substantiation of claims to legitimacy and centrality must address a twofold issue. First, a position must show that the guiding idea of good and the ensuing prescription of means is fundamental at the moment and that substantiation can be sustained between moments. In the light of earlier discussion, this would mean that the particular version of an appeal to common rationality and experience will hold in other momentary circumstances. Second, the theoretical position must exhibit a character of completeness by embracing other fundamental dimensions of architecture that it does not directly address.

The posing of these two criteria should not be construed as a call for the convergence of all positions on some "middle ground." For that to be practical, or even desirable, we would have to agree upon an "essence of things" that remains fixed, is incapable of variation, denies other experience, and is ahistoric. This hardly seems reasonable. Nevertheless, it is a call for assuming the responsibility of going beyond the realm of purely architectural categories and self-referential lines of argument in making claims to legitimacy.

Finally, one might ask what all this has to do with the guidance of practical inquiry, design thinking, or professional action. As we have seen, normative positions of the types examined, as well as those that are more idiosyncratic and personal, do in fact provide direction for action. There is an undeniable connection between design thinking, the artifacts from its practice, and theoretical pronouncements from the same or a nearby source.

Throughout, an appropriate balance must be struck between aloof abstractions providing for nearly infinite interpretations and concrete prescriptive principles. Without such a relationship theoretical positions would be inoperative in the practical realm. The point is, however, that when there are failures to provide sufficient substantiation, theoretical positions are vulnerable and practical inquiry based upon them is impaired. A plethora of positions arises, all of them making more or less equally valid claims, and decisions about which of them to look to for guidance become merely a matter of personal taste.

Architectural Positions and Their Realms of Inquiry

4

Within the various normative positions that seek to describe what constitutes proper architecture, two realms of inquiry can be discerned. Each derives its distinctive characteristics from both the locus of inquiry and the interpretative frameworks employed in seeking substantiation and grounding in meaning for architectural production. These interpretative frameworks, it will be argued, can have the effect of circumscribing interpretation within their methodological confines, sometimes with undesirable consequences. In the sense that they prescribe the exclusion or inclusion of certain data and kinds of observation, they are ideological; yet the oppositional relation in which they are often perceived to stand disguises common purposes and interpretative problems. Furthermore, architectural positions, although they may strongly favor one realm of inquiry, rarely show sole conformance with either. Rather, each realm provides a vantage point from which some measure of legitimation may be secured for a position's proposals and subsequent production.

Two Realms of Inquiry

In the first realm of inquiry architecture is seen in relationship to a hypothesized society or interpretation of man and his world.[1] Here the fundamental concern is with legitimating and validating architecture with reference to "nature" or to a set of events or presumed facts that lie outside architecture itself. Inquiry frequents this outside domain in an effort to erect or borrow the necessary interpretative scaffolding to explain, compare, and devise architectural design principles within the inside world of architectural objects and production.

In the second realm architecture is seen in relationship to itself and its constituent elements. As Vidler puts it in his exposition of neorationalism, "Columns, houses, and urban spaces, while linked in an unbreakable chain of continuity, refer only to their own nature as architectural elements, and their geometries are neither naturalistic nor technical but essentially architectural" (Vidler 1978, p. 31). The locus of inquiry is the architectural object—in Vidler's and the neorationalists' case, the form of the city. Such interpretative frameworks see the object world as already a domain of man's manifest being and enterprise, and thus as not requiring outside excursions for the purposes of validation and legitimation. Eisenman, for example, states that "much of the 'modernist' enterprise had to do with work on the language itself," by which he means the language of architectural form, "one that was concerned with its own objecthood" (Eisenman 1978, p. 22).

Within these two realms of inquiry, "grounding in meaning" itself takes on a number of constructions. It can mean the making of architecture that is understandable, intelligible, and useful, and thus congruent with man's needs and wants. Or it can mean an architecture that is rhetorical, argumentative, polemical, and thus capable of providing commentary on man and his world. It is generally the case that the first realm of inquiry, where architecture is seen in relationship to a nature outside itself, tends toward the former sense of "grounding in meaning," while the second view tends toward the latter sense. For instance, the grounding of architecture in a view of social behavior, institutional procedures, and the like allows discrete needs and wants to be addressed and a relatively direct connection to be made back to an architectural object. On the other hand, interplay within a palette of rhetorical architectural resources, especially when they exhibit historical continuity, allows for critical strategies of quotation, redefinition, and polemic, the idea being that architectural elements and fragments from the past, with all their associated cultural meanings, can be recombined to make new statements.

Architecture from a Naturalistic Interpretation of Man and His World

In seeking substantiation from outside the domain of architecture, recent and contemporary architectural and urban design positions have tended to look to three sources: human behavioral science, production technologies, and—later on—various fields of environmental management involving both technological means and controlling influences on choice behavior. The kind of interpretation that is involved has been described by Bernstein as "naturalistic" in the sense that it considers reality to be adequately described by concepts of "natural phenomena" (Bernstein 1976). It is a "scientific" interpretation of man and his world, after the natural sciences. It represents an epistemology and world view that are very definitely foundational in inclination, and it generally coincides with a positivist orthodoxy.[2] Consequently, this interpretative framework tends to recognize two legitimate models of knowledge—namely, natural science and formal disciplines such as mathematics and logic.

● Functionalism and the Modern Movement

Amid the postrevolutionary fervor of the early twentieth century, architects sought to define their role through an avant-garde stance. They espoused, as Barbara Miller put it, "an architecture of a new beginning and social order . . . a search for a new 'spirit' for a new community" (Lane 1968, p. 60). The modern movement was more than a transformation of past practices, such as the historicist styles of Behrens, Bonatz, and other late-nineteenth-century architects. It was a complete departure, even a rejection of such earlier orientations.

By now the history of the development of this departure is well known. Throughout, there was an embracing of the apparent opportunities presented by new building materials, new fabrication technologies, and new models in the form of artifacts of the machine age, particularly in the areas of flight, navigation, and overland travel (Le Corbusier 1959). "The architect is the organizer of the building sciences," asserted Hannes Meyer (Schnaidt 1965, p. 31).

The conception of a new social order became manifested in the stress that was placed, in housing for instance, on the individual unit—on the manipulation of the unit in direct conformance with the functions it was to perform and on the equitable apportionment of exterior site amenity among units. In public housing projects, or *Siedlungen*—such as those at Weissenhof, Magdeburg, Dessau, and Berlin, by the architects of Der Ring, the Bauhaus, and CIAM (see figure 50)—the individual units, sometimes detached, were carefully designed to accommodate the functions of day-to-day life, and each had a more or less equal share in a hierarchy of public and private spaces. Aggregation of units maximized benign solar orientation, and a relative independence from the ground plane was provided through the use of pilotes and other devices. This strategy again effectively preserved, if by a sort of denial, an equitable distribution among unit dwellers of amenity and opportunity with respect to the street and outdoor recreation areas.

As others have eloquently pointed out, what seems to underlie the distinctions that were made in these schemes is a kind of "naive functionalism" (Rossi 1982, pp. 46–48), in which a close and inevitably static fit between function and form was striven toward along the lines of a functional determination involving discrete classifications of working, dwelling, and playing activities. Laudable though the notions of equitable access to accommodations, sunlight, and the public domain may have been, in

50
Apartment buildings in Siemensstadt, Berlin, by
Walter Gropius (1929).

practice many projects, especially in the hands of lesser architects, exhibited a tendency toward homogeneity, standardization, and even monotony. This tendency may have been inevitable
under the pressures of equitable distribution of spaces;
a highly deterministic, and in many senses narrow, categoriza-
tion of function; and moves toward standardization of fabrication systems and materials for their promise of reduced costs.

These shortcomings were recognized early on. Emil Utitz and
Schultze-Naumberg, among others, began in the period 1923–
1926 to voice criticism of the "new architecture" (Utitz 1923, p.
144). In fact, the appellation "functionalism" (*Zweckmässigkeit*)[3]
was coined to describe an architecture of engineering and planning that, while workable, economical, and efficient, nevertheless lacked qualities of "coziness, individuality, warmth and a
general rejoicing in the act of dwelling" (Lane 1968, p. 131).
Criticism was also leveled at the universality of the "new style,"
which seemed to be built for anyone, anywhere. This visual characteristic is attributable to ideas taken from the three sources

mentioned earlier—a narrow interpretation of function, equality of access to site amenities, and the use of modern production technology. Propositions about choice behavior, conflated with ideas of "typical" and "rational" man that were becoming prevalent at the time in other spheres, such as the behavioral sciences, were particularly influential.

In one of those disastrous moments of collision with the forces of history, the new architecture, which the critiques of the early 1920s had identified as a "style of labor and social utility" having a direct association with proletarian movements and Bolshevism, became the target of the political right in the 1930s. The fate of the Bauhaus at the hands of the National Socialist government of Germany is well known (Lane 1968, p. 147f.).

Of course Gropius, Taut, and others did not see their architecture as a mere product of function and technological opportunity. To them it represented the possibility of a new aesthetic in which an abstract geometric order would emerge, symbolizing a new practical realism amid the chaotic ferment of modern life. "The old forms are in ruins," wrote Gropius; "we float in space and cannot yet perceive the new order. . . . What is architecture? The crystalline expression of man's noblest thoughts" (Conrads 1964, p. 46). Again to quote Gropius, "The ultimate aim of all visual arts is the complete building" (Wingler 1969, p. 31). Here we begin to step across the boundary between our two general views of architecture. The modernists were clearly expressing a concern for architecture in itself. Yet theirs was not a strategy that operated entirely within the rhetorical resources of architecture and its constituent elements. It was an effort to devise a new aesthetic order without reference to past orthodoxies and with an express interest in the materials, techniques, concepts of behavior and ethics, and political developments of the time. A paramount principle of the modern movement was the prohibition against all direct stylistic references. This point will be taken up later, however, in the discussion of architectural language.

The spirit of "form follows function" and the preoccupation with new building technologies were, of course, to live on and thrive beyond the early modern period. The CIAM (Congress Internationale d'Architecture Moderne) was to give way to, or become identified with, the so-called international style (figure 51). In the postwar years a reappraisal and considerable reaffirmation of earlier positions was to be found in the pronouncements, proposals, and projects of Team Ten (Smithson 1968). As Colin Rowe and Fred Koetter were to write much later in something of

51
Buildings in the central area of Brasilia (Plaza of the
Three Powers), by Oscar Niemeyer (1960).

an epitaph, "If the combination of fantasies about science—with
its objectivity—comprised one of the most appealing and
pathetic of late-nineteenth-century doctrines, then the decisive
twentieth-century embodiment of these themes in the form of
building could not fail to stimulate; and, the more it excited the
imagination, the more the conception of a scientific, progressive
and historically relevant architecture could only serve as a focus
for a still further concentration of fantasy" (Rowe and Koetter
1978, p. 4).

● **Planning Orthodoxy and the Form of Cities**
In other realms concerned with the building of environments,
orthodox approaches of a positivist stamp emerged with similar
traits to those of the modern movement in architecture. Indeed,
when we consider the extensive influence of town and regional
planning practices and resulting policy and legal instruments
such as zoning, systems of economic incentives and disincen-
tives, and similar land-use and building control mechanisms, the
issue of managing and shaping buildings, towns, and cities appears inextricably engaged with architecture. To be more accurate, modern forms of managerial intervention and development

predate the architectural movements of the early twentieth century; and to the extent that a reciprocal relationship existed between planning and architecture, the direction of influence was more pronounced from the former to the latter (Scott 1969, pp. 1–46). Urbanism was confidently viewed as essentially a case of functional description, analysis, mediation, and control, all predicated on good "scientifically based" methods of interpreting the world (Mies van der Rohe 1923, p. 89).

From relatively early in this century, at least within the Anglo-American tradition of planning, the promise of an emphatic knowledge of human behavior—a science of human behavior—fueled attempts to engage in what later became decried as "social engineering" (Scott 1969, ch. 3; Krueckeberg 1983; Clawson and Hall 1973). The terrain of cities was subdivided along the lines of distinct and discrete patterns of use, with very little opportunity for mixing (figure 52). Urban land and buildings became highly valuable commodities, owing to the placement of transportation systems and their associated gradients of accessibility, and to the separation and concentration of functions. After all, the home environment should be just that, a residential sector with support from services such as schooling, shopping, and recreation, while places of work should be aggregated and serviced with their appropriate supporting functions. Such plans were deemed efficient. Intervening corridors provided access and with it better and worse opportunities for diminishing times and other inconveniences of travel. The results of these exercises provided a certain predictable and manipulable order, setting the stage for further episodes of development and redevelopment.

The appropriate accommodation and celebration of special uses, such as monuments, became something of a problem amid the general tendency toward standardization and homogeneity of uses. Rossi, for one, eloquently criticizes this aspect of modern cities (Rossi 1982, p. 55f.). More often than not, the problem was addressed through strategies like "connectivity," in which certain routes that already existed for other functional reasons were accentuated in ways that allowed for the display of special uses. This strategy did not attempt to break in any way with the entrenched linear continuity of land use and movement patterns (Crane 1964). Finally, certain general norms of behavior and aspirations were adduced, with the consequence that all-inclusive social contracts were struck (zoning ordinances, for instance). The result was that people on one side of a city with no real relationship to those on another found themselves responsible

52
Suburban tract housing in the United States.

for each other. By the 1950s the modern city had come very much into being.

Behind the scenes the influence of "scientifically based" methods of interpreting man and his world can be seen at work in at least two ways. First, there is the general practice of formulating problems concerned with the built environment in terms of the empirical orthodoxy's accepted procedures. Here the results of what count as valid and reliable exercises in measurement and analysis tend to determine which problems are identified and how they are understood.

The second manifestation of this orthodoxy's influence may be found in the widespread practice of "mapping" scientific explanatory theory about the relationship between man and his world into "instrumental action." For example, empirically based explanations of the trip-making behavior of urban residents often become the bases on which strategies to solve various transportation problems are developed. Similarly, an inference about environmentally defined patterns of behavior may be used unquestioningly as a basis for architectural design.

Generally, instrumental action means either a form of social contract that is used to regulate the conduct of human affairs as they relate to the built environment, or a physical intervention in the urban landscape that is proposed for similar purposes. Mapping is the process by which information from the formulation of a problem serves as a basis for the development of a social contract, designed intervention, or other instrumental action. For instance, a housing problem might be understood as such through the systematic gathering of empirical data, followed by the promulgation of some policy instrument (such as economic incentives) or a specific proposal about buildings that has meaning within the particular problem formulation.

Both influences are evident in the typical technical paraphernalia of urban design and planning—various schemes and methods for performing quantitative analyses of empirical data, computer models of a statistical or logical variety that are intended to mirror the subject matter of interest, "quantitative indices" of performance that link some measurable part of the world to some abstract dimension of quality (Dickey and Watts 1978, Catanese 1972). Witness also the technical undertakings of government agencies, either in-house or through sponsorship, that support legislative activities directly concerned with building and urban issues.

● Systems Approaches to Interpretation

At the heart of these "scientific" methods for interpreting man and his world for design purposes are empirical *systems approaches*—more particularly, the concept of *model* and the activity of *operational modeling* (Chadwick 1972, La Patra 1973, Handler 1970, Ferguson 1975). For example, there is the common use of behavioral models, of one sort or another, that purport to characterize the habitual or special behavior of individuals and groups contingent upon a variety of environmental circumstances. In general, for the "social bases" of design contemporary practitioners place a heavy reliance on interpretative frameworks that come directly out of social sciences such as anthropology and sociology.

In the earlier work of the current era by researchers like Hall and Sommer we see "territoriality" introduced, or reintroduced, with its concomitant concepts of "personal distance," the effects of crowding on social behavior, and the perception of space (Hall 1969, Sommer 1969). Cross-cultural comparisons were included to reinforce the contingent and relative importance of these dimensions of man-environment relations, and detailed case studies were conducted around specific activities such as learning and recreation. Barker, in an influential work dealing with approaches for studying environments of human behavior, broadened the methodological range in the direction of ecological concepts for defining fundamental "environmental units" and their structural interrelationships (Barker 1968; Proshansky, Ittelson, and Riulin 1970). Lynch's early studies on the image of the city also gave considerable weight to empirically determined concepts of spatial perception, and the idea of "cognitive mapping" was to become highly influential in the theory and practice of urban design (Lynch 1960).

Subsequent investigations and proposals of design criteria by Rapaport, Craik, and Zube, as well as Moore and Golledge, elaborated on these themes, extended the range of methodological possibilities, and reiterated the importance of a detailed explicit understanding—a model—of man-environment relations (Rapaport 1969, 1977; Craik and Zube 1976; Moore and Golledge 1976). At the same time, texts appeared that brought these ideas and empirical findings to bear more directly on the design process. The anthology of Lang and colleagues was aimed at the practicing professional as much as the researcher and provided both prescriptive advice and conceptual frameworks for addressing the design of various settings (Lang, Burnette, Moleski, and Vachon 1974). Later works by Sanoff and Preiser were even more specific and specialized in the area of facility programming (Sanoff 1977, Preiser 1978).

The Concept of Model

A review of literature dealing with modeling reveals its kinship with the logical-empirical approach and the hypothetical-deductive system of theory construction (Krimerman 1969). Under this system scientific explanation has two major components, an *explanandum* describing the phenomenon to be explained and an *explanans* containing statements of antecedent conditions and of the all-important general laws that account for the phenomenon. For example, if a vessel containing a fluid explodes when heated, the event can be accounted for by physical conditions surrounding the event and by laws, such as that pressure is directly proportional to temperature (Hempel and Oppenheim 1948). The explanatory scheme incorporates logical deduction whereby the explanandum can be deduced from the explanans in a straightforward Aristotelean manner (Mitroff and Kilmann 1978, ch. 3).[4] In practice, the development of laws in the social sciences invariably involves methods of statistical reasoning by which a conformance between data and theoretical regularities is established. Here the aim is to ensure that a relationship between the hypothesized occurrence and the real-world occurrence of variables of interest can legitimately be struck under all conceivable conditions (Campbell and Stanley 1970). The approach is hypothetical insofar as no claim is made that any of the laws and premises involved are infallible (Hempel and Oppenheim 1948).

According to Echenique, "A model is simply a representation of relevant characteristics of a reality . . . a means of expressing certain characteristics of an object, or system, that exists, existed, or might exist" (Echenique 1963, p. 1). Clearly, further elaboration of this definition requires consideration of what is meant by "relevant characteristics of a reality" and consideration of alternative means of representation.

The first part of model making, the "selection of relevant characteristics," is seen to be a process framed by the intentions of the model maker (Echenique 1963, p. 2f.). In other words, it is the questions that the model is designed to answer that will determine the selection of relevant variables, antecedent conditions, and so on. In this regard the concept of model does not really differ from the idea of theory construction in the social sciences. Both situations must begin with intentions, even if these are not generally recognized—are, as Popper calls them, "private matters'' (Popper 1959). How the actual selection of relevant characteristics is appraised and verified is considered largely a technical matter, involving good practice within the logical-empirical system of theory construction.

Consideration of alternative means of representation is also taken to be a technical matter, dictated by the situation at hand. For example, the choice of means may be strongly determined by how time, location, or other characteristics of the behavioral setting under scrutiny either need to be represented or can be incorporated into the model structure. It is also here that difficulties can be encountered. For example, available means and modeling ''languages'' may constrain the model builder's intentions. Such constraints may also result in the reformulation of a problem in line with available techniques of representation, with a concomitant abandonment of certain fundamental aspects of the original problem under consideration. The problem focus thus becomes shifted, and in ways that might later prove quite damaging in the context of broader social areas of concern. For example, the planning and design of a transportation system within an urban area, based upon the analysis of data about past travel behavior, may ignore aspects of the system that are inherently socially regressive for certain groups (such as gasoline taxes for low-income groups). This ignorance may be due to an underrepresentation of pertinent qualitative data, or it may be the consequence of socially regressive effects that could not be adequately described within the systematic framework originally used for the planning and design exercise.

In summary, the process of model making generally conforms to the following five steps, although not necessarily in the outlined order. First, the existence of an object, setting, or system that is of interest. Second, an intention, clearly expressed, enabling the selection of appropriate characteristics of the object, setting, or system. Third, a process of observation and abstraction enabling the reality in question to be observed in relationship to selected variables. Fourth, a process of translation, enabling the creation of a suitable conceptual framework for organizing factual information. And fifth, a process for testing and making conclusions about the congruence between the model and reality. This last operation is often referred to as ''calibration,'' or the fitting of some previously determined regularity to the specific circumstances of the locale under scrutiny.

Models and Theory

To Echenique and others, the differences between models and theories are principally matters of degree or status rather than ones of kind. The intellectual orientation for both is clearly the same (Echenique 1963, p. 3f.; C. Lee 1973, ch. 1; Collins 1976). In fact, Echenique suggests that a model can stand as a theory to the extent that it is a system of ideas that is held as an explanation for a phenomenon or group of facts; he clearly means theory in the ideal scientific sense.

The conformity of this concept to social science's orthodox approach toward hypothetical-deductive theory construction is not surprising. The latter is, more often than not, the acknowledged ideal for the former. However, when it comes to the activities of operational modeling, involving practical application for design and policy planning, certain distinctions can be made between a theory and a model. Alternatively, one can distinguish between kinds of models, according to their predictive powers: theoretical models are idealizations and weakly predictive, whereas analog models based upon empirical data are not (Hesse 1963).

Operational Modeling

Ira Lowry, an early luminary in the field of modeling and land-use planning, makes the following distinction: "In formulating his constructs the theorist's overriding aims are logical coherence and generality. . . . He is ordinarily content to specify only the conceptual significance of his variables and the general form of their functional interrelationships. . . . The model builder, on the other hand, is concerned with application of theories to a concrete case, with the aim of generating empirically relevant output from empirically based input" (Lowry 1965, p. 160).

In certain respects Lowry's distinction can be seen as nothing more than an operational one—as accommodation to the demands of applying a model to specific situations. In effect, a concern for the identity and direction of relationships is shifted in operational model building to the joint specification of both direction and magnitude. In other respects, however, particularly in the practical realm, the distinction implies an extension of theory. It is a situation where extant theory provides the building blocks for model construction, but where the model is not necessarily fully subsumed under theory and therefore becomes something different. More precisely, the model is based on theory but extends beyond theory in some respect.

The kind and magnitude of the difference or distinction can be dictated by several circumstances (Lowry 1965, Steinitz and Rogers 1970). First, the resources available for model construction and application may not fully permit a faithful theoretical account of the phenomenon to be made. Second, theory may generally cover the case in question but lack precision in particular considerations of magnitude; for example, the direction of a relationship may be known, but its functional form, in the formal or mathematical sense, may not. Third, theory may not yet exist covering some parts of the modeling exercise that are at any rate deemed relatively insignificant, thus requiring a patching together of promising hypotheses that have not been tested. Finally, theory may be applied in a model, but under conditions of application that extend beyond the reasonable limits of the theory's antecedent conditions.

The extension from theory to operational models in Lowry's sense can also be seen when one examines a fairly commonly accepted hierarchical classification of models (Lowry 1965; Steinitz and Rogers 1970, p. 8). Typically, four types of models are identified, according to the general purposes of their application. They are (1) *descriptive models,* (2) *predictive models,* (3) *explorative models,* and (4) *planning models.*

The principal intention behind a descriptive model is explanation of phenomena in the domain of interest. For instance, in a building or urban context a good descriptive model would reveal much about the underlying structure of the building or urban environment. It would reduce the apparent complexity of the observed world to a coherent and rigorous framework. Furthermore, the descriptive model is logically essential for any of the other three types. We cannot predict, explore, or plan, at least in the view of this orthodoxy, in the absence of a fundamental description of the reality under study.

The merit of a descriptive model can be assessed according to three broad criteria. First, the required ratio of input data to output data must be small; that is, explanatory power must be high (Lowry 1965, p. 160). Second, the conformance of model output to direct observation must be high; that is, the model must be accurate. Third, the model should be generally applicable—applicable beyond a specific spatio-temporal domain.

The purpose of a predictive model is to give a forecast of the temporal disposition of the phenomenon under study. These models can be of two types. *Extrapolative predictive models* are those in which the spatio-temporal change process is represented by a continuation of past trends—for example, by using a "line of best fit" applied to historical data. The obvious disadvantage here is that the change process in the future, or even in the present, may be discontinued or radically changed unbeknownst to the model maker. Recent models of settlement and urban structure that make use of the "order by fluctuation" principles propounded by Prigogine in chemistry have shown the possibility of sudden "bifurcation" of phenomena due solely to the timing of events (Allen 1981). This is a situation where the system is capable of reaching an entirely different state, due not to the types of processes at work per se but to their temporal conjunction. For instance, an interaction of otherwise independent and conventional land development decisions may radically change the type and pattern of economic activities in a geographic location.

Conditional predictive models are those in which the mechanism of cause and effect governing the change process is specified in the general form "If X is present at time t_1, then Y will transpire at time t_2." Clearly, the advantage of this type of model is that the process of change, or a significant portion of it, is endogenously specified—specified within the model. It does not rely solely on translation of past events into the future.

Explorative models are usually designed to allow the discovery, by systematic speculation, of realities other than the one at hand that may be logically possible. Such speculation usually proceeds by exploiting the systematic variation of basic parameters used in a descriptive model. A case in point is Zwicky's celebrated "morphological analysis" that leads to the invention of a particular type of jet engine (Zwicky 1962). Similar examples may be found in Simon's discussion of a "science of design" regarding an instrument for telling the time (Simon 1969, p. 6f.).

Within the framework of this kind of model, a functional analysis is usually performed on the type of system under consideration. From this analysis various alternative means for achieving required functions are identified, such as means of combustion, torque conversion, and so on. Compatible means, technically or otherwise, are then combined covering the required functions. Sometimes the results are novel solutions. An analogous approach can be employed in examining behavioral and cultural settings of interest, particularly when there is a premium being placed on new insights about underlying structure or behavior patterns. The general approach has also been proposed and applied in architectural design situations, again principally for the purpose of reexamining conventional practices.

A planning model necessarily incorporates prediction, usually of the conditional kind, but is extended to allow for the evaluation of predicted outcomes in terms of goals. In other words, this type of model is primarily developed for simulating the effects of different decisions about an environmental and behavioral setting, and evaluating those decisions or strategies against a specified goal structure (an expression of "good" performance).

Typically, the structure of planning models has the following components. First, a specification is made of alternative programmatic or design interventions that might be applied through some course, or courses, of action. Second, a predictive model is developed, allowing the consequences of choosing any specified alternative to be revealed. Third, there is a method of scoring and ranking the consequences so revealed according to some metric of goal achievement; that is, against some objective function. Finally, there is a mechanism for making the choice of (presumably) the alternative that yields the highest score. For example, a planning model developed expressly for the purpose of resolving floor-plan layout problems requires specification of the type of allocation procedures to be considered. It must also allow various room arrangements to be evaluated against specific metrics of performance, such as adjacency and transportation cost.

Classification of the models is hierarchical because one model type forms the foundation for others, with planning models located at the furthest extremity (see figure 53). The hierarchy also illustrates the steps in the construction of a planning model, including the use of an explorative model to test variables for possible inclusion in the model of conditional prediction.

● **Problems of Interpretation**
Of the types of models examined, planning models would most frequently seem to be extensions beyond empirically based explanatory theory. They incorporate goals presumably based on normative positions, which are largely precluded from the idea of explanatory theory. They seem to draw, as it were, on information from elsewhere. In contrast, the other models appear to conform more strictly to the boundaries of the idea of theory advocated by a logical-empirical orthodoxy.

The question then becomes whether planning models can meaningfully transcend their inherently explanatory function of "scientific interpretation" to any significant degree. Can they incorporate other values and qualities not directly accounted for by this interpretation? The answer is probably no. For one thing,

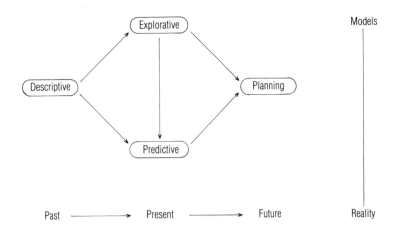

53
A hierarchy of model types.

a cursory survey of practical applications and experience with planning models would reveal an assortment of metrics for scoring achievements, each with its own requirements and limitations for accommodating the specification of goals. This would also apply to predictive models. For instance, cost-benefit analysis in its various guises, a mainstay for discriminating among various design alternatives, incorporates arcane formulae for what is counted versus what is not (Mishan 1976). The very strictures of these formulae, however, preclude any real advance beyond the realm of "facts" into the domain of "values," except in rather crude terms. For instance, affective aspects of choice behavior are largely precluded, and there is a tacit assumption of economically rational behavior.

Yet it is with a second, related characteristic of planning models that the in-principle restrictions imposed by the very ideals of scientific interpretation come into play. In such models, outcomes are evaluated in terms of goals. For this to be logically accomplished, a reasonable correspondence must be struck between an expression of an outcome and an expression of a goal. Given the inherent limitation of planning models as to movement away from strictly factual expressions, the goals inevitably become defined by, and therefore limited to, the currency of factual terminology. Furthermore, the converse also appears to be true in the process of model construction itself. For example, in econometrics and similar undertakings, there is the ubiquitous problem of appropriately representing various policy options in the "language" of a model (Domencich and McFadden 1975).

The central issue here is not so much whether planning models exhibit explanatory power or predictive accuracy as that a dependent relationship can very easily develop between the possibilities for formulating goals or design interventions and the technical exigencies of model development and application. Furthermore, these are exigencies that seem to be largely due to the pedigree, so to speak, of their "value-free" theoretical underpinnings. But if design and policy formulation is to be freed from the methodological restrictions that derive from the epistemology of the logical-empirical orthodoxy, to what other guiding theoretical orientation might it adhere? What are the alternatives to the science of human behavior?

● **Alternative Positions**

A number of authors have developed comprehensive and cogent criticisms of the empirical orthodoxy's idea of theory and the possibility of a science of man. For example, Bernstein in his classic work *The Restructuring of Social and Political Theory* brings to bear arguments from analytical philosophy, phenomenology, normative political theory, and critical rationalism (Bernstein 1976); Krimerman presents a well-organized anthology representing both sides of the debate (Krimerman 1969). The following brief account of critiques draws on these and other works and is intended to give a taste of the kinds of arguments that have been advanced, rather than anything approaching a thoroughgoing account.

A Humanist Critique

One kind of criticism revolves around drawing a distinction between the "outward" manifestations of human activity and "inner" systems of belief or thought that bear directly on this activity. For example, Isaiah Berlin challenges the claim that all real questions about man and his world can be answered through empirical and formal methods of the kind we have been discussing. To Berlin, "men's beliefs in the sphere of conduct are part of their conception of themselves and others. . . . This conception, whether conscious or not, is intrinsic to their picture of the world" and thus is central to social theory. Berlin does not merely conclude that social theory must embrace beliefs and convictions; he goes much further, asserting, "It is not simply a case of the existence of subjective states of mind but rather self-interpretation as constitutive of actions and practices" (Berlin 1963, pp. 13–15). As Bernstein observes, Berlin effectively provides a picture of social behavior in which we are dominated by models of what the world is like and these models determine both the content and the form of our beliefs, convictions, and behavior (Bernstein 1976, pp. 59–63). Any change in the guiding model necessarily results in changes in both belief and behavior.

The primary issue here is that dichotomies between the "objective" and the "subjective," between "fact" and "value," entirely misrepresent human action. Any proper description of objective action is internally related to interpretations of what constitutes action. This interpretation, in turn, is largely a matter of belief, self-awareness, and value. For Berlin there is "human action," and to speak of its factual and value sides is ridiculous (Bernstein 1976, p. 61).

Another critique, in a similar vein, is propounded by the historian Collingwood in his discussion of the "a priori impossibility of a science of man" (Collingwood 1946, pp. 205–231, 315–320; Krimerman 1969, pp. 7–25). Here he is referring to a science of man based on analogy with the methods of natural science and thus of the orthodox empirical variety. Collingwood makes a case for the primacy of history in these matters through its fundamental concern with events that are consequential beyond the realm of biological functions such as eating and sleeping. He also makes a distinction between the "outside" and the "inside" of an event, where the "outside" corresponds to all the documented circumstances about the event and the "inside" refers to the thought behind the event. In short, he advocates an interpretative scheme for history in which the aim is to see through the event to the thought that lies behind it. For Collingwood science and its methods are about "processes of events" and their interconnections, whereas history, or historical knowledge, is about "processes of thought." Therefore, while he seems more willing than Berlin to entertain a distinction between facts and thoughts, he clearly concludes that a science of man, in the orthodox empirical sense, is an impossibility.

Structuralist Similarities and Divergences
In many respects the salient features of structuralism resemble the idea of theory and general theory development advocated by the empirical orthodoxy. At least this seems to hold among common themes and approaches to be found in the works of Lévi-Strauss, Piaget, and Leach (Gardner 1981; Piaget 1970a, 1970b). Structuralism is founded in an "ardent and powerfully held conviction that there is structure underlying all human behavior and mental functioning." This structure "can be discovered by orderly analysis and . . . once discovered it has cohesiveness, meaning and generality" (Gardner 1981, p. 10). What proponents mean by structure takes on a variety of forms, usually expressed

in terms of the subject matter in which they are dealing. For Piaget in his developmental psychology, it is represented by the immutable stages of cognitive development from conception to adult life (Piaget 1965, 1970a, 1970b). For Chomsky it is the presence of a single deep structure that is the root of all language (Chomsky 1965). There is a strong adherence to a "universal base hypothesis," whereby all manner of human thought, activities, and experience can be traced to a common foundation, regardless of culture, economic position, or other surface manifestations of the human condition.

Apart from the similarity apparent in the foundational inclination of theory, parallels with the empirical orthodoxy are also evident within the framework of methods for theory construction. In simplified form, this framework may be depicted as follows (Gardner 1981, p. 15f.). First, if regularities are apparent, or seem likely to hold, then the behavioral phenomenon can be subject to structural analysis. Second, a diverse set of phenomena can be related to one another once common factors have been discovered. In the "developmental method" of structural analysis espoused by proponents such as Piaget, this means distinguishing between two kinds of factors. They are "synchronic elements," or factors that do not exhibit temporal variation, and "diachronic elements," or those within the domain of inquiry that change with time. These elements can be further distinguished into two subgroups, namely, "irreversible elements" that move solely in one direction and "reversible elements" that include shifts from one pole to another, actions and reactions, and cycles of events. In "nondevelopmental" or "agenetic approaches" it is assumed that all relevant factors are present in some form throughout the period and across the domain of interest. The third and final general step in the procedure is the devising of a formal or informal model of underlying structures. It is a model that must have the characteristics of accounting for the data in an economic and comprehensive fashion and being applicable to data yet to be collected. Thus, the model must be divorced from concrete reality, to the extent that it is possible; that is, it must not make specific reference to the particular case being investigated. Models cannot be mere empirical generalizations, although they must be reflections of observations made by empirical observation.

Clearly this framework coincides with the theoretical ideals of the empirical orthodoxy. Beyond these general working methods, however, structuralism in practice parts company with the positivist empirical temper. Its intellectual heritage is profoundly influenced by a Rousseauan opposition to Cartesian and other mainstream Enlightenment positions (Gardner 1981, pp. 15–47). Hence structuralism does concern itself with the affective and irrational nature of man. It has also placed considerable emphasis on nonempiricist intellectual activities of theorizing, such as "arm-chair" or "thought" experiments.

The Problem of Tacit Conventions

As proposed by Bernstein, yet another critique, or alternative position, comes from the direction of analytical philosophy and certain kinds of linguistic analysis closely associated with Wittgenstein and others (Bernstein 1976).[5] Here theorists such as Winch involve the notion of "forms of life" as being fundamental and given in any description of human behavior (Winch 1958, Wittgenstein 1969, Bloor 1983). Furthermore, it is these forms of life that constitute the essential questions to be pondered. The necessary and sufficient ingredients that define and distinguish forms of life are intersubjective conventions and agreements; for example, speech is understood via complex intersubjective agreements about language. These intersubjective conventions manifest themselves, in turn, by "rule following" behavior and hence are logically indispensable from the idea of "making a mistake" or the valuation of some things that count from those that do not. In short, Winch concludes that social relations are governed by the language, ideas, concepts, and beliefs, as well as the reflective and unreflective actions, that constitute institutional practices, and therefore cannot be separated from them in any meaningful manner (Bernstein 1976, pp. 63–74). Like Berlin, he seems to be arguing that a purely "objective" or "scientific" rendition of human behavior may run the risk of misunderstanding the appropriate concept of behavior, by divorcing this concept from a detailed explanation of outward manifestations.

The Phenomenological Alternative

The "phenomenological alternative," as Bernstein calls it, to the empirical orthodoxy interposes concepts such as Husserl's *Lebenswelt* in the "scientific" account of man and his world (Bernstein 1976, pp. 117–169). The alternative might also include Merleau-Ponty's idea of situations and Heidegger's being-in-the-world (Mallin 1979, chs. 1–2; Heidegger 1962). Roughly speaking, the *Lebenswelt* is the world we live in and the world of everyday experience (Husserl 1975; Kockelmans 1967, p. 31f.). In Husserl's earlier accounts, at least, it covers the circumstances surrounding commonplace events, including those that are affective and intentioned. All human thinking and behavior in this everyday world, argue the phenomenologists, has an indispensable core of conceptual equipment that has no history and embodies concepts, commonplaces, and views of the world corresponding to the time when man first encountered himself. This core does not change; as we might expect, the objective of phenomenological inquiry is to reveal it and thus to address questions about the "essence of things."

According to Bernstein, where the phenomenologists part company with the empirical orthodoxy is in their conclusion that it makes no sense to replace the core of conceptual equipment with a "scientific" account (Bernstein 1976, pp. 126–135). Science, like any other conceptual equipment, must presuppose this core. For people like Merleau-Ponty, science is thus a second-order expression of basic human experience and not ontological (Mallin 1979, p. 20f.). This is not to say that all phenomenologists necessarily assert ontological primacy for their concept of everyday experience; Heidegger, for instance, rejected Husserl's schema as reductionist (Kockelmans 1967, pp. 228–230). In general, they argue for the juxtaposition and interposition of this kind of concept with that of objective science and, therefore, a suspension of judgment about the reality of either. The "bracketing" of both worlds that comes about through such juxtaposition and interposition will result, so the argument goes, in understanding through pure reflection, or the enigmatic "transcendental turn." It is only through this transcendental turn that one reaches a complete phenomenological understanding of the affairs of man, and positivist science fails to make such a turn (Husserl 1970).

Logical Falsification and Ambiguity
Finally, in a more strictly logical vein, Duhem and later Feyerabend, both from the realm of the philosophy of science, have attacked the commonly accepted notion that application of the hypothetical-deductive method can result in falsification (Duhem 1914; Feyerabend 1978, p. 294; Mitroff and Kilmann 1978). In fact, both argue, scientific experiments and procedures cannot be decisively falsified.

Their argument begins with the assertion that scientists never test a single hypothesis in isolation from other hypotheses, but rather against a network of assumptions, auxiliary hypotheses, concepts, and so on. Therefore, relationships with regard to a hypothesis H_i and an observation O can only be regarded as taking place within a network of n hypotheses. Thus, when observation of *not O* or *O* is in disagreement with the predictions of theory, all one can legitimately conclude is that the hypothesis in question, H_i, is false. In fact, exactly which hypothesis is in error can never be determined with complete assurance (Mitroff and Kilmann 1978, p. 38f.).

Neither Duhem nor Feyerabend contend that falsification cannot occur. They do, however, raise the issue that in order to falsify a hypothesis, we have to assume the veracity of all the other hypotheses and auxiliaries entering into an experiment. Thus falsification is ambiguous. Moreover, in a case where one is considering the relationship between a hypothesis H and an observation O, if an experiment yields the result *not O*, the null hypothesis can be concluded if and only if there are no assumptions that serve the original hypothesis and are also compatible with *not O*. In other words, there would seem to be a certain open-endedness to gradual elimination of false ideas through experimentation (Feyerabend 1978, p. 35f.).

Arguments have been leveled at the "scientific interpretation" of man and his world from other quarters. The attack from "critical theorists" such as Habermas, for instance, has been omitted from this discussion (Habermas 1979). So too have the doubts expressed by otherwise staunch proponents of scientific interpretation, such as Weber in his discussion of *wertfrei* ("value-free") investigations (Weber 1957). The foregoing discussion should, however, have given at least some indication of the reasonableness of raising fundamental questions about this form of interpretation, in view of the plausible alternatives.

Architecture from a Referential Interpretation

Over the last few decades there has been a noticeable shift of emphasis in architectural discourse toward the world of architectural "objects" and the use of its constituent elements as the primary focus of design. "I really don't think that architecture is about social and political activity any more than I think politics is about architecture," remarked Michael Graves at a recent symposium. He went on to characterize architecture as "invention" that makes up its own "text" from the myths and rituals of society—a text that in turn provides impetus to further invention (Graves 1984). Such sentiments resonate with Wittgenstein's concept of "forms of life." Arithmetic is just that, arithmetic, and not a set of operations based upon mathematics and logic. To engage in arithmetic one has only to know its constituent elements and not those of some other form of life, such as logic (Diamond 1976, p. 271).

This kind of preoccupation is by no means new. Each architectural epoch has had its share of introspective interest in its own constituent elements and their meanings. In the baroque era, for example, precise architectural elements and compositional principles from the Renaissance were transfigured, even dematerialized, the baroque architects taking the principles of the Renaissance as givens for their more willful explorations (Millon 1983, pp. 9–10). The pluralism that is so characteristic of current interest undoubtedly owes much, if only by reaction, to the avant-garde stance of the modern movement, with its concentration on abstract formalism and its steadfast denial of stylistic reference or figural quality.

● **Strategies of Reinterpretation**
At least three strategies can be seen at work in contemporary efforts to reinterpret and develop the world of architectural objects. They are not styles in either the art-historical or the commonplace sense of the word. Rather, they may be regarded as modes of interpretation with an essentially methodological inclination: frames of reference with a judgmental as well as an objective dimension.

The three strategies will be referred to as *work on the language, bricolage,* and the use of *type.* This is a somewhat arbitrary classification and one that is not at all novel (Colquhoun 1978a; Vidler 1977, 1978; Rowe and Koetter 1978; Krier 1978; Dunster 1977). Work on the language encompasses both a consideration of the formal component of architectural language, or the "how," and a consideration of the figural component, or the "what" (Colquhoun 1978a, pp. 29–30). By contrast, bricolage and the use of type will be discussed chiefly in relation to the problem of choosing and reusing existing architectural objects, or constituent elements. The classification is arbitrary because the very applicability of the term *language* may be questioned, and because the use of type and bricolage may themselves be regarded as work on the language insofar as they deal with matters of both figure and form. Yet verbal language is normally regarded as capable of describing something outside itself, but with no particular agenda or purpose. People use the same language to express many different ideas, whereas type and bricolage are more ideological means of interpretation and expression. In short, they are ways of using the language, or more precisely, ways of appropriating and using constituent elements of architecture.

Work on the Language: The Formal and Figural Traditions

Alan Colquhoun makes the following distinction between *form* and *figure: form* applies to "a configuration with natural meaning or none at all" (here "natural meaning" signifies meaning without the overlay of intervening interpretative schema of a culture), whereas *figure* applies to "a configuration whose meaning is given by culture." Further, the figure organizes ideas and thus is expressive and didactic (Colquhoun 1978a, p. 30f.). The two components, he argues—and hence the formal and figural traditions in architecture—are not entirely disconnected, although during certain eras the preoccupation may be more with one component than with the other.

As is clear from the statement by Walter Gropius quoted earlier, the modern movement had an undeniable preoccupation with an abstract formalism. By denying any stylistic references of either a formal or a figurative kind, the meaningful content of architecture became indistinguishable from its form. This is not to say that it had no meaning at all. On the contrary, it had a kind of functional meaning that, as Colquhoun puts it, was "absorbed directly into form" (1978a, p. 29).

In the hands of a consummate architect like Louis Kahn, a lyrical architecture of the tectonic resulted from the use and expression of frame, masonry wall, slabs, and vault, as evidenced in the Kimball Art Museum in Fort Worth and the Salk Center in La Jolla (figure 54). His was also an architecture in which the hierarchical disposition of "served and servant spaces," very much a functional determination, played a considerable role in the overall organization. As Frampton and others have noted, when Kahn's architectural enterprise involved the need for an expression of monumentality or a question of saying "what," he resorted to the use of platonic arrangements such as squares and circles, in much the same manner as Enlightenment architects such as Ledoux and Boulée (Frampton 1985, Burton 1983). In comparison to other figural devices that might be employed, this seems like a last resort, and one that shows a certain discomfort outside modernist doctrine.

The work of the "New York Five" dramatized and extended the geometrical abstractions of the modern movement in general and of Le Corbusier in particular (Five Architects 1972). The complex spatial interplay of solid and planar elements, beams, and columns seemed more concerned with the very possibilities presented by the world of such architectural objects than with any other kind of meaning. As Peter Eisenman, one of the Five,

54
The Jonas B. Salk Center in La Jolla, by Louis I.
Kahn (1962–1966).

55
House II, by Peter Eisenman (1969).

was to comment later, "It [the formal language] changed the relationship between man and object away from an object whose
primary purpose was to speak about man to one that was concerned with its own objecthood" (Eisenman 1978, pp. 21–22).

Eisenman's own work seemed so completely to absorb functional meaning into form that the architecture became a "pure"
work of art orchestrated according to its own internally consistent formal rules (figure 55). Form seemed to be running the risk
of so totally subsuming function that it would transgress any reasonable bounds. The "bedroom suite" in House VI, for example,
deconstructs the normal planar surfaces of wall and floor to the
point where questions can be raised about the suite's actual
commonplace use (Gutman 1977). Eisenman's work pushes Colquhoun's definitions of form and figure to the limit. If the didactic purpose is to explore architectural form for the sake of
art, then the work certainly can have a significant cultural meaning beyond a "natural" one. As Eliot observed with respect to
the changing of meaning within a literary tradition, it is the effect
of new works to simultaneously rearrange the tradition and bring
about an alteration in the meaning of each text (Hirsch 1967, p.
215). Eisenman's work would certainly seem to have accomplished this shift, to the extent that it calls for reexamination of
accepted traditions.

The figural tradition has a long standing in architecture. Panofsky eloquently describes the connection between Gothic and Scholasticism and the synthetic power Gothic cathedrals had for the purposes of transfixing, instructing, and transporting the hearts and minds of the people (Panofsky 1967). The rich iconography and allegorical elements of baroque architecture formed a text whose meaning was also readily construed (Norberg-Schulz 1980b). And classicism has spoken to us about order and harmony as well as the place of man in the universe (Kaufmann 1968).

After the hiatus represented by modernism a recovery of the figural tradition can be discerned. In fact, as Colquhoun argues, such a tradition never fully disappeared. He cites oblique references to the Beaux Arts on the part of modernists, as well as the "neoclassicism" of many American works during the 1950s (Colquhoun 1978a, p. 29). Currently, however, the references are far more literal and complete.

In the work of Venturi, Scott Brown, and others the recovery of popular symbols is very much a hallmark. During a discourse on the architecture of the American commercial strip—to continue a discussion begun in the last chapter—various principles for recovering a figural tradition were established (Venturi, Scott Brown, and Izenour 1972). Buildings were classified as either "ducks" or "decorated sheds." A duck is a building whose conformation is a complete symbol or icon. A decorated shed is a building to which symbols, often commonplace signs, have been attached. All such signs and symbols were in common usage and part of the "vernacular" of the culture. It was argued that a figural component to architecture could be developed that drew upon "the ugly and the ordinary" as a legitimate rhetorical resource.

The Venturi office has produced a number of decorated sheds. It is both the distinctive and the ordinary features of the Guild House in Philadelphia that demonstrate its figural qualities. Windows look unabashedly like windows and, together with the brickwork on the exterior, are quite suggestive in their ordinariness. The ornamental horizontal white stripes near the top of the building and the broad white panels are applied decoration for the purpose of helping to organize the facade. The large arched windows at the top center of the facade also help to organize the composition; in addition, they call attention to the unique occurrence of a large common room (Venturi, Scott Brown, and Izenour 1972, pp. 90–103). The recent proposals for the Laguna Gloria Art Museum, to be constructed in Austin, Texas, are of a similar stamp (figure 56; Venturi, Rauch, and Scott Brown 1985). The shed represents a very skillfully organized plan, and its exterior is decorated through the use of ornament and appliqué, with such things as "stars of Texas" and rather classical pilasters, a presumed commentary on Texas culture.

The work of Charles Moore also employs figurative fragments— particular roof forms, colonnades, alcoves, and niches—although less as appliqué or shed decoration. For the most part these elements are composed in a modern, albeit picturesque, manner as an integral part of the overall work. Kresge College in Santa Cruz exemplifies these characteristics (Moore 1967).

As Colquhoun points out, the strategy that seems to be most involved in Venturi's work and in Moore's early work amounts to "quotation" (Colquhoun 1978b, p. 35). Isolated figural elements or motifs from outside the rest of the work itself are deliberately introduced either to qualify or to offer additional commentary. The interest of Venturi's work derives from the intellectual foundation of the choice of quotation and from the skill with which the quotation is integrated into the architectural work. The problem of "misreading" is minimized by the currency and vernacular quality of the decoration or quotation. The Lone Star cannot be completely misconstrued. Still, the inevitable parochialism of today's commonplaces would seem to limit the inherent power of the strategy of quotation to unearth more universal meanings. Can it be said of architecture, as of literature, that certain motifs, figures, or tropes are handed down across the ages? If so, then these would seem to represent the treasure trove for quotation. The weakness of the vernacular is its more momentary meaning.

The recent scheme by Cesar Pelli for Robert R. Herring Hall, housing the Jesse H. Jones Graduate School of Administration (1982–1984), makes use of quotation, although the reach of the references is far more modest and indeed is confined to the architecture of the Rice University campus (figure 57). Here Pelli's renowned ability for systematic articulation and surface rendering of buildings (Pastier 1980) takes its cue from the intricate patterns of masonry work and inlaid decoration that abound on nearby buildings. As one reviewer remarked, however, the project "reinterprets that tradition and reveals richer aspects of [Pelli's] design vocabulary" (Papademetriou 1985, p. 86). This is not a case of mere contextual conformance but one in which the architect's already distinctive approach is enriched by quotation

56
The Laguna Gloria Art Museum in Austin, by
Venturi, Rauch, and Scott Brown (1985): sketch
and model.

57

Robert R. Herring Hall at Rice University in Houston,
by Cesar Pelli and Associates (1982–1984).

and a strong sense of what it is to make a building. The result at once provides a sense of continuity with the campus's earlier architectural tradition and offers a new statement about the manner in which the tradition can be celebrated. As Pelli has stated in a recent article with regard to the legitimacy of an existing building context, "The hope is that by repeating their forms . . . somehow the value of the past will rub off. . . . This cannot be a lasting condition. . . . For me the solid ground . . . is given by the basic relationship between the art of our buildings and their system of construction" (Papademetriou 1985, p. 86).

The spatial organization of Herring Hall recognizes another building tradition at Rice, namely, the creation of formalized courts appropriated for use by surrounding departments. As did Stirling and Wilford in their earlier addition to M. D. Anderson Hall (1979–1981), Pelli "wraps" or rather "layers" the building around an outdoor garden to much the same effect as that of the courtyard of the student center located opposite (figure 57). A clear formal and figural relationship is thus struck, across an open field, between the two building complexes.

In addition to quotation, more full-fledged deployment of a figural tradition in architecture is to be found in the historicist styling and conformation of a number of contemporary works. Many might be dismissed as simply exercises in eclecticism that do little to advance work on the language and the meaningful uses to which it can be put. They might be seen as mere associative uses of history—rifled, often indiscriminately, for the purposes of styling. The recent work of Bofill and the Taller de Arquitectura, however, is not to be taken lightly. Particularly in their new town and other urban projects in France—in Saint-Quentin-en-Yvelines, Paris, and Montpelier—a thoroughly Beaux-Arts interest in classicism and a strongly rational sense of spatial organization are pervasive. The interesting turn, however, is in the manner of construction with which these figurative elements are produced, and the types of accommodations to which they are quite grandiosely applied.

The type of construction is close to the ultimate in sophistication and efficiency. It employs industrial precast concrete produced in specially prepared forms for the cladding, as well as highly mechanized on-site "tunnel system" techniques for the shell of the building (Dixon 1981). Rather than the design process being subordinated to technical capacities for the production of desired forms, the sophistication of the casting techniques is such that the designer is released, so to speak, to consider other matters.

In most of the projects, such as Le Viaduc and Les Arcades du Lac, the type of accommodation is predominantly mass housing for middle-income wage earners. What one finds are several inversions of expected doctrine, especially of the modernist kind. First, the mass housing has the conformation of a palace. It is monumental, grand, and compositionally complete in a classical sense (figure 58). Second, rather than a tectonic aesthetic orthodoxy that strives to absorb or express a fabrication technology, the very sophistication of the technology has removed it from matters of expression, as epitomized by the explosion of unexpected figural forms. The resulting architecture is indeed rhetorical in both a technical and a sociopolitical sense.

Certain problems emerge with this approach, particularly when attempts are made to integrate domestic architecture with other special and, one might say, more monumental uses. The expected hierarchy among institutional uses, which is normally expressed through an ascending scale of grandeur, material quality, and monumentality, becomes difficult to achieve. This dilemma is evident in the proposals for a largely nonresidential civic complex to be placed on the other side of the lake from the Arcades du Lac and Le Viaduc projects (Taller de Arquitectura 1984). The sheer monumentality of the existing housing threatens to overwhelm the newer project proposal and makes the design exercise that much tougher to resolve.

Bricolage

According to Lévi-Strauss, "a bricoleur is adept at performing a large number of diverse tasks. . . . His universe of instruments is closed and the rules of his game are always to make do with whatever is at hand, that is to say, with a set of tools and materials which is always finite and is also heterogeneous, because what it contains bears no relation to the current project, or indeed to any particular project, but is the contingent result of all the occasions there have been to renew or enrich the stock" (Lévi-Strauss 1966, p. 16). Colin Rowe and Fred Koetter in *Collage City* call for the recovery of the bricoleur's craft as a more meaningful alternative to what they see as the emasculating influences of positivist planning and urban design doctrine (Rowe and Koetter 1978). We are presented with the idea of making use of past forms, fragments, and edifices in our cities, not as mere sympathetic contextualism whereby one designs after the fashion of what is around and about, but as a strategy that provides

58

Le Viaduc and Les Arcades du Lac in Saint-
Quentin-en-Yvelines, by Ricardo Bofill and the
Taller de Arquitectura (detail view of Le Viaduc and
general plan of both complexes, 1974–1978).

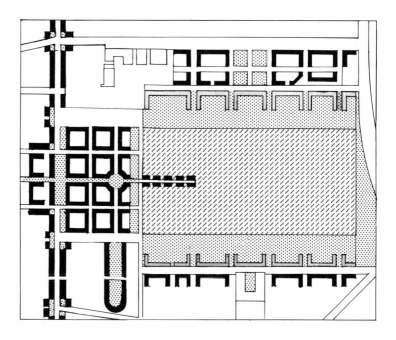

both continuity with the past and access to novel future works. For after all, if we admit the possibility of recombining, reusing, and reconstruing the old parts that are laid at architecture's doorstep, as it were, some measure of continuity is assured and the new use to which the old parts are put advances the possibility of new meanings.

Colquhoun, in analyzing the work of Michael Graves, depicts a shift away from an earlier preoccupation with abstract formalism toward the expressive use and reinterpretation of traditional architectural elements: "Columns developed capitals, doors became qualified with architraves and pediments, and ornamentation adorned surfaces" (Colquhoun 1978b, p. 25). Certainly in the Portland Public Services Building of 1979–1982 a bricolage can be seen (figure 59). The exterior, organized according to a classical tripartite division, borrows heavily from the Beaux-Arts facades in surrounding old Portland. The small roof pavilions, obscuring mechanical equipment and the like, appear quite literally as a collection of public buildings from a bygone era. The overall appearance is very much in keeping with American city halls built during the 1920s and 1930s. In part this is due to the classical compositional principles involved, but it is also due in large measure to the reinterpretation that has been placed upon borrowed motifs and decorative elements (Jencks 1980, p. 133f.).

59
The Portland Public Services Building in Portland,
Oregon, by Michael Graves (1979–1982): model
and sketches.

Of course, the bricoleur's craft, if it is to be of service to society as a real alternative in matters of city planning and architecture, must "address [itself] to a collection of oddments left over from human endeavors" (Lévi-Strauss 1966, p. 17) and transcend both imitation and Rube Goldbergian invention. The product of the bricoleur's labors must have contemporary meaning. This requirement raises issues of the choice of fragments or parts, their integration, and their articulation, whether the purpose is polemical or not.

In addressing these issues, Hirsch's four criteria for good interpretation seem most appropriate (Hirsch 1967, p. 236f.). For the bricoleur must interpret the situation of the moment, even if only through the "oddments" he has at hand. The four criteria are *legitimacy, correspondence, generic appropriateness,* and *coherence.* By legitimacy is meant the permissibility of the use of the oddments within prevailing public norms. Here some latitude may be extended. What stands as accepted convention might be quite far-ranging. And unlike those attempting to make new formal or figural extensions to an architectural language, the bricoleur faces the likelihood of public understanding based on past experience. As one Portland resident said of Graves's projected building, "I look forward to a public building that offers more than the blank facades and mirror walls of modern architecture. . . . The 'temple' design shows sensitivity to the design of neighboring buildings" (Jencks 1980, p. 138).

The criterion of correspondence requires that the bricoleur account for all the conditions inherent in the situation of application and in the oddments themselves. The choice, integration, and articulation of architectural elements must resolve all the problems at hand and do so in a legitimate manner. The criterion of generic appropriateness is most simply illustrated by a linguistic example: You don't use the standards of, say, scientific discourse to measure or interpret casual conversation. In architecture, the bricoleur must be careful not to use forms that are inappropriate to their situations. The exterior of worker housing that looks like a palace might be such a transgression. Alternatively, the interpretative framework that allows such transgressions to be made must be apparent and consistently applied. In the work of Bofill cited earlier, sociopolitical commentary might well be the appropriate basis for polemical articulation of grand neoclassical facades on mass housing.

The fourth criterion is perhaps the hardest to meet. Coherence requires that the meaning be obvious and make sense: more sense in fact than an alternative arrangement of architectural elements. As we have seen in earlier chapters dealing with such matters as "satisficing decisions" and the unbounded nature of design problems, knowledge that a given proposal is the best is well-nigh impossible to attain. Nevertheless, such a quality, should it prevail, would ensure conformance with the other three criteria.

The danger of an architecture of bricolage is that legitimacy, correspondence, and generic appropriateness cannot be maintained in the light of contemporary situational conditions that have little or no congruence with past experience. The modern urban world is notable for the rise of new institutions and means of transaction. To equate the conditions of modern transportation, for example, with the streets, roads, and byways of old, even if in a consciously polemical vein, is to deny the relevance and ignore the opportunities of these conditions.

The undeniable strength of an architecture of bricolage is the sense of cultural continuity, which may serve as a stabilizing influence in the face of sharp disjunctions with tradition or caprice. This strength does not entirely lie in the preservation of the status quo or "remembrance of things past," however. Bricolage offers the opportunity for new kinds of meaning by direct reference to and use of old, familiar, and rediscovered architectural elements, fragments, and edifices. The strategy depends, in large measure, on architectural elements' retaining their meanings. Nothing would confound the strategy more than if these meanings were to shift and change on a whim, or during the passage of time. The elements would surely lose their identity as tools and materials in the bricoleur's craft shop.

Type

The "type idea" has exercised the minds of many in the Western philosophical tradition. From Plato's "ideas" to modern linguistic conceptions of a type as a shared mental object, the relationship of the "one and the many" inherent in the type idea has been a subject for profound contemplation and impassioned dispute for centuries (Hirsch 1967, p. 265f.). A central issue concerns the ability of a type, which is one thing, to stand for or represent more than one thing. Our trees and their trees are all "tree."

In architecture today, type often stands at the center of debate. It is widely recognized as fundamental to the formulation of significant and legible work, both for its "one and the many" properties and, by extension, for the sense of continuity of tradition that is offered. According to the definition promulgated by the eighteenth-century theorist Quatremère de Quincy, "the art of regular building is born of a preexisting source," and that preexisting source is the idea of type. "The word type presents less the image of a thing to copy or imitate completely than the idea of an element which ought itself to serve as a rule for the model. Thus one should not say . . . that a statue or the composition of a finished and rendered picture has served as a type for the copy that one made. But when a fragment, a sketch, a thought of a master, a more or less vague description has given birth to a work of art in the imagination of an artist, one will say that the type has been furnished for him by such-and-such an idea, motif or intention" (Quatremère de Quincy 1977, p. 148).

In this discussion Quatremère de Quincy is careful to distinguish between type and model, the latter being possessed of precisely identifiable properties. He also, however, makes a distinction between "idea, motif, or intention" and type, in which type has the quality of a definable rule that is provided by the idea, motif, or intention. Consequently, while type definitely belongs to the realm of ideas, it is not to be seen as something altogether vague and fuzzy.

This kind of lofty abstraction is little different from definitions to be found in disciplines other than architecture,[6] and does little to influence architecture of its own accord. For that we might turn to the group known as the neorationalists and their program of inquiry centered on the city, or what Vidler has referred to as the "Third Typology" (Vidler 1978).

In seeking to overcome the difficulties of positivist interpretations of cities according to their functional elements (such as land uses) and technical characteristics (such as infrastructure systems), the neorationalists see the city as being most meaningfully composed of "fragments," or architectural elements. These elements, in turn, are not reinventions of past architectural types and not just repetitions of past typological forms. According to Vidler, such elements can only be defined, assembled, or reassembled if they meet the following three criteria of meaning: first, meaning "inherited from ascribed meanings of the past existence of the forms"; second, meaning "derived from the specific fragment and its boundaries and often crossing between previous types"; and third, meaning "proposed by a recomposition of those fragments in a new context" (Vidler 1978, p. 31).

With the first criterion Vidler echoes Rossi's idea of the "city type" as "the collective memory of its people made up of objects and spaces, . . . a memory which in turn shapes the future, . . . for when a group is introduced to a space they transform it into their own image, but at the same time they yield and adapt to material things [objects and spaces of the city] which resist this transformation" (Rossi 1982, p. 130). It is a criterion that allows quite heavy reliance to be placed on collective past meaning(s) to ground and validate the work. As will be discussed later in this chapter, the multiplicity of meanings with which a fragment is imbued can sometimes confuse significance with meaning and deny the very grounding that is being sought.

The work of the brothers Krier and others provides insight into the second criterion by suggesting how the fragments should be defined (Krier 1979, AAM 1978). For example, there is the "conception of urban space"—streets and squares—"as the primary organizing element of an urban morphology," from which it follows that buildings alone do not form a describable (meaningful) space (figure 60). There is the dictum that housing zones must be "transformed into complex parts of the city, into cities within the city, into 'quartiers' which integrate all the functions of urban life." According to this vision of the city, "the street and square are precise spatial types, the block is a result" (Krier 1978). Many if not all these blocks are zones of mixed use in which the perceived modern tendency toward separation of function is deliberately denied. The resulting idea of city form is reminiscent of certain eighteenth-century accomplishments, although for different reasons; as critics have argued, it does not follow that the spatial conformities of one way of life are applicable to those of another (Frampton 1980, p. 292). Neorationalist proposals are viewed by some as having a faintly reactionary orientation, removed from the sociopolitical locus of contemporary urban conditions.

The third criterion for assembly, that meaning be imparted by the "recomposition of . . . fragments in a new context," recalls the standard definition for another sort of human activity. The genre of spoken language called the joke requires just such a comprehension of new meaning through a shift in context. In the hands of someone like Rossi, assembly in this manner takes on a critical sociopolitical stance. According to Vidler's interpretation, Rossi's Regional Hall project for Trieste of 1974 (figure 61), with its references to eighteenth-century prisons assigned to the seat of local government, raises questions regarding the ambiguous condition of civic government (Vidler 1978, p. 32). The juxtaposition of an open arcade suggests a lack of confinement and is thus a contradiction of a prison. Other such metaphysical op-

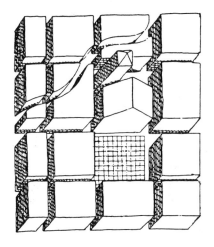

1

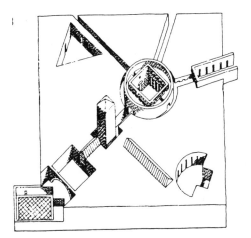

2

60

Three models (types) of urban space: 1. blocks resulting from a street-and-square pattern, 2. streets and squares as a result of positioning blocks, and 3. streets and squares as precise spatial types.

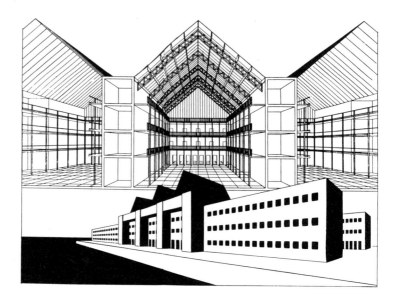

61
Project for the Regional Hall in Trieste, by Aldo
Rossi (1974).

positions can be seen deployed in Rossi's work ("prisons and
schools," for instance), whereby past fragments are used to
strive toward new meanings (Braghieri 1982).

● **Problems of Meaningful Interpretation**
In this second realm of inquiry, where architecture is seen
primarily in relationship to itself and its constituent elements, a
number of general issues of interpretation arise. Several specific
examples have already been noted in passing, and the criteria
for "good" interpretation raised in connection with the bricoleur
could well be applied to other strategies. Three issues in particular stand out, however—issues that in one way or another attend
architectural form making of the introspective and referential
kind under discussion. They are the question of privacy versus
accessibility in the employment of an architectural language; the
confusion between "significance" and "meaning"; and the problem of adequately integrating new formal constructs, as well as
expressing new social institutions.

The Privacy of Language
With regard to written text material, the evolving field of hermeneutics—roughly speaking, the science of interpretation—has
dwelt upon a paradoxical situation that confronts a reader in
obtaining knowledge from the material (Gadamer 1982, p. 113f.;

Bernstein 1983, pp. 30–48). This paradox is sometimes referred to as the "hermeneutic circle" and can be described in the following manner (Hirsch 1967, p. 259; Rickman 1976, p. 246f.). "The meaning of a text is a complex of submeanings or parts which hang together." Further, "it is not merely a mechanical collocation but a relational unity in which the relations of the parts to one another and to the whole constitute an essential aspect of their character as parts . . . and [of] the character of the whole" (Hirsch 1967, pp. 258–259). It follows "that we cannot perceive the meaning of a part until we have grasped the meaning of a whole" (Hirsch 1967, p. 259), and vice versa. A genuine dialectic can be seen to occur between our idea of the whole and our perception of the parts that constitute it. Once the dialectic, or "circle," has been entered into, neither the "parts-side" nor the "whole-side" is totally determined by the other, and of course for meaningful interpretation to ensue, the circle must not be a vicious one.

A great deal of scholarship has been developed around this paradox and the way in which the circle might be broken so as to arrive at a plane of real understanding—if it can be broken at all. Some, like Gadamer, hold that the process of grappling with the paradox is inherently open-ended (Gadamer 1975, p. 251f.). For our immediate purposes, however, this description of the paradox serves to establish an important dilemma posed by a work, such as a piece of architecture, with regard to meaning.

In the dialectical relationship between parts and whole in a work of architecture, the parts must be apprehended and understood if one is to make sense of the whole, and the whole must be apprehended in some manner that facilitates understanding of the parts. Understanding, then, requires intelligibility on the part of the overall organization and composition of the work and on the part of its surfaces, framing devices, material, and decoration. In the absence of a truly expressive capacity, the architectural object will remain mute and thus have no meaning.

As described earlier, one of the problems of an artificially contrived abstract formalism is that it can stretch the public expressive capacity of the architectural work toward a limit at which meaning is difficult to sustain. By the same token, rampant ad hoc use of figural devices, like adjectives and nouns composed on a page in some private way, can also fail to make public sense. This is not to say that either abstract formalism or figural devices have no place in architectural expression. On the contrary, to deny their place is to deny architecture. For example,

geometries of various kinds are certainly abstract and fundamentally concerned with the ordering of spatial objects, including architecture. They should and must be explored for their
formal expressive possibilities. But like the idea of types mentioned earlier, geometries do have rules, and because of this
they can be held up to a more public scrutiny and accountability.

The real dilemma is where the boundary line might be drawn
between the public realm and a more private world—assuming,
as this discussion does, that architecture is a broadly based cultural enterprise and hence that the accessibility of a work is important. Several criteria, on the order of "balancing tests," were
proposed in the last chapter in connection with the issue of the
"engagement" of a work. One was that architecture should not
be considered arbitrary if it provides the means for obtaining
understanding. Nevertheless, the difference between a mere provision of means and real understanding can be considerable; the
work must gain meaningful substantiation in the "real world"
outside itself if it is not to be "relegated to virtual worlds created
in the image of private languages and meanings" (Colquhoun
1978b, p. 37).

Significance and Meaning

A popular contention today is that architecture is autonomous,
effectively leading a "life of its own." More precisely, what is
proposed is that architecture, like other cultural works such as
literature, can have a meaning independent of authorial intention and that such meaning can change during the course of
time. This raises the question whether meaning can be sustained
in the absence of permanent norms on which to base judgment.
In other words, if we can have as many different meanings as
spectators, then are we not likely to have no lasting meaning at
all?

The obvious counter to this is that at any given moment there is
some unanimity about meaning on the part of spectators (Hirsch
1967, p. 212f.). They are all part of the same culture, read the
same books, breathe the same air, and so on. As Hirsch points
out, however, even if we accept this as so, it still leaves unan-
swered whether the meaning of the work has changed or
whether the meaning of collective interpretations has changed
(Hirsch 1967, p. 213). In fact it seems quite possible that any
original meaning that the work may have had must be understood in order for it to have any further meanings. As Hirsch
argues, it is clear that "significance"—that is, present relevance—cannot readily be fused with meaning. Furthermore, an

autonomous, "living" work does not really free the specator from the "shackles of historicism," it only destroys the basis for agreement and objective study (Hirsch 1967, p. 214). On the contrary, to paraphrase Husserl, it would seem that the meaning of a work of architecture must be an "intentional object," corresponding to the designer's intentions, which remains unchanging through the course of time (Husserl 1913, p. 96f.).[7] In short, the meaning of an architectural work is that aspect of the designer's intention which, under architectural conventions, may be shared by others.

Of course this kind of declarative statement does not settle the matter; what is actually shared by others may be unintentional. But it does mean that architecture is not a purely public object, whose character is solely determined by public norms. This would imply the operation of some system of probabilities in the adjudication of meaning; or, as Cassirer put it, meaning arises from the "reciprocal determination" of "public [conventional] possibilities and subjective specification of those possibilities" (Cassirer 1975, p. 178; Hirsch 1967, p. 225). Returning to the interpretative paradox, at least some semblance of architectural convention must be present in order to constrain or otherwise direct the knowing gaze of the spectator. As we have seen, many form-making strategies, such as the use of formal and figural devices, bricolage, quotation, and type, axiomatically require a substantial measure of fixity of meaning; otherwise, the rhetoric and cultural continuity to which designers aspire would be totally ineffective. The presence of this fixity of meaning also suggests that mistakes, misquotations, and misappropriations can be made, and that the history and the original circumstances of the architectural device, fragment, or oddment in question are consequential to its contemporary use.

New Constructs and Institutions

As societies move through time, discoveries are made, new functions and sociopolitical arrangements are instituted alongside the old, and the complexion of how natural resources are harnessed undergoes change. The results are frequently laid at the doorstep of man's cultural enterprise. New institutions emerge, requiring expression through architecture; some severely tax or transcend traditional practice. For example, the modern automobile city presents institutional arrangements and movement rituals that are materially if not radically different from those of cities of earlier times. The problem of interest to us here is how to provide appropriate expression to these entities, arrangements, and rituals. This, as modern functionalism was to discover, involves more than merely housing the new functions and providing basic systems of movement.

The enterprise of cultural interpretation and integration is an essential part of a living tradition. We have seen many failures, either in the guise of the emasculated, mechanistic, and fragmented forms of functionalism or in anachronistic and whimsical uses of architectural elements and devices of other epochs. The problem seems to call for concerted development and extension into new dimensions and new forms of architectural expression. So might we regard the heroic efforts of the modern movement. On the other hand, the integrating aspect of tradition seems to require the establishment of continuity with the past; and in any case, since cities are not built in a day, newcomers have a responsibility to make a nod toward old-timers. It is not at all clear that the existing constituent elements of architecture can be regarded, after the pattern of language, as a more or less complete set of words and grammatical rules with which texts may be written and novel thoughts expressed. In any event, natural languages change through time and become themselves the objects of changing needs and institutional rearrangements.

Architecture is also susceptible to changes in the very material and dimensional aspects that fundamentally determine its constitution. Advances or discoveries in material and fabrication technologies can have import. Similarly, as suggested earlier, geometry itself by now offers many different systems for organizing space. In certain brands, the system immediately moves beyond three-dimensional Euclidean space into the realm of "hyperspaces." The representational schemes that go with these geometries also affect the view of space and therefore its conformation.

The directions in which such discoveries and inventions might influence architecture are difficult to predict and even sometimes difficult to discern after the fact. In some cases, such as that of new geometries, they seem to represent opportunities and promising lines of investigation for work on the language. Nevertheless, exploration of this kind for its own sake, although it may eventually suggest some important contributions, at the moment is not necessarily architecture. Furthermore, it seems unlikely that the new contributions can be appreciated without reference to tried and true procedures, again raising the issue of the necessarily integrative aspect of tradition and its advancement.

A Convergence of Issues

To summarize, we have two realms of inquiry. One is concerned with the making of architecture in the light of an external vision of man and his world. The other is concerned with architecture in itself.

At the risk of caricature, interpretation in the first realm can be described as tending to adhere to the hypothetical-deductive system of theory construction and empirical observation favored by the social sciences. As pointed out earlier in the chapter, the emerging idea of theory is one that makes categorical distinctions between facts and values. Indeed, some purists would argue that value aspects of propositions about man and his world can be neither true nor false and therefore cannot be included in the realm of theory at all. Others might treat the same propositions about values as disguised factual claims and thus misplace them within factual rather than normative discourse. Below the loftier heights of such theoretical speculation, prevalent logical-empirical orthodoxies have tended to bequeath a reductionist and naive functionalism to the design and physical planning professions. As Bernstein persuasively argues, it is also a theoretical perspective that in more extreme cases fosters an attitude of disinterested observer, with a concomitant faith in "value-free" objectivity as the inevitable avenue for social progress (Bernstein 1976). What has resulted is a disguised form of ideology in which a dependent relationship is often unwittingly struck between methodological exigencies and limitations and the formulation of courses of action: ends become defined by means instead of by some other standard. The horizon of policy formulation, planning, and design is determined by a "scientific view" of man and his world and not by some other vision. When such a view is inappropriate or ignores many dimensions of the situation at hand, the consequences can be dire indeed.

That a certain disenchantment would occur within the areas of planning, urban design, and architecture was probably inevitable. There has been a growing suspicion of the kind of "liberal faith" implicit in the role of urban theorists and practitioners as aloof observers and dispensers of information and technical know-how. "Value-free" research and application have become open to criticism as masked ideology that lends false legitimacy to technical control (Schön 1983, ch. 1). On a more practical level, a sense of professional crisis has developed. At first this appeared to be just a problem of technique, quality of data, analytical methods, and so on. Surely with a little more perseverance and added resources such problems could be overcome. Repeated failures of planning and design applications to live up to expectations, however, pronounced a requiem, first for large-scale models in planning (Lee 1973, Harris 1967), then for quantitative techniques to be found more squarely within design disciplines, and finally for the naive functional form making of architects.

Not surprisingly, perceptions of these kinds of difficulties have had mixed professional and institutional responses. Technical shifts and more radical reorientations toward the possibility of other interpretative frameworks have occurred. For example, the inherent pluralism of irreducible concepts about tradition, culture, and "forms of life" has been expounded in so-called ethno-methodologies and especially in hermeneutic critiques of the modern era (Winters and Peckham 1984). These themes, however, are beyond our present scope.

Within the second realm of inquiry there is a tendency to adhere to the rhetorical domain of architectural objects and organizing compositional principles. Thus the distinction between architecture and other disciplines is sharply and narrowly drawn. In more extreme cases the kind of theory that is advanced fosters an introspective attitude that is disengaged from technology and architecture's social purpose. Here "art for art's sake" can become an operative maxim that threatens to relegate architecture to the rarefied fringes of consumer culture.

Means-ends and fact-value dichotomies, so evident in theorizing of the logical-empirical variety, are also to be found among theoretical positions of a recognizably normative kind. Many normative speculations about architecture fail to find sufficient grounding outside the immediate realm of architectural categories and the private languages of design. The result is that questions of ends, surely the heart of normative discourse, remain implicit and vague. Consequently, these normative positions are actually cast only in the form of means. Such discourse, if it remains centered solely on prescriptive devices and architectural categories—on questions of "right" rather than on questions of "good"—seems certain to fail to generate sustaining normative doctrines. It will also suffer many of the same problems as do theoretical perspectives that confuse ends and means under the influence of more "scientific" kinds of interpretation. Even if the confusion is not so blatant, the theoretical discourse may suffer from a certain self-referential quality that might well confound efforts to provide adequate substantiation for the positions involved. If one position seems to be more or less as good as another and choosing between them is merely a matter of taste, why bother much with fundamental considerations of appropriateness, comprehensiveness, or validity?

Disenchantment with the expressive possibility of abstract modern formalisms has led to attempts to recover a figural tradition in architecture. These attempts involve a number of strategies, including quotation, bricolage, and certain uses of type, all of which turn on the resurrection and reintroduction of architectural elements from past eras. Meanwhile, other formal exercises continue, in a seemingly endless quest for different ordering systems and means of manipulating spatial geometries.

Grounding the meaning of an architectural work has become very much an issue, as a consequence of the dismantling of the confidence placed in the doctrine of "form follows function." The idea of architecture as a language, capable of a broad repertoire of referential and rhetorical statements, has taken on a new vitality, and acknowledgment of the importance of preserving cultural continuity with the past has further reinforced an already introspective and backward-looking theoretical stance. But the spectre of cities cluttered with self-referential ironic statements, or simply architecture for architecture's sake, looms large in this orientation. Neither of these would seem to advance our cultural enterprise.

Again not surprisingly, we are looking at what might more reasonably be regarded as two sides of the same coin. For architecture, with its unique pedigree of art and science, plays between the two realms. Furthermore, if we set aside the procedural strictures of both realms in favor of their enabling prejudices, a common problem may be seen. It is the problem of recovering the social purpose of architecture beyond the often insightful but emasculated and reductive constructs from our logical-empirical interpretation of man and his world. It is also the problem of making the ennobling aspect and substance of architecture more accessible and a part of society. The two facets of the problem are clearly intertwined. Without social purpose it is difficult to imagine how a broad understanding of and meaning for architecture can be established. On the other hand, without engagement it is difficult to see how architecture can be conveyed in the cultural mainstream, even with a strong sense of purpose.

Notes

Chapter 1

1

Procedure for the protocols took the following format. First, subjects were invited to participate with the promise, unless waived, of having their identity and association with the experiments remain confidential. Second, interview sessions were conducted with each subject from the beginning to the end of a particular design project. Except at the start and the end, these sessions were largely self-scheduled by the subjects to coincide with points at which they felt comfortable discussing their work. The general aim of the protocol analyses was in the direction of "validity of measurement" rather than "reliability." Third, each subject was asked to keep a "sketchbook," or set of working notes and drawings, and to record the sequence of design ideas of any other jottings about the project. Fourth, each interview was tape-recorded in two parts. The first part allowed the subject to describe and explain the work to date. The second part allowed questions to be asked for the purpose of clarification. At no time was an overtly critical attitude taken toward the subjects' work. Finally, the tape recordings and drawings were analyzed for the purpose of reconstructing the design protocols that are presented here in summary form.

The reasons why real-time protocol analysis was not used include the limited availability of resources and the interference that real-time recording procedures would seem to impose on the process itself. For example, it is unusual for designers to describe aloud what they are doing as they do it. Also, the technical paraphernalia that would be required for real-time recorded observation would be obtrusive, unless carefully masked. The aims of the protocol analyses were more modest and more in the direction of capturing the broader contours of design rather than specific relationships such as time of response to the problem encountered, levels of anxiety, and the like.

2

Prejudices in Gadamer's sense of the word (Gadamer 1975). "Prejudices [*Vorurteile*] are biases of our openness to the world. They

are simply conditions whereby we experience something—whereby what we encounter says something to us" (Gadamer 1976, p. 9). As Hirsch observed, *Vorurteil* is Gadamer's version of the hermeneutic principle that was first clearly perceived by Schleiermacher and then elaborated by Dilthey and Husserl (Hirsch 1967, p. 258). *Vorurteil* should be translated as "prejudgment" in order to avoid the pejorative sense that "prejudice" takes on in English; I use the term *enabling prejudice* to convey this positive construction.

Chapter 2

1

Bazjanac and Rittel cite eleven properties of wicked problems. In addition to the four described in the text, there are the following: no exhaustive list of admissible operators for solving such problems; for every wicked problem there is more than one possible explanation; every wicked problem is a symptom of another higher-level problem; no wicked problem and no solution to one has a definitive test; each wicked problem is a "one-shot" operation; every wicked problem is unique; and the wicked-problem solver has no right to be wrong (Rittel and Webber 1972; Bazjanac 1974, pp. 9–10).

2

David Hartley (1705–1757) is generally recognized as the founder of the school of psychology known as associationism. In 1749 he published his *Observations on Man*. Other leading figures of the movement that held sway for some two hundred years were John Gay, John Stuart Mill, and Alexander Bain.

3

Embodiment of this view is hardly an accident, since associationism grew out of the philosophy of John Locke (1632–1704), especially as expressed in his *Essay Concerning Human Understanding* (1690).

4

Wundt (1832–1920), often referred to as the founder of modern experimental psychology, was the pioneer of introspective techniques whereby subjects' sense data could be indirectly observed.

5

The mental state was referred to as *Bewusstseinslage,* or "imageless thought" (Humphrey 1963, ch. 3).

6

This corresponds to Wallas's four steps (Wallas 1926), which were extended by researchers such as Rossman (Rossman 1931) to (1) observation of a need, (2) analysis of the need, (3) survey of available information, (4) formulation of objective solutions, (5) critical analysis of solutions, (6) birth of a new idea, and (7) experimentation and testing.

7

Perkins quarrels with this idea as an explanation of creativity on the basis that bisociation is not a distinctive psychological process. Hence it does not clarify creativity but rather begs the question (Perkins 1981, pp. 91–99).

8

The term "chunk" was introduced by Miller (1956, p. 93) to denote a grouped set of input data in a familiar unit—that is, a familiar unit of information. Simon (1979, pp. 50–61) presents an extended discussion of chunks, concluding among other things that the size of chunks may vary depending upon context (word chunks, chunks of poetry, etc.).

9

The term derives from the Greek *heuriskein,* "to discover."

10

In other words, it is a view that runs against the Cartesian concept of objective foundational knowledge that stands, as it were, by itself.

11

Utzon's own commentary indicates an additional purpose for the superstructure of sail-like buildings: "In the Sydney Opera House, the idea has been to let the platform cut through like a knife and separate primary and secondary functions completely" (Utzon 1963, p. 117).

12

Let us assume a decision-making process with the following general form:

$$R_t^i \rightarrow s_t^i; [S - s_t^i] \rightarrow R_{t+1}^{j \neq i}; \text{ etc.},$$

R_t^i = the ith rule chosen at time t;

s_t^i = observed characteristics of the proposed solution from application of the ith rule at time t;

S = characteristics, or properties, of the required solution as known to the designer; and

[ ] = the difference between the proposed and required solution properties at time t (episode t), as it appears to the designer.

In the case of a well-defined problem (that is, S are unambiguous) a particular rule R_t^i is applied and a proposed solution s_t^i is obtained. Any resulting discrepancies (through the comparison $[S - s_t^i]$) are used in order to select another rule $R_{t+1}^{j \neq i}$ during the next episode, or to subsequently modify the rule under consideration.

For the case of an extremely ill-defined problem, however, where S are largely unknown, such an evaluation between S and s_t^i cannot be sustained with any confidence. Here $R_t^i \rightarrow s_t^i \rightarrow S$ by definition. Hence $[S - s_t^i] = 0$. In other words, no discrepancies are likely to be found and s_t^i may or may not be a solution to the problem at hand. Furthermore, problem solving can only continue by simply starting again.

If we admit a certain "selective inattention" in the constancy of appreciation with which rule R_t^i is applied to yield proposed solution s_t^i, then the switching model might take the following form:

$$R_t^i \rightarrow s_t^i \text{ and } \rightarrow S$$
$$\therefore [S - s_t^i] = 0$$
$$\text{but } R_t^i \rightarrow R_{t+1}^{j \neq i}, \dots, \text{ etc.}$$

In short, even in ill-defined problem-solving situations, rule R_t^i, upon reflection by the designer, is likely to be considered part of a constellation of rules that are linked or related in some manner (ΣR_t^j), and problem solving could continue with the use of one of these related rules.

During the subsequent application of rules in this manner, even under conditions of trial-and-error, the required solution properties (S) will become clearer. Thus something approximating the first kind of rule application can take place. In fact, for the solution of wicked problems, where there is no definitive stopping rule (that is, S is poorly defined), only this type of sequence seems plausible.

Chapter 3

1
"The office building is a house of work of organization, of clarity, of economy . . . the maximum effect with the minimum expenditure of means" (Mies van der Rohe 1923, p. 89).

2
First enunciated succinctly by Louis Sullivan: "Form is everything and anything. . . . According to their nature . . . some forms are definite and some are nebulous . . . the form exists because of the function" (Sullivan 1934, pp. 40–41).

3
These terms are borrowed from Paul Frankl (*Raumzellen* as "space cells" and *Körperformen* as "mass forms") and represent a conceptual scheme for the analysis of architectural compositions (Frankl 1914).

4
The *Existenzminimum* of lodging was a preoccupation of "Der Ring" architects, the Bauhaus, and later the CIAM. For instance, the CIAM II in Frankfurt (1929) was devoted to "minimum-living-standard housing." Le Corbusier developed the notion of the "biological unit" of housing, corresponding to a standard of 14 square meters per occupant. And at the same CIAM congress of 1929 he was to repudiate the idea of the "minimum house" as being possible with traditional techniques (Le Corbusier 1967, p. 29).

5
After Wittgenstein, *Investigations,* in which, for instance, the matter of a musical theme and its variations is analyzed. "In short,

what makes something a correct step in composing a variation . . . is that it is connected pertinently with what precedes it; what makes a connection pertinent is settled by the reaction of practitioners" (Mounce 1981, pp. 116–118).

6
"Vernacular" in the sense of a derivative of a more formal language. To a certain extent the term "popular" might seem synonymous with vernacular. For instance, "popular architecture" is a term often used to refer to indigenous local forms of building, to local materials and production systems. Yet vernacular expressions are variations of "high style," while popular architecture is concerned with the development of forms outside high style.

7
For example, Stern's assertion that contemporary architecture "represents a complex interaction between the often conflicting issues that characterize the modern world." "It is difficult," he continues, "to sustain a belief in Modernism's struggle to reestablish a monolithic style, because such a style would possess an intolerably inadequate palette with which to address the complexities of modern life" (Stern 1980, p. 39).

8
In making this kind of point Eisenman noted that the development of the formal language of architecture "fundamentally changed the relationship between man and object away from an object whose primary purpose was to speak about man to one which was concerned with its own objecthood" (Eisenman 1978, p. 22).

9
[We] can . . . represent a corpus of knowledge . . . by a deductively clcsed set of sentences . . . containing a set [to be called the 'urcorpus']. The [urcorpus] consists of all logical truths, etc. . . . [in the corpus of knowledge] . . . as well as any other items . . . which might qualify as incorrigible in the sense that they are immune from removal from the standard of serious possibility" (Levi 1980, pp. 7, 12–13). The concept also has much in common with Landau's notion of the "hard core" (after Lakatos) in the

context of "architectural programmes," except here the hard core seems to take on a more explicit presence in programme development (Landau 1982, pp. 303–309).

Chapter 4

1

The distinction of the two realms is by no means novel. In certain respects it coincides with Simon's definition of an artifact as the meeting point ("interface") between the "inner" environment, described according to "the substance and organization of the artifact itself," and an "outer" environment, "the surroundings in which it operates" (Simon 1969, p. 7). In quite a different vein, it coincides with Vidler's distinction between his "second typology"—"architecture as simply a matter of technique"—and his "third typology," in which architecture "stresses its continuity of form and history" (Vidler 1978, pp. 23–32).

2

"Generally coincides" in the sense that few proponents of the view are positivists in the strict sense of Ernst Mach and the Vienna Circle. They have nonetheless been profoundly influenced by the positivist temper. For instance, a central role is assigned to empirically based explanatory theory very similar to Comte's idea of a "positive science" based on precise observation, hypothesis making, experimentation, and regularities of natural cause and effect (Bernstein 1976).

3

Or more precisely, *Zweckmässigkeit und die neue Sachlichkeit*—"purposiveness/expediency/functionalism and the new objectivity/practicality."

4

Such a system of logic primarily involves three principles. First, there is the *Law of Contradiction,* under which no proposition can be true and false at the same time (i.e., if *p* then *q*). Second, there is the *Law of the Excluded Middle,* under which proposition *p* and *q* is either true or false but not both.

Third, there is the *Law of Implication* (*Modus Ponens*): if *p* then *q*; *p* is true; therefore *q* is true (Mitroff and Kilmann 1978).

5

Bernstein groups together philosophers like Wittgenstein, Ryle, and Austin as providing the basis for this position; to them we might add Russell and Moore.

6

For example, "I consider type to be a mental object or, if one prefers, an idea. The essential feature of a type idea is its ability to subsume more than one experience and therefore to represent more than one experience" (Hirsch 1967, p. 265).

7

In very contracted form Husserl's analysis proceeds as follows: (1) different intentional acts (for instance, acts by which I perceive objects) can exist; (2) different intentional objects (for instance, the object I am perceiving) can exist but each is unchanging; (3) intentional objects may be reproduced by different intentional acts and remain self-identical (the same) through these reproductions; (4) meaning is the sharable content of an author's intentional object; and (5) since this meaning is unchanging and interpersonal, it may be reproduced by the mental acts (appreciation) of other persons (Husserl 1913; Hirsch 1967, p. 217f.).

Bibliography

AAM, ed. (1978). *Rational Architecture: The Reconstruction of the European City.* Bruxelles: Editions des Archives d'Architecture Moderne.

Akin, Ömer (1978). "How Do Architects Design?" In G. Latombe, ed., *Artificial Intelligence and Recognition in Computer-Aided Design,* pp. 27–34. New York: North Holland.

Akin, Ömer (1982 [1979]). *Models of Architectural Knowledge: An Information Processing View of Architectural Design.* Ann Arbor, Michigan: University Microfilms International.

Alberti, L. B. (1955 [1726]). *Ten Books on Architecture (De Re Aedificatoria).* London: A. Tiranti.

Alexander, Christopher (1964). *Notes on the Synthesis of Form.* Cambridge, Massachusetts: Harvard University Press.

Alexander, Christopher (1965). "A City Is Not a Tree." *Architectural Forum,* April.

Alexander, Christopher (1981). *The Linz Cafe.* New York: Oxford University Press.

Alexander, C., S. Ishikawa, and M. Silverstein (1968). *A Pattern Language Which Generates Multi-Service Centers.* Berkeley, California: Center for Environmental Structure.

Alexander, Christopher, et al. (1975). *The Oregon Experiment.* New York: Oxford University Press.

Alexander, Christopher, et al. (1977). *A Pattern Language.* New York: Oxford University Press.

Alexander, Christopher (1979). *A Timeless Way of Building.* New York: Oxford University Press.

Alexander, C., and M. Manheim (1962). "HIDECS 2: A Computer Program for the Hierarchical Decomposition of a Set within an Associated Graph." *Civil Engineering Systems Laboratory Publication No. 160,* MIT, Cambridge, Massachusetts.

Allen, Gerald, and Richard Oliver, eds. (1981). *Architectual Drawing: The Art and the Process.* New York: Whitney Library of Design.

Allen, P. M. (et al.) (1981). *Models of Urban Settlement and Structure as Dynamic Self-Organizing Systems.* Washington, D.C.: U.S. Department of Transportation, Systems Analysis Division, February.

Anderson, Stanford (1984) "Architectural Design as a System of Research Programmes." *Design Research.*

Archer, Bruce (1963–1964). "Systematic Methods for Designers." *Design, 172,174, 176,179,181,185,188,* April–August.

Arieti, Silvano (1976). *Creativity: A Magic Synthesis.* New York: Basic Books.

Asimow, M. (1962). *Introduction to Design,* Englewood Cliffs, New Jersey: Prentice-Hall.

Attoe, Wayne (1978). *Architecture and Critical Imagination.* New York: John Wiley and Sons.

Bachelard, Gaston (1979). *The Poetics of Space.* Boston: Beacon Press.

Barker, Roger G. (1968). *Ecological Psychology: Concepts and Methods for Studying the Environment of Human Behavior.* Stanford, California: Stanford University Press.

Bartlett, Sir F. (1961). *Remembering.* London: Cambridge University Press.

Batty, M. (1971). "A Rational Approach to Design." *Architectural Design, 41,* pp. 436–439, 498–501.

Bazjanac, Vladimir (1974). "Architectural Design Theory: Models of the Design Process." In William R. Spillers, ed., *Basic Questions of Design Theory,* pp. 8–16. New York: North-Holland.

Berlin, Isaiah (1962). "Does Political Theory Still Exist?" In Peter Laslett and W. G. Runciman, eds., *Philosophy, Politics and Society* (second series). Oxford: Blackwell.

Bernstein, Richard L. (1976). *The Restructuring of Social and Political Theory.* New York: Harcourt Brace Jovanovich.

Bernstein, Richard L. (1983). *Beyond Objectivism and Relativism: Science, Hermeneutics and Praxis.* Philadelphia: University of Pennsylvania Press.

Blondel, Jacques-François (1771–1777). *Cours d'architecture, Ou traité de la décora-*

tion, distribution et construction des bâtiments. Paris (9 vols.).

Bloomer, Kent C., and Charles W. Moore (1977) *Body, Memory and Architecture.* New Haven, Connecticut: Yale University Press.

Bloor, David (1983). *Wittgenstein: A Social Theory of Knowledge.* New York: Columbia University Press.

Bonta, J. P. (1979). *Architecture and Its Interpretation: A Study of Expressive Systems in Architecture.* New York: Rizzoli.

Boring, E. (1950). *A History of Experimental Psychology.* New York: Appleton-Crofts.

Braghieri, Gianni (1982). *Aldo Rossi.* Barcelona: Estudio.

Broadbent, Geoffrey H. (1966). "Creativity." In S. A. Gregory, ed., *The Design Method.* London: Butterworths.

Broadbent, Geoffrey (1973). *Design in Architecture: Architecture and the Human Sciences.* New York: John Wiley and Sons.

Broadbent, G., and A. Ward, eds. (1969). *Design Methods in Architecture.* New York: Wittenborn.

Bruner, Jerome S. (1961). "The Act of Discovery." *Harvard Educational Review,* Winter.

Bruner, Jerome S. (1967). "The Conditions of Creative Thinking." In H. Gruber, G. Tewell, and M. Wertheimer, eds., *Contemporary Approaches to Creative Thinking.* New York: Atherton Press.

Bruner, Jerome S., Jacqueline J. Goodnow, and George A. Austin (1967). *A Study of Thinking.* New York: John Wiley and Sons.

Burton, Joseph (1983). "Notes from Volume Zero." *Yale Architectural Journal, 20,* pp. 70–91.

Campbell, Donald T., and Julian C. Stanley (1970 [1963]). *Experimental and Quasi-Experimental Designs for Research.* Chicago: Rand McNally.

Carlian, Jean Paul (1979). "The Ecole des Beaux-Arts: Modes and Manners." *Journal of Architectural Education, 23,* no. 2, November, pp. 7–17.

Cassirer, Ernest (1975 [1955]). *The Philosophy of Symbolic Forms, Vol. 1: Language.* New Haven, Connecticut: Yale University Press.

Catanese, Anthony J. (1972). *Scientific Methods of Urban Analysis.* Urbana, Illinois: University of Illinois Press.

Chadwick, George (1972). *A Systems View of Planning.* New York: Pergamon Press.

Chomsky, Noam (1965). *Aspects of the Theory of Syntax.* Cambridge, Massachusetts: MIT Press.

Churchman, C. West (1967). "Wicked Problems." *Management Science, 4,* no. 14, pp. B-141, and B-142.

Clawson, Marion, and Peter Hall (1973). *Planning and Urban Growth: An Anglo-American Comparison.* London: Johns Hopkins University Press.

Collingwood, R. G. (1946). *The Idea of History.* New York: Oxford University Press.

Collins, Lyndhurst, ed. (1976). *The Use of Models in the Social Sciences.* Boulder, Colorado: West-View Press.

Colquhoun, Alan (1967). "Typology and Design Method." *Perspecta, 12,* pp. 71–74.

Colquhoun, Alan (1978). "Form and Figure." *Oppositions, 12,* Spring, pp. 29–37.

Colquhoun, Alan (1978b). "From Bricolage to Myth: Or How to Put Humpty-Dumpty Together Again." *Oppositions, 12,* Spring, pp. 1–18.

Conrads, Ulrich (1964). *Programs and Manifestos on 20th-Century Architecture* (translated by Michael Bullock). Cambridge, Massachusetts: MIT Press.

Consortium of East Coast Schools of Architecture (1981). *Architectural Education Study, Vols. 1 and 2.* New York: Andrew W. Mellon Foundation.

Craik, Kenneth H., and Ervin H. Zube, eds. (1976). *Perceiving Environmental Quality.* New York: Plenum Press.

Crane, David A. (1964). "The Public Art of City Building." *Annals of the American Academy of Political and Social Sciences,* March.

Davis, Albert J., and Robert P. Schubert (1976 [1974]). *Alternative Natural Energy Sources in Building Design.* New York: Van Nostrand Reinhold.

De Leon, Augusto (1972). *A Computer-Aided Markovian Model of the Design Process.* Houston, Texas: Rice Architecture Computer Laboratory.

Diamond, C., ed. (1976). *Wittgenstein's Lectures on the Foundations of Mathematics, Cambridge 1939.* Brighton: Harvester Press.

Dickey, John W., and Thomas M. Watts (1978). *Analytical Techniques in Urban and Regional Planning.* New York: McGraw-Hill.

Dietz, Albert G. H., and Lawrence S. Cutler (1971). *Industrial Building Systems for Housing.* Cambridge, Massachusetts: MIT Press.

Dixon, John Morris (1981). "Wage-Earner's Versailles." *Progressive Architecture,* October, pp. 94–97.

Domencich, Thomas A., and Daniel McFadden (1975). *Urban Travel Demand: A Behavioral Analysis.* New York: North-Holland.

Duhem, Pierre (1914). *La théorie physique: Son objet, sa structure.* Paris.

Dunster, David (1977). "A Comeback for Architectural Theory." *Progressive Architecture,* May, pp. 80–83.

Durand, J. N. L. (1802). *Précis de leçons d'architecture.* Paris.

Eastman, Charles (1969). "Towards a Theory of Automated Design." *Proceedings, Interdisciplinary Conference on Decision-Aids, Ohio State University,* May 16, p. 30.

Eastman, C. M. (1975). *Spatial Synthesis in Computer-Aided Building Design.* New York: John Wiley and Sons.

Echenique, M. (1963). *Models: A Discussion.* Working Paper No. 6, Land Use and Built Form Studies, University of Cambridge, March.

Egber, Donald Drew (1980). *The Beaux-Arts Tradition in French Architecture.* Princeton, New Jersey: Princeton University Press.

Eisenman, Peter (1978). "Postscript: Graves of Modernism." *Oppositions, 12,* Spring, p. 22f.

Eisenman, Peter (1979). "Aspects of Modernism: Maison Domino and the Self-Referential Sign." *Oppositions, 15/16,* pp. 118–129.

Fann, K. T. (1970). *Peirce's Theory of Abduction.* The Hague: Martinusnijhoff.

Ferguson, Francis (1975). *Architecture, Cities and the Systems Approach.* New York: George Braziller.

Feyerabend, Paul (1978 [1975]). *Against Method: Outline of an Anarchistic Theory of Knowledge.* London: Verso.

Five Architects (1972). *Five Architects: Eisenman, Graves, Gwathmey, Hejduk and Meier.* New York: Wittenborn Art Books, Inc.

Frampton, Kenneth (1974). "Apropos Ulm: Curriculum and Critical Theory". *Oppositions, 3,* pp. 17–36.

Frampton, Kenneth (1980). *Modern Architecture: A Critical History.* New York: Oxford University Press.

Frampton, Kenneth (1982). *Modern Architecture and the Critical Present.* London: Architectural Design Press.

Frampton, Kenneth (1983). "Towards a Critical Regionalism: Six Points for an Architecture of Resistance." In Hal Foster, ed., *The Anti-Aesthetic: Essays on Postmodern Culture,* pp. 16–30. Port Townsend, Washington: Bay Press.

Frampton, Kenneth (1985). "Architecture and the Tectonic Culture." *Lecture Series at the School of Architecture, Rice University,* Spring.

Frankena, W. K. (1963). *Ethics.* Englewood Cliffs, New Jersey: Prentice-Hall.

Frankl, P. (1914). *Die Entwicklungsphasen der neuen Baukunst.* Leipzig.

Gadamer, Hans-Georg (1975). *Truth and Method.* New York: Crossroad.

Gadamer, Hans-Georg (1976). *Philosophical Hermeneutics* (translated by David E. Linge). Berkeley, California: University of California Press.

Gadamer, Hans-Georg (1982). *Reason in the Age of Science* (translated by Frederick G.

Lawrence). Cambridge, Massachusetts: MIT Press.

Gardner, Howard (1981). *The Quest for Mind: Piaget, Lévi-Strauss and the Structuralist Movement.* Chicago: University of Chicago Press.

Ghiselin, Brewster, ed. (1952). *The Creative Process.* Berkeley, California: University of California Press.

Gombrich, E. H. (1965). *Art and Illusion: A Study in the Psychology of Pictorial Representation.* New York: Pantheon.

Gordon, W. J. (1961). *Synectics.* New York: Collier Books.

Graves, Michael (1977). "The Necessity of Drawing: Tangible Speculation." *Architectural Design, 47,* no. 6, pp. 384–394.

Graves, Michael (1984). "Monumentality and the City: Forum Transcript, December 12, 1981." *Harvard Architecture Review, 4,* Spring, p. 40.

Gregory, S. A., ed. (1966). *The Design Method.* London: Butterworths.

Gutman, Robert (1977). "House VI." *Progressive Architecture,* June, pp. 57–68.

Habermas, Jürgen (1979). *Communication and the Evolution of Society* (translated by Thomas McCarthy). Boston: Beacon Press.

Habraken, N. J. (1972). *Supports: An Alternative to Mass Housing.* New York: Praeger.

Halfpenny, William (facs. ed. 1968 [1724]). *Practical Architecture.* London: Bowles.

Hall, Edward T. (1969). *The Hidden Dimension.* Garden City, New York: Anchor Books.

Handa, Rumiko (1983). "Abduction Theory and Its Application to Bruno Taut's Interpretation of Japanese Architecture." Unpublished paper, Ph.D. Program in Architecture, University of Pennsylvania, December.

Handler, A. B. (1970). *Systems Approach to Architecture.* New York: Elsevier.

Harris, Britton (1967). "The Limits of Science and Humanism in Planning." *American Institute of Planners Journal,* September, pp. 324–335.

Harrison, Andrew (1978). *Making and Thinking: A Study of Intelligent Activities.* Sussex: Harvester Press.

Hayes, J. R. (1978). *Cognitive Psychology: Thinking and Creating.* Homewood, Illinois: Dorsey.

Hayes, John R. (1981). *The Complete Problem Solver.* Philadelphia: Franklin Institute Press.

Heidegger, Martin (1962). *Being and Time* (translated by John Macquarie and Edward Robinson). London: SCM Press.

Hempel, Carl G., and Paul Oppenheim (1948). "The Covering Law of Scientific Explanation." *Philosophy of Science, 15,* no. 2, April, pp. 135–146, 172–174.

Herdeg, Klaus (1983). *The Decorated Diagram.* Cambridge, Massachusetts: MIT Press.

Hesse, Mary (1963). *Models and Analogues in Science.* Brighton: Harvester Press.

Hillier, Bill, John Musgrove, and Pat O'Sullivan (1972). "Knowledge and Design." In W. J. Mitchell, ed., *Environmental Design: Research and Practice,* pp. 29–33. Los Angeles: EDRA.

Hirsch, E. D., Jr. (1967). *Validity in Interpretation.* New Haven, Connecticut: Yale University Press.

Holmes, Ann (1985). "New Austin Museum Shown as Work in Progress." *Houston Chronicle,* April 23.

Hubbard, William (1981). *Complicity and Conviction: Steps toward an Architecture of Convention.* Cambridge, Massachusetts: MIT Press.

Huet, Bernard (1978). "Small Manifesto." In AAM, ed., *Rational Architecture: The Reconstruction of the European City,* p. 54. Bruxelles: Editions des Archives d'Architecture Moderne.

Humphrey, G. (1963). *Thinking: An Introduction to Its Experimental Psychology.* New York: John Wiley and Sons.

Hunt, Morton (1982). *The Universe Within: A New Science Explores the Human Mind.* New York: Simon and Schuster.

Husserl, Edmund (1913). *Logische Untersuchungen*. Halle: Max Niemeyer.

Husserl, Edmund (1970). *The Crisis of European Sciences and Transcendental Phenomenology* (translated by David Carr). Evanston, Illinois: Northwestern University Press.

Husserl, Edmund (1975 [1962]). *Ideas: General Introduction to Pure Phenomenology* (translated by W. R. Boyce Gibson). New York: Collier.

Ingram, Gregory K. (1979). "Simulation and Econometric Approaches to Modeling Urban Areas." In Peter Mieskowski and Mahlon Straszheim, eds., *Current Issues in Urban Economics*, pp. 130–164. Baltimore: John Hopkins University Press.

Ivins, William M. (1973). *On the Rationalization of Sight*. New York: Da Capo Press.

Jencks, Charles, and George Baird, eds. (1969). *Meaning in Architecture*. New York: George Braziller.

Jencks, Charles, ed. (1980). *Post-Modern Classicism*. London: Garden House Press.

Jones, J. C. (1970). *Design Methods*. New York: John Wiley and Sons.

Julian de la Fuente, Guillermo (1968). "The Venice Hospital Project of Le Corbusier." *Architecture at Rice, 23,* April.

Kahn, Louis I. (1961). "Order Is. . . ." *Zodiac, 8,* June, p. 20.

Kaliski, John (1983). "Learning from the Park Regency." *Cite,* Spring, pp. 8–13.

Kaufmann, Emil (1968 [1955]). *Architecture in the Age of Humanism*. New York: Dover.

Kockelmans, Joseph K., ed. (1967). *Phenomenology: The Philosophy of Edmund Husserl and Its Interpretation*. Garden City, New York: Anchor Books.

Koestler, A. (1964). *The Act of Creation*. London: Hutchinson.

Koffka, K. (1935). *Principles of Gestalt Psychology*. New York: Harcourt, Brace.

Köhler, Wolfgang (1929). *Gestalt Psychology*. New York: Liveright.

Kostof, Spiro, ed. (1977). *The Architect: Chapters in the History of the Profession*. New York: Oxford University Press.

Krier, Leon (1978). "The Reconstruction of the City." In AAM, ed., *Rational Architecture: The Reconstruction of the European City*, pp. 38–42. Bruxelles: Editions des Archives d'Architecture Moderne.

Krier, Rob (1979). *Urban Space (Stadtraum)*. New York: Rizzoli.

Krimerman, Leonard I. (1969). *The Nature and Scope of Social Science: A Critical Anthology*. New York: Appleton-Century-Crofts.

Krueckeberg, Donald A., ed. (1983). *Introduction to Planning History in the United States*. New Brunswick, New Jersey: The Center for Urban Policy Research.

Landau, Royston (1968). *New Directions in British Architecture*. New York: George Braziller.

Landau, Royston (1982). "Methodology of Research Programmes." In B. Evans, T. A. Powell, and R. J. Talbot, eds., *Changing Design*, pp. 303–309. New York: John Wiley and Sons.

Lane, Barbara Miller (1968). *Architecture and Politics in Germany, 1918–1945*. Cambridge, Massachusetts: Harvard University Press.

Lang, Jon, Charles Burnette, Walter Moleski, and David Vachon (1974). *Designing for Human Behavior: Architecture and the Behavioral Sciences*. Stroudsburg, Pennsylvania: Dowden, Hutchinson, and Ross.

La Patra, J. W. (1973). *Applying the Systems Approach to Urban Development*. Stroudsburg, Pennsylvania: Dowden, Hutchinson, and Ross.

Le Corbusier (1951). *The Modulor*. London: Faber and Faber.

Le Corbusier (1958). *The Chapel at Ronchamp*. London: Architectural Press.

Le Corbusier (1959) *Towards a New Architecture*. London: Architectual Press.

Le Corbusier (1965). *Oeuvre complète: 1910–1929*. Zurich: H. Girsberger.

Le Corbusier (1967). *The Radiant City.* New York: Orion Press.

Le Corbusier and Pierre Jeanneret (1926). "Five Points towards a New Architecture." *Almanach de l'Architecture Moderne,* Paris.

Lee, Colin (1973). *Models in Planning.* New York: Pergamon Press.

Lee, Douglas B. (1973). "Requiem for Large-Scale Models." *American Institute of Planners Journal,* May, pp. 163–178.

Levi, Isaac (1980). *The Enterprise of Knowledge: An Essay on Knowledge, Credal Probability and Chance.* Cambridge, Massachusetts: MIT Press.

Lévi-Strauss, Claude (1966). *The Savage Mind.* Chicago: University of Chicago Press.

Lowry, Ira S. (1965). "A Short Course in Model Design." *American Institute of Planners Journal,* May, pp. 158–166.

Lynch, Kevin (1960). *The Image of the City.* Cambridge, Massachusetts: MIT Press.

Lynch, Kevin (1981). *A Theory of Good City Form.* Cambridge, Massachusetts: MIT Press.

Maldonado, T. (1972). *Design, Nature and Revolution: Toward a Critical Ecology.* New York: Harper and Row.

Maldonado, T., and G. Bonsiepe (1964). "Science and Design." *Ulm, 10/11,* May.

Mallin, Samuel B. (1979). *Merleau-Ponty's Philosophy.* New Haven, Connecticut: Yale University Press.

Merleau-Ponty, Maurice (1962). *Phenomenology of Perception* (translated by Colin Smith). London: Routledge and Kegan Paul.

Mesarovic, M. D. (1964). *Views on General Systems Theory.* New York: John Wiley and Sons.

Meyer, Hannes (1928). "Building." Bauhaus, *Zeitschrift für Gestaltung (Dessau), 2,* no. 4, p. 153f.

Mies van der Rohe, Ludwig (1923). "Working Theses." *De Stijl, 6,* p. 89.

Miller, George A. (1956). "The Magical Number Seven, Plus or Minus Two: Some Limits on Our Capacity for Processing Information." *Psychology Review, 63,* pp. 81–97.

Millon, Henry A. (1983). *Baroque and Rococo Architecture.* New York: George Braziller.

Milne, Murray (1970). "CLUSTER: A Structure-Finding Algorithm." In Gary T. Moore, ed., *Emerging Methods in Environmental Design and Planning.* Cambridge, Massachusetts: MIT Press.

Mishan, E. J. (1976). *Cost-Benefit Analysis.* New York: Praeger Special Studies.

Mitchell, William J. (1970). "Switching On the Seven Lamps." In Henry Sanoff and Sidney Cohn, eds., *EDRA-1.* Chapel Hill, North Carolina: University of North Carolina.

Mitchell, William J. (1977). *Computer-Aided Architectural Design.* New York: Petrocelli-Charter.

Mitroff, Ian I., and Ralph H. Kilmann (1978). *Methodological Approaches to Social Sciences.* Washington, D.C.: Jossey-Bass.

Moore, Charles (1967). "Portfolio: Architecture." *Perspecta, 11,* pp. 178–218.

Moore, Gary T., and Reginald G. Golledge (1976). *Environmental Knowing.* Stroudsburg, Pennsylvania: Dowden, Hutchinson and Ross.

Morris, Robert (facs. ed. 1971 [1734]). *Lectures on Architecture Consisting of Rules Founded upon Harmonic and Arithmetical Properties in Buildings, etc.* London: Bowles.

Mounce, H. O. (1981). *Wittgenstein's Tractatus: An Introduction.* Chicago: University of Chicago Press.

Negroponte, N. (1970). *The Architecture Machine.* Cambridge, Massachusetts: MIT Press.

Negroponte, N. (1972). *The Soft Architecture Machine.* Cambridge, Massachusetts: MIT Press.

Negroponte, N., ed. (1974). *Reflections on Computer Aids to Design and Architecture.* New York: Mason and Lipscomb.

Newell, A., J. C. Shaw, and H. A. Simon (1957). "Elements of a Theory of Problem Solving." *Rand Corporation Report P-971,* March.

Newell, Allen, J. C. Shaw, and Herbert A. Simon (1967). "The Process of Creative Thinking." In H. Gruber, G. Terrell, and M. Wertheimer, eds., *Contemporary Approaches to Creative Thinking,* pp. 63–119. New York: Atherton Press.

Newell, Alan, and Herbert A. Simon (1972). *Human Problem Solving.* Englewood Cliffs, New Jersey: Prentice-Hall.

Norberg-Schulz, Christian (1965). *Intentions in Architecture.* Cambridge, Massachusetts: MIT Press.

Norberg-Schulz, Christian (1968). "Less or More?" *Architectural Review,* April, pp. 257–258.

Norberg-Schulz, Christian (1980a). *Genius Loci.* New York: Rizzoli.

Norberg-Schulz, C. (1980b). *Architettura tardabarocca.* Milan: Electa.

Owen, Charles L. (1970). "DCMPOS: An Algorithm for the Decomposition of Non-Directed Graphs." In Gary T. Moore, ed., *Emerging Methods in Environmental Design and Planning.* Cambridge, Massachusetts: MIT Press.

Panofsky, Erwin (1967 [1951]). *Gothic Architecture and Scholasticism.* Cleveland, Ohio: Meridian Books.

Papademetriou, Peter C. (1980). "Putting Up a Good Front." *Progressive Architecture,* July, pp. 58–59.

Papademetriou, Peter C. (1985). "Pattern and Principle." *Progressive Architecture,* April, p. 86.

Pastier, John (1980). *Cesar Peli.* New York: Whitney Library of Design.

Peirce, C. S. (1965). *Collected Papers of Charles Peirce* (edited by C. Hartshorne and P. Wiess). Cambridge, Massachusetts: Harvard University Press.

Peña, William M. (1977). *Problem Seeking: An Architectural Programming Primer.* Boston: Cahner Books.

Perez-Gomez, Alberto (1983). *Architecture and the Crisis of Modern Science.* Cambridge, Massachusetts: MIT Press.

Perkins, P. N. (1981). *The Mind's Best Work.* Cambridge, Massachusetts: Harvard University Press.

Perrault, Claude (1683). *Ordonnance des cinq espaces de colonnes selon la méthode des anciens.* Paris: Jean Baptiste Coignard.

Pevsner, Sir Nikolaus (1961). *An Outline of European Architecture.* London: Pelican Books.

Piaget, J. (1965). *The Child's Conception of the World.* Totowa, New Jersey: Littlefield Adams.

Piaget, J. (1970a). *Structuralism.* New York: Basic Books.

Piaget, Jean (1970b). *Genetic Epistemology.* New York: W. W. Norton.

Pohlman, Richard W. (1982). "A System for Recording Behavior and Occupying Design." In Ömer Akin and Eleanor F. Weinel, eds., *Representation in Architecture,* pp. 121–138. Silver Springs, Maryland: Information Dynamics.

Polya, Gyorgy (1954). *Mathematics and Plausible Reasoning,* 2 vols. Princeton, New Jersey: Princeton University Press.

Polya, G. (1957). *How to Solve It.* London: Doubleday.

Popper, Karl R. (1959 [1934]). *Logic of Scientific Discovery.* London: Hutchinson.

Portoghesi, Paolo (1983). *Postmodern: The Architecture of the Post-Industrial Society.* New York: Rizzoli.

Preiser, Wolfgang, ed. (1978). *Facility Programming.* Stroudsburg, Pennsylvania: Dowden, Hutchinson and Ross.

Price, Cedric (1965). "Non-Plan." *Architectural Design,* May.

Price, Cedric (1966a). "Ptb Life Conditioning." *Architectural Design,* October.

Price, Cedric (1966b). "Potteries Thinkbelt." *New Society, 2,* June.

Proshansky, Harold M., William H. Ittelson, and Leanne G. Riulin, eds. (1970). *Environmental Psychology: Man and His Physical Setting.* New York: Holt, Rinehart and Winston.

Quatremère de Quincy (1977 [1825]). "Type" (translated from an essay in the *Encyclopédie méthodique*, Paris). *Oppositions, 9*, p. 148f.

Rapaport, Amos (1969). *House, Form and Culture.* Englewood Cliffs, New Jersey: Prentice-Hall.

Rapaport, Amos (1977). *Human Aspects of Urban Form: Towards a Man-Environment Approach to Urban Form and Design.* New York: Pergamon Press.

Rawls, John (1971). *A Theory of Justice.* Cambridge, Massachusetts: Harvard University Press.

Rickman, H., ed. (1976). *Dilthey: Selected Writings.* New York: Cambridge University Press.

Rittel, Horst W. J. (1972). "On the Planning Crisis: Systems Analysis of the First and Second Generations." *Bedrifsøkonomen, 8,* pp. 390–396.

Rittel, Horst W. J., and Melvin M. Webber (1972). *Dilemmas in a General Theory of Planning.* Working Paper No. 194, Institute of Urban and Regional Development, University of California, Berkelely.

Rossi, Aldo (1982). *The Architecture of the City* (translated by Dianne Ghirardo and Joan Ockman). Cambridge, Massachusetts: MIT Press.

Rossman, J. (1931). *The Psychology of the Inventor.* Washington, D.C.: Inventors Publishing.

Rowe, Colin, and Fred Koetter (1978). *Collage City.* Cambridge, Massachusetts: MIT Press.

Rowe, Peter G. (1972). "A Question of Architecture, a Matter of Style." *Architectural Design*, August, p. 466f.

Rowe, Peter G. (1982). "A Priori Knowledge and Heuristic Reasoning in Architectural Design." *Journal of Architectural Education, 36,* no. 1, pp. 18–23.

Ryle, Gilbert (1949). "On Knowing How and Knowing That." In *The Concept of Mind.* London: Hutcheson.

Sanoff, Henry (1977). *Methods of Architectural Programming.* Stroudsburg, Pennsylvania: Dowden, Hutchinson and Ross.

Schnaidt, Claude (1965). *Hannes Meyer: Building Projects and Writings.* New York: Architectural Book Publishing.

Schön, Donald A. (1983). *The Reflective Practitioner: How Professionals Think in Action.* New York: Basic Books.

Schön, Donald A. (1984). "Problems, Frames and Perspectives on Design." *Design Research.*

Scott, Mel (1969). *American City Planning since 1890.* Berkeley, California: University of California Press.

Scott Brown, Denise (1977). "Suburban Space, Scale and Symbols." *Via, 3,* pp. 41–47.

Scully, V., Jr. (1979). *Modern Architecture.* New York: George Braziller.

Silverstein, Murray, and Max Jacobson (1978). "Restructuring the Hidden Program: Toward an Architecture of Social Change." In Wolfgang F. E. Preiser, ed., *Facility Programming.* Stroudsburg, Pennsylvania: Dowden, Hutchinson and Ross.

Simon, H. A. (1957). *Models of Man.* New York: John Wiley and Sons.

Simon, Herbert A. (1969). *The Sciences of the Artificial.* Cambridge, Massachusetts: MIT Press.

Simon, Herbert A. (1970). "Style in Design." In John Archae and Charles Eastman, eds., *EDRA-Two: Proceedings of the Second Annual Environmental Design Association Conference,* Pittsburgh, Pennsylvania, pp. 1–10.

Simon, Herbert A. (1973a). "Does Scientific Discovery Have a Logic?" *Philosophy of Science,* December, pp. 471–480.

Simon, Herbert A. (1973b). "Structure of Ill-Structured Problems." *Artificial Intelligence, 4,* pp. 181–201.

Simon, H. A. (1979). *Models of Thought.* New Haven, Connecticut: Yale University Press.

Skinner, B. F. (1953). *Science and Human Behavior.* New York: Free Press.

Smithson, Alison, ed. (1968). *Team 10 Primer*. London: Studio Vista.

Sommer, Robert (1969). *Personal Space: The Behavioral Basis for Design*. Englewood Cliffs, New Jersey: Prentice-Hall.

Steinitz, Carl, and Peter Rogers (1970). *A Systems Analysis Model of Urbanization and Change*. Cambridge, Massachusetts: MIT Press.

Stern, Robert (1980). "Classicism in Context." In Charles Jencks, ed., *Post-Modern Classicism*. London: Garden House Press, pp. 89–91.

Studer, R. (1965). "Christopher Alexander's *Notes on the Synthesis of Form*." *Architecture Association Journal*, March.

Suckle, Abbey (1980). *By Their Own Design: Ten Architects Discuss Their Process of Design and Construction*. New York: Whitney Library of Design.

Sullivan, Louis H. (1934). *Kindergarten Chats*. Chicago: Scarab Fraternity Press.

Summerson, John (1979). *The Classical Language of Architecture*. Cambridge, Massachusetts: MIT Press.

Tafuri, Manfredo (1976). *Architecture and Utopia: Design and Capitalist Development*. Cambridge, Massachusetts: MIT Press.

Taller de Arquitectura (1984). Lecture presentation of work, School of Architecture, Rice University, November.

Thorndike, E. L. (1931). *Human Learning*. Cambridge, Massachusetts: MIT Press.

Thornley, D. G. (1963). "Design Method in Architectural Education." In J. C. Jones and D. G. Thornley, eds., *Conference on Design Methods*. Oxford: Pergamon.

Tolman, E. C. (1938). "The Determiners of Behavior at a Choice Point." *Psychology Review*, 435, pp. 1–41.

Utitz, Emil (1923). "Zweckmässigkeit und Sachlichkeit." *Dekorative Kunst*, 26, p. 144.

Utzon, Jørn (1963). "Platforms and Plateaus." *Zodiac*, 10, p. 117.

Van der Velde, Henry (1907). "Credo." *Vom Neuen Stil*, p. 150.

Venturi, Robert (1966). *Complexity and Contradiction in Architecture*. New York: Museum of Modern Art.

Venturi, Rauch and Scott Brown (1985). "The Laguna Gloria Art Museum: An Exhibition of a Work in Progress." Farish Gallery, Rice University, April 8–24.

Venturi, Robert, and Denise Scott Brown (1968). "A Significance for A&P Parking Lots, or Learning from Las Vegas." *Architectural Forum*, March, pp. 37–43f.

Venturi, Robert, and Denise Scott Brown (1971). "Ugly and Ordinary Architecture, or the Decorated Shed (Parts 1 and 2)." *Architectural Forum*, November, pp. 64–67, and December, pp. 48–53.

Venturi, Robert, Denise Scott Brown, and Steven Izenour (1972). *Learning from Las Vegas*. Cambridge, Massachusetts: MIT Press.

Vickers, Sir G. (1983). *Human Systems Are Different*. New York: Harper and Row.

Vidler, Anthony (1977). "The Idea of Type: The Transformation of the Academic Ideal, 1750–1830." *Oppositions*, 8, pp. 95–115.

Vidler, Anthony (1978). "The Third Typology." In AAM, ed., *Rational Architecture: The Reconstruction of the European City*, pp. 28–32. Bruxelles: Editions des Archives d'Architecture Moderne.

Wade, John W. (1977). *Architecture, Problems and Purposes: Architectural Design as a Basis Problem-Solving Process*. New York: John Wiley and Sons.

Waldman, Peter D. (1982). "The Design Narrative." *Journal of Architectural Education*, 35, no. 4.

Wallas, G. (1926). *The Art of Thought*. New York: Harcourt, Brace.

Watson, J. B. (1930 [1924]). *Behaviorism*. New York: W. W. Norton.

Watts, Ronald D. (1966). "The Elements of Design." In S. A. Gregory, *The Design Method*, p. 85. London: Butterworths.

Weber, Max (1957 [1922]). *The Theory of Social and Economic Organization* (translated by A. H. Henderson and Talcott Parsons). Glencoe, Illinois: Free Press.

Wertheimer, Max (1945). *Productive Thinking*. New York: Harper and Row.

Wiebenson, Dora, ed. (1982). *Architectural Theory and Practice from Alberti to Ledoux*. Chicago: Architectural Publications.

Winch, Peter (1958). *The Idea of a Social Science and Its Relation to Philosophy*. London: Routledge and Kegan Paul.

Wingler, Hans M., ed. (1969). *The Bauhaus*. Cambridge, Massachusetts: MIT Press.

Winters, Ed, and Andrew Peckham, eds. (1984). "Architecture and Hermeneutics." *Issue, 4,* March.

Wittgenstein, L. (1969 [1933–1935]). *Blue and Brown Books*. Oxford: Blackwell.

Wittkower, Rudolf (1971 [1962]). *Architectural Principles in the Age of Humanism*. New York: W. W. Norton.

Woods, Shadrach (1964). "Project for the Free University of Berlin." *Architectural Design,* August.

Woods, Shadrach (1965). "Free University, Berlin." In *World Architecture,* vol. 2. New York: Viking Press.

Wright, F. L. (1943 [1932]). *Autobiography*. New York: Hawthorn.

Ziegler, Oswald L. (1973). *Sydney Builds an Opera House*. Sydney: Oswald Ziegler Publications.

Zwicky, Fritz (1962). "Morphology of Propulsive Power." *Monograph on Morphological Research No. 1,* Society for Morphological Research, Pasadena, California.

Illustration Credits

12
Julian de la Fuente, Guillermo (1968). "The Venice Hospital Project of Le Corbusier." *Architecture at Rice, 23,* April, composite from pp. 8, 12, 16, 27.

13
After Watts 1966, p. 85.

14
After Archer 1963, p. 6.

17–21, 26
Basic drawing of the facade of San Sebastiano after Wittkower 1971 (1962), p. 52.

22
Le Corbusier (1951). *The Modulor,* p. 117. London: Faber and Faber.

27
Alexander, Christopher (1964). *Notes on the Synthesis of Form,* composite from pp. 137, 142, 151, 153. Cambridge, Massachusetts: Harvard University Press.

29
After Ziegler 1973, p. 28.

30
Jencks, Charles, ed. (1980). *Post-Modern Classicism,* p. 64. London: Architectural Design and Academy Editions.

32
Davis, Allen J., and Robert P. Schubert (1976). *Alternative Natural Energy Sources in Building Design,* p. 78. New York: Van Nostrand Reinhold.

33
AAM (1978). *Rational Architecture: The Reconstruction of the European City,* p. 70. Bruxelles: Editions des Archives d'Architecture Moderne.

34
Alexander, Christopher, Sara Ishikawa, and Murray Silverstein (1968). *A Pattern Language Which Generates Multi-Service Centers,* p. 18. Berkeley, California: Center for Environmental Structure.

36
Five Architects: Eisenman, Graves, Gwathmey, Hejduk, Meier (1972), pp. 32, 34. New York: Wittenborn Art Books, Inc.

37
Paraline and perspective drawings after Allen and Oliver 1981, pp. 19, 20.

41
Schnaidt, Claude (1965). *Hannes Meyer: Buildings, Projects and Writings,* p. 18. New York: Architectural Book Publishing Co.

42
Le Corbusier (1965). *Oeuvre complète,* p. 191. Zurich: H. Girsberger.

43
Plan redrawn from *Process Architecture, 8,* no. 9, 1979, p. 62.

48
Progressive Architecture, 1, January 1979, p. 85.

49
Landau, Royston (1968). *New Directions in British Architecture,* p. 72. New York: George Braziller.

50
Lane, Barbara Miller (1968). *Architecture and Politics in Germany 1918–1945,* p. 110. Cambridge, Massachusetts: Harvard University Press.

51
Photograph by L. G. Rowe.

55
Five Architects: Eisenman, Graves, Gwathmey, Hejduk, Meier (1972), p. 37. New York: Wittenborn Art Books, Inc.

56
Model photograph and sketch reproduced with permission of Venturi, Rauch and Scott Brown.

58
Plan abstracted and redrawn from Jencks 1980, p. 54, and photograph a detail from *Progressive Architecture,* October 1981, p. 95. (Original photograph by Deidi von Schaewen.)

59

Model photograph from *Architectural Record, 8,* August 1980, p. 100. Sketches from Wheeler, Karen Vogel, ed. (1982), *Michael Graves: Buildings and Projects 1966–1981.* New York: Rizzoli International.

60

AAM (1978). *Rational Architecture: The Reconstruction of the European City,* p. 58. Bruxelles: Editions des Archives d'Architecture Moderne.

61

Braghieri, Gianni (1982). *Aldo Rossi,* pp. 120, 121. Barcelona: Editorial Gustavo Gili, S.A.

Index